D1595883

THE EUROPEAN IDEA IN HISTORY IN THE NINETEENTH AND TWENTIETH CENTURIES

THE EUROPEAN IDEA IN HISTORY IN THE NINETEENTH AND TWENTIETH CENTURIES:
A View from Moscow

Alexander Tchoubarian
Institute of Universal History, Moscow

FRANK CASS

First published in 1994 in Great Britain by
FRANK CASS & CO. LTD.
Newbury House, 890–900 Eastern Avenue,
Ilford, Essex IG2 7HH, England

and in the United States of America by
FRANK CASS
c/o International Specialized Book Services, Inc.
5804 N.E. Hassalo Street, Portland, Oregon 97213-3644

British Library Cataloguing in Publication Data

Tchoubarian, Alexander
  The European Idea in History in the
  Nineteenth and Twentieth Centuries: View
  from Moscow
  I. Title
  940.28
  ISBN 0-7146-4503-6

Library of Congress Cataloging-in-Publication Data

Tchoubarian, Alexander.
    The European idea in history in the nineteenth and twentieth
  centuries : a view from Moscow / Alexander Tchoubarian.
      p. cm.
    ISBN 0-7146-4503-6
      1. Europe—History—1789–1900. 2. Europe—History—20th century.
    3. Europe—Relations—Russia. 4. Russia—Relations—Europe.
    I. Title.
    D359.T36 1994
    940.2′8—dc20
                                                          92-41954
                                                          CIP

Typeset by Vitaset, Paddock Wood, Kent
Printed in Great Britain by Bookcraft (Bath) Ltd, Midsomer Norton

CONTENTS

1

WHAT IS EUROPE – IDEA, SPIRIT, REALITY?

The problem of how the notion of Europe should be defined, its geographical boundaries and its political and cultural–historical meaning, has been an object of heated debate and lively discussion for many decades. Currently we have what may be described as a mythology of Europe, a European way of thinking, a European tradition and a European syndrome. The aim of this book is to present a view of the European idea, its sources and evolution, as seen from Moscow and to determine, probably for the first time in Russian historiography, the way a Russian historiographer sees the problem of European unity.

Should we define Europe by adopting the notion of European civilization, or is it a broader or more formal phenomenon? Is the term 'civilization' to be identified with culture, or should civilization include many other factors and phenomena?

Man, his material life and spiritual principles, his passions and everyday reality form the nucleus of civilization (including European civilization). However, apart from the type of culture, the notion of civilization presupposes a certain stage in industrial development. In this sense European civilization has its own standards and special features and has developed according to its own logic.

The concept of Europe and Europeans, of their mentality and appearance has been formed over a long period, so that gradually, and especially in the nineteenth and twentieth centuries, the conclusion was drawn that the notion of Europeans presupposes not only people residing in a certain geographical region but also a certain way of thinking, mentality, lifestyle and type of culture. One may object that there are elements of something mystical and irrational in such an approach – a European mythology. That may well be so. However, at the same time, Europe and Europeans are an obvious reality, a specific geographical space, comprising scores of states; Europe is a conglomeration of various social and political systems, as well as dozens of nationalities and ethnic groups; it has its own historical traditions, cultural heritage and complex economic contacts.

If we take this approach, the 'European idea' will be seen as a complicated and conditional notion; that is why we have a wide range of definitions of the European idea, from very broad, including almost all aspects of the European reality and its residents, to purely specific projects of Europe's unification. In its broadest sense 'the European idea' or 'the idea of Europe' means the attitude to Europe as a certain community, as well as its analysis from the viewpoint of internal unity and as something different from other parts of the world.

A number of studies on the history of the European idea associate it exclusively with the history of various projects of unification either of Europe as a whole or some of its parts. Many attempts have been made to take a broader approach to this problem. There is a desire to see in the European idea various aspects of the European community, including mutual economic contacts, the common cultural–historical heritage and factors of political development on the international scene. Such an approach also naturally presupposes an analysis of a great number of versions of the unification of Europe, as well as specific plans for setting up various pan-European bodies and alliances.

The history of the European idea is the history of the formation of European theories and views, but it is also a history of attempts at practical realization of those theories. This interpretation of the European idea inevitably involves various aspects of the specific European history in the sphere of research. On the one hand, this history serves as a permanent background of studies into all-European theories and reality and, on the other, makes it possible for us to analyse the struggle of various classes and political forces on the issues of unity and variety of European development.

The European idea is neither an eternal and invariable notion nor an abstract logical or psychological category. Ideas of European identity, and ways to realize it, changed at various stages of world and European history.

The purpose of this present study is to analyse the history of the European idea in so far as it concerns issues of war and peace. In doing this, it cannot help but touch on general aspects of interpretation and assessment of the European idea. Nevertheless, many important elements of this idea, relating to historico-cultural processes or economic factors, for instance, are not dealt with here. The main stress is on the issues of war and peace, which reflect our belief that the European idea has always included, as an important component, the notion of European responsibility for the continent's destiny and for the preservation of peace in Europe.

'Europeanism' as a trend of political thought and as an objective reality was multifaceted and heterogeneous, remaining a field of permanent and sharp struggle of conservative, bourgeois-liberal and revolutionary-democratic ideas and views.

Numerous plans for permanent peace, put forward by European thinkers in past centuries, which reflected clashing humanistic and reactionary views, are evidence of this. Of equal importance were those international systems that emerged in Europe in the seventeenth–twentieth centuries, the so-called 'European equilibrium' as a pan-European institution and phenomenon.

RUSSIA AND EUROPE

To what extent Russia belongs to Europe (in geographical, political, cultural and historical aspects) is a problem that has for many decades served as a subject of controversy in Russian society and provoked numerous discussions in Europe.

Special importance is attached to the way European states have developed in different ways and at different times, on the one hand, and, on the other, how this development has enriched European civilization as a whole.

The indisputable fact that Russia belongs to Europe, but at the same time not only to Europe, underlies numerous discussions. In this case it is not even so important that vast areas of Russia are situated in Asia. By virtue of its civilization, social structure, political organization and spiritual values Russia represents a special, unique community. It is an original alloy of two great civilizations, Europe and Asia, an inimitable type of culture, which is a kind of synthesis of Western and Eastern values. In turning to the specific history of the nineteenth and twentieth centuries, we shall again discuss the so-called Eurasian idea whose advocates put forward the idea of Russia as a specific Eurasian civilization and community.

For many centuries Russia has been regarded in Europe as a source of permanent danger, posing a threat of aggression and expansion. At the same time Russia has always been an inexhaustible commodity market and supplier of natural resources, attracting travellers and merchants. In the nineteenth century Russia served as a source of spiritual inspiration for Europe, through the ideas and genius of Dostoyevsky, Chekhov and Tolstoy, and in the twentieth century this mission was carried on in literature and the arts by

3

writers such as Bulgakov, Pasternak and Solzhenitsyn, artists like Shagal and Kandinsky and composers such as Shostakovich and Prokofiev.

In the early centuries and in the early Middle Ages Russia was actively involved in the general current of European development, although for many decades following the Tatar–Mongol invasion its social progress was retarded, thus leaving Russia far behind Europe. It was only in the fifteenth to seventeenth centuries that the process of renaissance of Russian statehood and culture set in, although later Russia's development was rather contradictory. On the one hand, the trend for Russia's *rapprochement* with Europe and the adoption of its values and the European political system was growing ever stronger and, on the other, that trend has always been opposed by 'healthy Russian principles' whose advocates criticized Western decadent culture and the harmful influence of Western Europe. In the twentieth century such moods were in every way encouraged by the government and the ideological machine of the socialist state. The idea of Russia as some sort of synthesis, as an original country lying in between two civilizations – Europe and Asia – often emerged as a result of the clash of those two trends.

The Western tradition has also in many respects contributed to the isolation of Russia and the USSR, by excluding Russia from the geographical notion of Europe. Classical works by A. Brugmans, J.L. Chabod, J.J. Duroselle and others served as a foundation for modern studies in Europeanism, for understanding its cultural–historical, international and psychological principles.

Interest in the European idea varies in different European countries. In France, for instance, this subject is relatively popular and is discussed both in academic textbooks and in popular current affairs literature. It also evokes widespread interest in Italy, but as in Germany and the United Kingdom there are very few publications on the subject. When I met students, intellectuals, journalists and diplomats in Paris, Geneva, Rome or Florence, the European idea provoked interest and understanding, whereas it provoked hardly any interest among those I met in London and Berlin.

The attitude among the public and in academic circles to pan-European subjects in East European countries is equally very different. In the USSR, in particular, the subject was almost unknown and hence has come as some sort of revelation.

While mentioning the Soviet historiography of Europeanism, it should be noted that the very notion of 'Europeanism' has always been frowned upon by Soviet historians and was discussed only in the context of so-called cosmopolitan ideas strictly in a negative sense. This approach only added to the conviction of those Western scholars who discussed Europeanism that such a concept should not include Russia or the Soviet Union.

For many years Soviet historiography gave the same negative assessment to the meaning and importance of West European integration. This approach reflected the stage in Soviet historical studies when all events were interpreted from narrow class positions and in an over-ideologized form, with common humanistic values and historical traditions either underestimated or passed over in silence.

Thus, Europeanism as a trend of political and social thought and the reality of European history was in fact non-existent as a scientific subject in Russia. For that reason Soviet readers had no opportunity to familiarize themselves with the important works on this subject published in Europe. The word 'Europeanism' itself was interpreted in a negative sense, as something alien to Marxism–Leninism and the interests of the revolutionary movement on the continent.

This approach reflected a distorted view of the interconnection between national and international, specific and universal factors in history as a whole and in European history in particular. It was the radical changes in the USSR, the renunciation of stereotyped views of the past, the recognition of the priority of common human values and a fundamentally new approach to the political realities of Europe that have made possible a new assessment of Europeanism, its interpretation as an objective and age-long process of historical development and as a separate trend in European political thought and the civic movement that organically incorporates Russia and what used to be the Soviet Union.

EVOLUTION OF THE EUROPEAN IDEA: FROM ANTIQUITY TO THE FRENCH REVOLUTION

In etymology the word 'Europe' is often traced back to the town of that name, situated in the Karia area, in the south-eastern part of Asia Minor. The legend of Europa, daughter of King Agenor of Phoenicia who was abducted by Zeus in the form of a Cretan bull, was well-known from classical times. According to some versions, however, Europe's etymology can be traced to the word 'ereb' meaning dark and also the land of the setting sun, or the west, as distinct from the east, the land of the rising sun. In Ancient Greece Europe meant 'wide-eyed', 'seeing (hearing) far'.

Classical writers and philosphers such as Hesiod, Hecataeus of

Miletus, Herodotus, Thucydides, Aristotle, Isocrates, Srabo, Pliny the Elder, Polibus and Ptolemy referred to Europe as a geographic notion. Many Greek and Roman authors held almost identical views on Europe's geographic boundaries. They described it as the land stretching between the Azov Sea and the Don River (or the Caucasus) in the east and the Iberian Peninsula and the Atlantic in the west. Britain was then regarded as an island in the north of Europe. Europe's southern border ran along Asia Minor, the Black Sea and the Mediterranean, and its northern border ran along the Danube.

Europe was thus regarded in the ancient world as land surrounding the Mediterranean, which was viewed as its nucleus. New areas in central and northern Europe were drawn into the continent's political, economic and spiritual sphere, but Europe's eastern borders were defined only in the seventeenth century. *Cosmography*, published in Russia in 1682–86, and many simple Russian geography books of that period described the Don as the natural border between Europe and Asia. Soon after, Count Vassili Tatishchev, an outstanding Russian historian and geographer, wrote in the article 'Europe', included in his *Russian Lexicon*, that Europe's border ran along the Ural range. Europe's eastern border was also shown by the Swedish traveller Stralenberg as running along the Urals.

Arguments on geographical boundaries naturally did not involve any other aspects of the notion of 'Europe', although geographical unity is the necessary basis for cultural–historical, political and economic unity.

Classical Europe exerted a notable influence on subsequent concepts of European unity, the ancient culture in many respects serving as a common heritage in the later development of European peoples. Classical Europe gave political lessons to future generations which are now regarded as the first manifestations of the contest between principles of universalism and particularism that for many centuries have been a constant element of European political thought and practice. Historians often refer in this respect to *amphictyons*, the alliances of tribes and city-states in the Aetolian and Achaean regions in Ancient Greece.

In the Middle Ages the development of European ideas and concepts was primarily associated with the development of Christianity. From the early years of this period the Christian Church acted as an important connecting link and a unifying element of life in Europe. So the appearance of various treatises and studies advocating universalist ideas, which served as a basis for approaching Europe from

6

positions of universality and integrity (quite understandable in view of the feudal and religious mentality), was not accidental.

The feudal epoch was marked by a long political and ideological struggle between secular and religious elements for European domination. In the course of that struggle, the two sides strove not only to substantiate their claims to hegemony but also to express their view of European unity. The contest between universalist and particularist trends was manifested in clashes between the ideas and practice of national statehood in Europe, on the one hand, and claims to supranational hegemony made by the papal and imperial authorities, on the other.

Those ideas were reflected in writings by P. Crassus, a royal judge of Ravenna, treatises by Marcilius of Padua and William Occham, a work by M. von Lautenbach, and decrees and encyclicals by Popes Gregory VII and Innocent III. The conflict between the secular and religious authorities for domination in Europe was brilliantly described by the Italian poet and thinker Dante Alighieri in his treatise *Monarchy* (1312–13). Central to it is the idea of unity of the whole world, incarnated in a world state which, in the medieval period, naturally enough, primarily meant Europe.

At a time when the religious and secular authorities were locked in bitter struggles and the popes were trying to implement their theocratic programme, Dante denounced their claims of world domination, thus reflecting the interests of the city circles which were gaining strength at that period, and advocated a strong secular power that would be able to protect the people from the omnipotence of the Church, hoping that this would help establish eternal peace.

Ecumenical councils, held in the twelfth to fifteenth centuries, were a manifestation of the rivalry between the religious and secular authorities. The councils of the twelfth to fourteenth centuries largely reflected the desire of the Catholic Church to retain its hold on and extend the sphere of its influence in Europe and outside it, whereas in the fifteenth century they became a scene of fierce clashes between the universalist claims laid by the popes and the system of national statehood that was gaining strength in Europe. The most typical in this respect was the 1414–18 Constanta Council. An attempt to modernize these councils and set up some sort of new pan-European initiative was made by Pope Aeneus Silvio Piccolomini who also offered a new interpretation of the notion of Europe in his writings, for he wrote not only of Christian but of European peoples.

However, the role of Christianity was most pronounced in the cultural–historical sphere. It was Christianity which supplied the basis for Europe's spiritual unity and made it possible for many thinkers and philosophers to speak about a united Christian Europe. The idea of union was felt especially acutely in Europe during the Crusades, when the Catholic Church, under the banner of Christianity and in alliance with secular rulers, sought to conquer new lands in the Middle East and North Africa.

The thirteenth and fourteenth centuries saw the first European plans that reflected, on the one hand, stronger European national statehood and, on the other, persistent attempts by the popes to supranational domination. Those plans gave birth to new trends in the development of the idea of European unity.

First, there was a clear-cut desire to substantiate the possibility of Europe's unification under the hegemony of a European state. The project of the French Royal Procurator, Pierre Dubois (fourteenth century), proceeded from the idea of unifying most of the European countries under the banner of the French king. Dubois was among the first European political thinkers to base a project on the idea that European unity was to be interpreted as a form of and means towards state domination (in this case, France) on the European continent.

Second, only the initial steps were then being made to introduce a humanistic approach to the European idea. The plan of King Podebrad of Bohemia (fifteenth century) holds a notable place in the history of European political thought. It was the first ever ardent call to stop wars and internecine strife in Europe and establish relations of fraternal co-operation instead. In his plan, King Podebrad made European peace conditional on the unification of the European states and peoples into 'an alliance of nations'. As distinct from the universalist ideas of Catholicism, King Podebrad in fact spoke about restructuring the life of European peoples on federalist principles.

The humanist trend was vividly manifested in a treatise by Erasmus of Rotterdam (1469–1536), an outstanding thinker of the Renaissance, entitled *A Complaint to the World*. Here he first broached the idea of eternal peace as a common human ideal. Imbued with the progressive ideas of the Renaissance, the treatise gave birth to a stable tradition of European thought, based on a humanistic and, in essence, democratic approach to the issues of war and peace which are closely interconnected with those of relationships among European states.

The history of relations between Russia and Europe also has deep roots. In the Middle Ages the Russian state maintained permanent contact and co-operation with the numerous tribes that inhabited

Asia and areas adjacent to the Near and Middle East. (It should be recalled that the whole of Europe and the western Mediterranean had also for many centuries maintained contacts with the peoples of North Africa and Asia Minor.) However, the notion of Europe is often referred to in *The Tales of Old Years*, the oldest monument of Russian literacy. Its author was well informed about Herodotus's system of the world's division into three parts.

In the eighth and ninth centuries the Slavs made their appearance among the peoples who shaped European policy. There were two Slavonic tribes in Eastern Europe in the ninth century: the Great Moravian State (which preserved its independence until the early tenth century) and Kievan Rus. Numerous studies have been devoted in Soviet historical literature to various aspects of the history of Kievan Rus and its place in European history. They testify that Kievan Rus was a European state with a developed economy and culture that maintained lively trade relations with other European and Western states, including Moravia, Bohemia, Poland and Germany. From the viewpoint of its social structure and the level of development of feudal relations, the Kiev state hardly differed in any respect from those of Western and Central Europe. Archaeological excavations have shown that Russian coins and handcrafted artefacts were to be found in practically all European countries. The marriages of Russian princes may serve as an indirect proof of the contact between Kievan Rus and the European states. Many rulers of West European countries were quite willing to establish dynastic and family relations with Russian princes.

Along with the Kiev state, other Russian princedoms also advanced to the political foreground and gained strength. After Kiev had lost its former glory, Kievan Rus was split into a number of rivalling princedoms including Rostov-Suzdal, Novgorod-Pskov, Galich-Volyn and Podolsk-Minsk. Studies carried out over many years during a lengthy expedition to Novgorod, headed first by Artemy Artsikhovsky and later by Valentin Yanin, helped to reveal the true nature of life in medieval Novgorod. Excavations in Novgorod clearly testify that the Novgorod feudal republic had many features in common with West European medieval republics.

The high level of old Russian culture is confirmed by Russian architecture of the period. Cathedrals of that period are real gems of old Russian architecture, manifesting perfect artistic taste.

Russian society's progressive development was, as is known, cut short in the early thirteenth century by the invasion of the Golden Horde. In this connection a general, although very important, question of principle arises.

9

The first problem was connected with the struggle against nomads even in earlier periods. Battles, fought against the Pechenegi, Polovtsi and other steppe peoples, put Russian tribes of that period in the forefront of the struggle to protect Europeans against nomadic raids. Russia played the role of a protective buffer zone against nomadic hordes which were ready to overrun Central Europe.

At the same time, in the thirteenth century Russia had a great role to play in protecting East European people from aggression by German feudal lords and papal forces. The Grand Lithuanian Princedom, with Russian assistance, successfully rebuffed the onslaught of the German feudal lords. Polish princedoms also received effective assistance from Russia.

Russo-Byzantine contacts had since time immemorial been a substantial factor behind the development of Eastern Europe. The two countries maintained lively trade, and their cultures were thus mutually enriched. Russia was baptized on the Byzantine model, which was a major contribution to the two countries' contacts. Assisted by the Galich and other old Russian princedoms, Byzantium fought against the Pechenegi and Seljuk Turks.

In the early thirteenth century the Golden Horde forces invaded Russia. In 1223 the Russian army was defeated in the Battle of Kalka River by the Mongol detachments. In 1226 the Horde, led by Khan Batyi, again overran Russia. By 1240 the whole of Russia languished under the yoke of the Golden Horde. This process was accompanied by the introduction of a ramified network of oppression and exploitation. The political structure of Russian princedoms was undermined, with the consequent economic enslavement of the Russian people, devastation of towns, degradation of handicrafts, etc. Outstanding monuments of Russian culture and art were destroyed in the course of the Golden Horde's invasion and scores of towns were burned down with the result that the external relations of Russian princedoms were cut short and trade between Russia and other countries came to a standstill.

The situation went from bad to worse with Sweden's seizure of Finland and Western Karelia, leaving Russia cut off from the Baltic Sea. At the same time Russian princedoms lost their positions in the Volga and the Black Sea areas. Contacts were no longer maintained with Central Asia and the Caucasus. The pressure exerted by the papal forces, German feudal lords and the Teutonic Order on Russian lands has already been mentioned. Although in the 1240s the Teutonic troops were defeated, that had not put an end to their attempts at capturing Russia's western lands. As a result Russia found itself in a sad plight in the early fourteenth century. In essence, it had been hurtled many decades backwards in its economic and social development, and its political consolidation was delayed.

As noted above, Russia and the other peoples living in the areas bordering on Europe served as buffers against the nomadic raids. During the fourteenth century their mission was carried out on an even broader scale. There were two aspects to it. First, the Golden Horde's strength had been thoroughly undermined in the battles against Russia. In 1241 the Horde detachments overran Poland and captured Krakow, then the Polish army was defeated at Lignica and the Horde moved on to Hungary, overran it and reached Croatia. Many European cities were then panic-stricken. England and France also went in fear of the Horde's invasion. However, the Horde's strength had been exhausted by its incessant advance and by the battles it had been fighting for many years against Russian troops. Thus, by having borne the brunt of the Horde's main blow the nascent Russian power, which had been operating within the system of European states, in fact protected the rest of Europe.

This is what Valery Bryusov, an outstanding twentieth-century Russian poet, wrote about it in his expressive and precise style:

> Russia! In Batyi's evil days,
> Wasn't that you who built a dam
> To the Mongol flood?
> Who, languishing under the yoke
> Of slavery, saved Europe
> From Genghis Khan's oppression?

The second aspect related to the removal of that threat. In spite of their dwindling strength, the nomads lorded it over Russian territory and still posed a threat to the whole of Europe. Although internecine strife prevented Russian princes from overthrowing the Golden Horde's yoke, the Russian people's resistance was mounting all the time. The unification of Russian lands that had started around Moscow, ushered in a new stage in the history of the Russian state. In 1380 the Horde was at last defeated in the Battle of Kulikovo Field, which touched off the process of Russia's liberation and that of the whole of Eastern Europe.

In essence it was a matter of removing the threat of aggression against the whole of Europe. Although Moscow was ravaged by Khan Tokhtamysh's troops in 1382 and the Golden Horde from time to time renewed its attempts at an offensive on Russia, on the whole the

Horde was losing its strength and soon disintegrated into a number of khanates. 1480 was the last year of the Horde's rule in Russia. This historic event was associated with the process of unification of Russian lands around Moscow, which culminated in the establishment of the Russian centralized state.

Consequently, by the late fifteenth century Russia had carried out its second mission by having finally overthrown the Golden Horde's yoke and thereby completely removing its threat to Europe. That threat was removed in East Europe, not outside it, by a state which previously had been developing approximately on a par with other European states.

The Horde's invasion set Russia centuries back in its development and, naturally, this could not but handicap its further development. It was then that synchronism and asymmetry with Europe in its development were born and, just as at the present time, there were grounds to speak about Russia's backwardness and the difference between it and Europe.

Historical experience shows and proves that social development has never been synchronous or simultaneous. Difference and variety of form are inevitable even within the framework of the same community. The same rule applies to Europe. The view of Europe as a community presupposes due account being taken of different forms and periods of the formation of some social process or other, so this community can hardly be uniform. In this case backwardness in some sphere is compensated for by advances made in another. It should be stressed that all this was happening within the framework of the emerging European communities and all-European realities that were connected with the specific of Europe's western and eastern parts, to which the religious schism added to no small extent.

Vladimir Pashuto, a Soviet historian, wrote in his study *Ancient Rus in the History of Europe*:

> Old Rus played an outstanding part in the shaping of Europe's political map; it was making an active contribution to the people's struggle against Arab, Byzantine and German domination; it bore the main brunt of attacks by Turkic nomads; finally, the victory of Rus, and the Russian people in their fight against the crusade of six powers, which coincided with the Mongol invasion, proved to be a turning point in Europe's historical destiny.

All the above-mentioned processes do not make the Russia–Europe problem less complicated in view of the fact that Russia had been

12

maintaining permanent contacts with the Asian continent. In ethnic and political respects, it was a state whose territory stretched over vast expanses in Europe and Asia and, consequently, it reflected both continents' special development features as well as the lifestyles and mentalities of the peoples.

The late fifteenth and sixteenth centuries saw a renaissance of the Russian people, the establishment and consolidation of its statehood and political system, the rehabilitation and development of its economy, its spiritual and cultural renaissance and the creation of an active Russian policy on the international scene.

In the fifteenth to seventeenth centuries there was much in common, just as before, in the socio-political processes that were under way in Russia and Western Europe. According to studies by Soviet historians, this similarity could be observed in many spheres of spiritual culture and political thought. In particular, there was a certain similarity in the reformation projects of Ivan Peresvetov, Feder Karpov and Yermolai-Erasm, on the one hand, and Thomas More's *Utopia*, on the other. The activity of Feodosi Kosoi, a most radical critic of the Orthodox faith and Christian dogma as a whole, was conducted in contact with Reformation circles in Poland, Lithuania, Switzerland, Italy, Germany and other countries. The activities of Maxim the Greek and Quirin Kumman served as a connecting link in the development of socio-political thought in Russia and Western Europe. There was much in common in the ideas that were put forward in the course of popular movements in Western and Eastern Europe.

So no matter how original the historical and cultural development of the Russian state was in the fifteenth and seventeenth centuries, it went on in close contact with other European regions and states. At the same time, the influence of the East and its traditions, the schism in the Christian Church and the Byzantine influence, in combination with the horrible aftermath of the Tatar–Mongol oppression, had produced a specific type of Russian organization and Russian culture. Slowly but surely Russia was making up for the damage through its desire to catch up with the general development of European states and peoples which was most vividly manifested during the reign of Peter the Great. However, Russia's general backwardness compared with the level of European development determined Russia's future for many ages that followed, and affected its political and economic development.

The period of the Enlightenment proved a most important stage in the evolution of the European idea. The problem of future reforms in Europe was discussed in many treatises of the late seventeenth to early nineteenth centuries in close interconnection with the ideas of democracy and people's power, social charters and freedom and the issues of war and peace. Moreover, it was precisely the problems of war and peace underlying many Enlightenment projects that paved the way for the elaboration of legal norms and the analysis of the political aspects of war and peace. Many ideas that were later borrowed by European political thinkers in the nineteenth and twentieth centuries were first formulated in the theories of the Enlightenment period. Characteristically, the ideas of the Enlightenment, no matter in which European country they originated, had much in common. The same subjects and ideas frequently appear in the works of Abbé Saint-Pierre and Jean-Jacques Rousseau in France, William Penn in England, Immanuel Kant, Johann von Herder and Johann Fichte in Germany, and Vassili Malinovsky, Yakov Kozelsky and Semyon Desnitsky in Russia.

It should be noted that the ideas of Enlightenment in Russia were formed within the general framework of trends which were also typical of the West European Enlightenment movement. The process of mutual influence and exchange of ideas in Europe occurred at an accelerated pace, becoming a permanent factor of European history. Although there were special national features, attributable to the asynchronous nature of social development and the special features of the people's cultural-historical traditions, in the European peace projects of the Enlightenment period, there was a certain similarity in the main aspects and trends. The ideas of Enlightenment represented a general European phenomenon, thus showing the common destiny and traditions of the European nations.

Almost all treatises on and projects for eternal peace in the Enlightenment period suggested setting up all-European bodies that would guarantee peace on the continent. Some authors gave only vague descriptions of such bodies, while others supplied full details for their structure and function, as well as the mechanism for their formation and activity.

Those plans may be assessed in various ways. Some of them were of a general humanistic/philosophic nature, whereas others were of an openly pragmatic nature and included ideas and plans that were meant to ensure privileges and advantages for some European countries at the expense of others. Nevertheless, most of the proposals were based on recognition of the rights and sovereignty of national states. Humanistic projects associated common European principles and a desire for peace with a fundamental social restructuring on the entire continent. This trend was further developed in the nineteenth century in the practical activities of revolutionary and liberation movements, the ideas of revolutionary democrats and socialist theories, and in the numerous European projects planned by the liberal bourgeoisie.

Although subsequent historical development revealed the utopian and unrealistic nature of many of the plans to reform European society and establish universal peace, the contribution of Enlightenment thinkers to the humanistic traditions of the peace movement on the European continent is quite clear.

The victory of the French revolution ushered in a new stage of development in the European idea. Indeed theories and plans that were formed at the turn of the eighteenth century have largely determined the destiny of Europe in the nineteenth and twentieth centuries. We will now concentrate on these centuries to show the evolution of thought on an all-European scale, the formation of Europeanism and the way this was received in Russia, how these trends were accommodated in the general European context and what hot debate and discussions were triggered off in Russian society by the words 'Russia and Europe'.

The topicality of those issues and the great interest shown in those periods today are attributable to the fact that throughout the twentieth century, up to the present time, we have been confronted with the same problems. On such problems hinge Russia's future and Europe's destiny and they are closely associated with the question of a European civilization and cultural heritage. However, it also includes the issues of the continent's security, war and peace in Europe, and European responsibility for a possible split in Europe or for its unity.

An in-depth analysis of Europe in the nineteenth and twentieth centuries may offer many arguments and lessons to help understand the Europe of today and may supply answers to questions about what the future has in store for Europeans at the turn of the twentieth century.

Present-day developments are a fresh warning that humankind should learn the lessons of history. Society must realize that it cannot possibly develop without looking back at the experience of the past, at its own history.

2

THE FRENCH REVOLUTION AND EUROPE

In the seventeenth and eighteenth centuries Europe was shaken by several bourgeois revolutions. The English revolution of the mid-seventeenth century and the French Revolution of the late eighteenth century revealed one of the most remarkable regularities of European development. The similarity of socio-economic and political develop-ment processes in Western, Central and Eastern Europe had deter-mined similar revolutionary action in various European countries.

The nature and motive forces of revolutionary processes, typical of the whole of Europe, were especially vividly manifested in the align-ment of political and international forces in Europe during the period of bourgeois revolutions. Attempts at establishing a certain social 'equilibrium' in feudal Europe was a typical feature of 'the European equilibrium' that was attained in the seventeenth and eighteenth centuries, with any changes in this 'equilibrium' leading to clashes between 'new' and 'old' forces. In the European revolutions this was apparent in the establishment of counter-revolutionary alliances and coalitions spearheaded against revolutionary changes in Europe.

The seventeenth-century English revolution was the first revolution to have reverberations all over Europe. Its distinctive features were then perceived in the French Revolution, as well as in revolutionary battles fought in Europe in later periods.

Having carried out its mission in world and European history, the English revolution failed to polarize forces on an all-European scale. On the one hand, no consolidation of revolutionary forces took place on the continent. Although we know about the reverberations the English revolution had in other countries, Europe as a whole was not yet ready for a bourgeois revolution. On the other hand, the English revolution failed to provoke any consolidation of European feudal reactionary forces either. Those forces had not united in an effort

16

to rebuff the English bourgeoisie which was gaining in stature and represented, on a broader scale, a trend for the triumph of the bourgeoisie system throughout Europe. However, the English ruling circles managed to curb the revolutionary forces and later forced them to take a rather limited course.

A radically different picture was observed in Europe in the late eighteenth century, when the French Revolution broke out. Its ideas and practice had a great impact both on European political thought (including Russia's) and on the specific course of historical development in Europe. Here we will look exclusively at aspects which influenced the evolution of the European idea.

Some of the problems associated with the French Revolution and central to it consisted of the establishment of new and revolutionary institutions, principles and norms of international law and a realignment of political forces in Europe and throughout the world. Many theories and projects of the period concentrated on the substantiation of the republic and a republican form of government.

The source of many of the new ideas and concepts of the time may be found in writings by the great French thinkers Voltaire and Montesquieu and others of the eighteenth-century Enlightenment, while Jean-Jacques Rousseau was the true spiritual father of the revolutionary ideals, with his ideas of a social treaty, his interpretation of 'common will' and his stress on the primary role to be played by 'ordinary people'. The notion of national sovereignty was also formulated in this period. Proceeding from those basic postulates, ideologists of the French Revolution immediately tried to formulate new laws and principles for international relations.

The most consistent ideologists of the French Revolution regarded it from the outset as the beginning of a European revolutionary process. Hence the calls by prominent leaders of the first revolutionary stage for the need to spread the revolutionary process, started in France, to other countries. The old idea of 'sister-revolutions', put forward by Helvetius in his time, became very popular in the 1780s–90s. Along with this, universalist ideas were canvassed in every possible way and attempts were made to introduce new norms of international law and new rules for relations between peoples. Interpretation of the issues of war and peace was closely bound up with an understanding of the continent-wide importance of the French Revolution and its ideologists' desire to stimulate development of the revolutionary process in other European countries.

It should be remembered, however, that the revolutionary camp was far from homogeneous. The split in the revolutionary forces

17

during the subsequent revolutionary stages had an immediate effect on the attitude of various political forces and parties to the issues of war and peace, to revolutions in other countries, to the formulation of legal principles and norms, as well as to universalist ideas and concepts.

All monarchists and opponents of the Revolution staked their hopes on the possibility that the war France was waging against other European states would lead to the collapse of the revolutionary forces as a result of the protracted nature of that war. In their turn, the Girondists, who heeded the French revolutionary forces in the first stage of the Revolution, were energetic advocates of war in the hope that it would help trigger off revolutions in other countries. On the other hand, moderate revolutionary leaders staked their hopes on war for entirely different reasons, since they planned to divert the revolutionary energy of the masses and lower classes out of France, thus distracting their attention from domestic affairs and avoiding excessive radicalization.

However, the situation was clearly changing as the Revolution entered a new stage. Jacobins led by Maximilien Robespierre, were firm opponents of wars of aggression. Robespierre denounced such wars and advocated peace. The newspaper *Revolutions de Paris* urged the revolutionary masses not to lose time in establishing in France the reign of law and freedom in order to strengthen peace, which was needed by foreign countries and by themselves.

Thus, the political thought of the French Revolution was far from unanimous on the issues of war and peace. The clashes of theories and actual political practice reflected the interests of various groups and parties involved in the Revolution and the degree of pressure exerted by the masses. Universalism was manifested in the desire to spread the ideas and goals of the French Revolution to other European countries, presenting them as a demonstration of common human needs and man's right to freedom from tyranny and oppression. At the same time, there were substantial nuances and shades in this general programme, and even contradictory propositions, reflecting the interests of various social strata, political parties and groups, a situation which gave rise to a number of contradictory trends in the revolutionary process. It was due to this that the effect of the French Revolution on Europe's development in the nineteenth and twentieth centuries was highly variegated, and often went in mutually exclusive directions.

The universal nature and worldwide importance of the French Revolution was based on its leaders' conviction, the philosophical and

18

legal concepts of humanity's unity, as well as on the idea that 'liberty, equality and fraternity' are the birthright of citizens not only of France but also of other countries. One of the declarations adopted by the French National Assembly proclaimed that

> humanity is regarded as a united community whose goal is peace and the welfare of all its members and of each person; that in this large united community, peoples and states are regarded as individuals who enjoy equal and natural rights and are governed by the same legal norms as individuals; that, as a consequence, not a single person has either the right to lay claim to other people's property or deny them freedom and normal means of assistance; that each military action, undertaken for some other reason and purpose than upholding a just cause, is an act of violence that should be rejected by the whole of society, since aggression by one state against another creates a threat to the freedom and safety of all. (*The French Bourgeois Revolution, 1789–1799*, Moscow-Leningrad, 1941, p.453)

The 1791 French Constitution stated unequivocally that 'the French nation renounces the idea of any wars of aggression and shall never direct its weapons against some other nation's freedom'.

The events of the French Revolution testify clearly that its leaders had no intention of imposing it by force or violence on other nations. Robespierre said that revolutionary principles should be spread through the triumph of reason, not by force of arms. The foreign policy pursued by the First French Republic was evidence of this. The Republic reaffirmed its loyalty to the country's existing treaties and its respect for the territories and interests of other countries. To oppose the policy aimed at suppressing the revolution and establishing anti-republican coalitions, the National Convention set out its programme, the essence of which was explained to other countries and peoples on 5 December 1793:

> Peoples, if you are unable to make your contribution to the national wealth, if you are as yet unable to make use of the rights, restored to you by us, take care at least not to violate our rights or calumniate our courage. French people are by no means obsessed with the idea of making some nation free and happy against its will. All kings might well have hibernated or died on their blood-stained thrones had they shown respect for the French people's independence. (Ibid., p.454)

19

Progressive ideologists of the period formulated the ideal of 'people's sovereignty', the rights of man and citizen and the principle of 'the division of powers', among others, which were expressed in the Declaration of the Rights of Man and Citizen (August 1789) and the 1791 and 1793 Constitutions. Drawn up at the height of the Revolution, at a time of major social upheavals – a period of humanity's transition to a new socio-economic system – they reflected the way the new revolutionary strata saw the world and Europe.

The distinction of the eighteenth-century French Revolution is the fact that it revealed a revolutionary passion of a greater degree than all previous or many subsequent revolutions did and that the interests, views and ideas of the masses influenced to some extent the course of the Revolution and many of its events and legislative acts. That is why that epoch's documents are permeated with a great spirit of democracy and served as a basis for many new democratic international laws.

Many of the principles of the French Revolution (including those fixed in the Declaration of the Rights of Man and Citizen) served as a basis and a point of departure for various nineteenth- and twentieth-century European theories. Numerous subsequent concepts, having for their goal the unification of Europe, were proclaimed by their proponents on the social and geographical plane (largely in a West European version) as the projection of the ideas and practice of the French Revolution of the late eighteenth century.

The heritage of the French Revolution on the issues of war and peace is highly variegated. Before the Revolution, war was largely viewed as an indispensable tool for the solution of dynastic disputes, the enlargement of a state's territory and the preservation of what had been established, particularly in Europe in the seventeenth and eighteenth centuries, with monarchs posing as supreme judges and arbitrators. They usurped the right of decision-making on all issues, including those of war and peace. For instance, in the wars for the Spanish and Austrian successions Frederick II, Louis XIV, Catherine II and Charles V did not bother to look for any legal pretexts to start military operations. However, the French Revolution introduced entirely new principles of international law. Decrees dated 22–27 May 1790 stated that

> any war, waged for purposes and goals other than the protection of a just cause, is an act of oppression which should be

suppressed by any great society, for the invasion of some state by another creates a threat to the freedom and security of all.

Article VI of the 1791 Constitution declared: 'Humankind is a united community whose goal is the peace and happiness of all and each of its members.'

Two years later the Convention further specified the principles of international law, among which, I would stress, are the independence and sovereignty of the people (irrespective of the strength of the population and size of the territory), non-interference in the affairs and government of other states and peoples, the right to wage just wars and to uphold a country's sovereignty, freedom and property, and the inviolability of treaties and agreements.

New principles and norms of international law by the leaders of the French Revolution were regarded in later epochs as universalist principles regulating the rules of existence throughout the world, especially on the European continent. Thus was formed the tradition of interdependence between the problems of revolution and the issues of war and peace, and also the beginning of the idea of European unity. However, revolutionary France operated within national boundaries so it had never given itself the task of setting up other revolutionary governments in Europe. Neither were there any illusions nourished about possible major changes in other European states. Proponents of the French Revolution were more concerned with laying the foundations for traditions that would be developed in the future. Traditions stemming from the French Revolution were especially vividly manifested in the second half of the nineteenth century, when the principles of the eighteenth century were resorted to at numerous peace congresses and served as a means and an argument to prove that the way to peace in Europe lay through versions of the continent's unification.

The period of the French Revolution was marked by a polarization of forces, parties and states elsewhere in Europe, a polarization that gradually assumed a regular place in European development. The first anti-revolutionary coalition was formed which set itself the task of barring the way to revolution in other countries and, moreover, of putting down the French Revolution. It should be stressed that this was an attempt to create a *European* counter-revolutionary alliance rather than just some private initiative by individual European powers or governments.

In July 1791, Austria and Russia signed an agreement on joint action against revolutionary France; at the same time King Leopold II of Prussia sent a message to many European monarchs with an offer to convene a pan-European congress for the purpose of launching armed intervention in France. However, these plans came to naught because of the wait-and-see policy pursued by England and Russia (which, however, did not prevent Catherine II from approving the plans to suppress the French Revolution).

A year later, in 1792, an Austrian–Prussian treaty against revolutionary France was signed. Characteristically, the struggle against revolutionary France was not the only aim pursued by the signatories to the treaty, for they were also planning to expand their territory at the expense of France. In later periods, too, European powers have combined their fight against revolutionary and liberation movements with far-reaching plans for redrawing the map both of Europe and of its colonies.

The development of the revolutionary process in France and the downfall of the monarchy in August 1792 produced considerable activity among the counter-revolutionary forces. This time British Prime Minister William Pitt (the Younger) was the mastermind behind the anti-French coalition, which also included Austria, Prussia, Spain, Holland, Russia and a number of minor states.

European monarchs were increasingly concerned about the show of sympathy for the ideas and events of the French Revolution from many regions of Europe. Democratic circles in England and Russia were stepping up their activities and by this time French revolutionary forces, which acted under the motto 'Peace to huts, war to palaces', were advancing through Belgium, where most of the population openly sympathized with the revolutionary reforms.

However, developments in France were drawing to their tragic end. The policy of terror conducted by Robespierre and his associates to suppress counter-revolution backfired on the revolution's supporters. Mass reprisals were launched against thousands of people, with all norms and legal principles violated. As a result the masses lost all their illusions about the revolutionary authorities. Eventually the Jacobins found themselves in a political vacuum, which was soon taken advantage of by counter-revolutionaries.

In general, the problem of terror has come to be regarded on a broader, European and even a world-wide scale. Terror as a form and method of settling social and other conflicts was widely used in Europe in the nineteenth and (especially) the twentieth centuries. In this sense the negative experience of the French Revolution has left a sad trace in the history of Europe.

The 1799 counter-revolutionary coup that catapulted Napoleon

Bonaparte into power led to sharp changes in France's foreign policy, with the result that France started making attempts to establish domination in Europe.

The period of the French Revolution revealed the dialectic of the European revolutionary process. Placed on the agenda then was the issue of correlation between national and international tasks. The issues of correlation between national interests and supranational goals were raised in an atmosphere of complicated interaction of social and political forces and clashes between domestic and international interests. The French Revolution dealt a mighty blow to the social status quo in Europe in the seventeenth and eighteenth centuries. The European feudal monarchist, reactionary forces set themselves exclusively the task of restoring the former equilibrium and preventing the establishment of the revolutionary forces' power in France and other countries.

The importance of the French Revolution for Europe lay in the fact that during this time the essential principles of democracy, freedom and human rights were formulated and proclaimed. It may be safely stated that civic society and a rule-of-law state were formed in Europe on the basis of the norms, laws and principles adopted in the course of the French Revolution.

It was after the French Revolution that Europeanism assumed its basic principles such as human rights, sovereignty, freedom and democracy. Those principles have occupied an important and stable place in the development of Europeanist social and political thought, and are associated with the triumph of the freedoms, rights and obligations of an individual, of a civic society and of a rule-of-law state.

In later epochs, while putting forward various projects for Europe's unification, European democratic circles turned to the ideas and practice of the eighteenth-century French Revolution. One may, of course, speak about the contradictory and inconsistent nature of the revolutionary leaders' activities, about the fact that its gains were later renounced in the policies of France and other European countries, but even in those tumultuous years the liberation movement turned to revolutionary ideas. And in the decades of the nineteenth and twentieth centuries, too, the principles of people's power and sovereignty, human and civic rights, democratic laws and legal norms have served as a mighty inspiration to supporters of democratic reforms and of Europeanist concepts. Therein lies the eternal significance of the ideas and practice of the French Revolution for Europe and the whole world.

At the turn of the eighteenth century Europeanism was taking shape and for many subsequent decades it exerted great influence on European political thought and the activity of philosophers, historians, politicians and public leaders who were devoted to the idea of a united Europe and who were inspired by the ideas of freedom and human rights.

The French Revolution and its ideas also had a considerable effect on Russian public thought, which we shall discuss after an analysis of European developments in the period of Napoleon's rule.

3

NAPOLEON'S VERSION OF THE UNIFICATION OF EUROPE

The epoch of Napoleon's rule gave birth to a new version of the realization of the European idea. This time the issue in question was an attempt to conquer and subordinate European countries by force of arms, thus 'unifying' it. During the Middle Ages the Catholic Church had toyed with the idea of subordinating Europe to the theocratic design of papal power. Later, during the period of the emergence and consolidation of European statehood, projects had been put forward to introduce national (to be more precise, French) domination, incarnated in the Great Project of Henri IV and the duc de Sully.

It might have been thought that the practice of the French Revolution and the ideas of equality and brotherhood would put an end to such designs, but history proves differently. On coming to power in France, the bourgeoisie sought to realize the project of Henri IV. Paradoxically enough, liberation and just wars were transformed into aggressive ones, and the ideas of brotherhood into hegemonistic designs. Napoleon's 'great' experiment showed that the French bourgeoisie was not prepared to fight for European domination in alliance with the feudal nobility. The winds of change of the French Revolution were followed by the Napoleonic Wars which, in their train, carried slavery to the peoples of Europe.

Much is known about the details of the Napoleonic Wars, but what we are more concerned with is Napoleon's vision of Europe, that is to what extent and how Napoleon wanted to 'unify' a conquered Europe. It should be pointed out that while acting as the French Emperor and achieving his aim of European domination, Napoleon said almost nothing about it in public. He rectified this only much later, *post factum* so to speak, when he was in exile on the island of St Helena.

So let us first examine the facts. The Peace of Amiens in 1802 indicated that Napoleon had started implementing his project, called Greater France, which presupposed the establishment of sister-republics (to use Helvetius's words) around France. In fact, these were really to become satellite-states, Italy and Holland being the first. The years 1805–6 saw Napoleon's victories over Austria and Russia. At that time European countries were being literally transformed by Napoleon into sister-republics – the imperial domain of his family, with Napoleon proclaimed as King of Italy and Eugène de Beauharnais as viceroy. Jérôme, Napoleon's second brother, was appointed King of Westphalia, and his third brother, Louis, King of Holland. Joachim Murat, who had married Napoleon's sister, became the King of Naples, and Joseph Bonaparte, King of Spain. Ironically enough, all these 'sister-states' in no way resembled republics. Just like France, they were ruled by imperial or royal authority. Napoleon's relations, who occupied the thrones, acted more like regents, ruling on behalf of, and to the glory of, the Emperor.

Apart from the kingdoms ruled by Napoleon's relations, the so-called allied states were formed, such as the Grand Dukedom of Warsaw, the Confederation of Rhine States and the Imperial Provinces in France. However, France was by no means dwarfed into insignificance by these: it held the central place in the vast Empire. Napoleon wrote to his sister, Murat's wife, that everything should be done for the welfare of France and that France should be offered every privilege.

In 1809–10 Napoleon transformed many of the conquered states into ordinary provinces, so that Portugal, Spain, Holland and the Illyrian Provinces found themselves totally subordinate to France. Napoleon's Empire now stretched from the Baltic to the Black Sea. In fact, the whole of Europe, except Russia and England (the latter being regarded by Napoleon as situated outside Europe), found itself under the thumb of France. Any slight difference in the status and names of the once independent European states was really of little consequence.

The French army, many thousands strong, which invaded Russia in 1812 seemed like the incarnation of Napoleon's hegemonistic plans. Apart from Frenchmen, the army incorporated military units from all the European countries conquered by Napoleon. The formation of a joint imperial army served as the main feature of the unification imposed by Napoleon on Europe, but its multinational composition only emphasized its temporary nature. Foreign units fought against their will and with minimum effort and, of course, never missed an opportunity to desert from the *Grande Armée*. The Emperor did not manage to introduce any unity into his armed forces

26

largely because, first, the soldiers had no stake in the goals of the Napoleonic Wars and, second, those soldiers came from countries and represented peoples who had been conquered by the French army, so they could not help viewing their oppressors with hostility.

However, Napoleon's unification of Europe was not confined to the formation of a multinational army. The Emperor planned to make his Code, then effective in France, the law for the whole of Europe, but that was easier said than done. The subjugated countries and allied states had their own laws, customs and legal and moral norms. They were united only by their subjugation to the same authority, in the person of the Emperor, and, in essence, that 'unity' was neither stable nor lasting. Moreover, it was a permanent source of hatred for foreign domination and the danger of liberation movements against the invaders was omnipresent.

Napoleon had quite definite plans for reforms in Europe, but before the reforms he had to complete the conquest. Neither the Emperor nor his associates concealed the fact that Russia was the main obstacle to the establishment of French domination in Europe. One may safely state that it was to be after the conquest of Russia that Napoleon planned to have the final settlement of the issues of European reform and unification. The débâcle of Napoleon's army in Russia and the subsequent liberation of European peoples from Napoleon's oppression completely thwarted the plan for Europe's unification by force and violence.

While in exile after his defeat, Napoleon recollected his original project of reforms for Europe and his vision of a post-reform Europe. The *Supplementary Act to the Constitution of the Empire* by Benjamin Constant was published in Paris in the period of the Hundred Days. According to some sources, the Preamble to the Act was written by Napoleon himself and stated:

> Our goal was to set up a vast federative European system that would, as we believed, correspond to the spirit of the century and promote progress and civilization. To improve that system and make it widespread and stable, we set up some intrapolitical institutions, especially in order to uphold the citizens' freedom. (*Les Constitutions de la France*, Paris, 1925, p.190)

After the final collapse of the Empire, while in exile on St Helena, Napoleon on many occasions analysed in restrospect the goals and details of his project. In one of his many talks with his friend, Las Cases, Napoleon said that if his Russian campaign had ended in victory, he would have stopped all military actions and operations. After that, Napoleon averred, he would have set about establishing a pan-European system that would have been much like a holy alliance. The ex-Emperor mentioned in this context his former intentions to draft a single pan-European Code, to set up a Court of Appeal and to introduce a uniform monetary system and a universal system of weights and measures. Europe, he believed, would have become a united nation, so that travellers would have felt at home wherever they went.

Napoleon asserted that one of his greatest ideas was the unification and concentration of all peoples who geographically belonged to the same nation, but who were later fragmented for political reasons. About 15 million French people, 15 million Italians and 30 million Germans lived in Europe at that time, and all of them, according to Napoleon's project, were to form a united nation. He believed it would then be possible to set about working on the project of setting up a community of European peoples in an organization that would be something like the United States Congress or the Chamber of Judges of the Greek amphictyons.

So, Napoleon dreamt about a united Europe, formed on a confederal basis, with a common system of legislation, a uniform monetary system, united armed forces, and so on. His Europe, however, was to be ruled by an Emperor. Back in 1809, Prince Metternich had outlined a picture of the Europe of the future as seen by Napoleon. This Europe would have to undergo common reforms, with the central government, acting as the supreme authority, exerting pressure on its subjects: a subjugated Spain, an Ottoman Empire placed beyond the Bosporus Strait, the Great French Empire stretching from the Baltic to the Black Sea, with Russia squeezed out of Europe into Asia. From Napoleon's notes and his talks with Las Cases it is clear that the ambitious French Emperor had dreamed about European domination. On many occasions he put himself on a par with George Washington.

Naturally, the truth of Napoleon's confessions after the collapse of his Empire should not be taken for granted, although his project for setting up a European federation under his thumb is, of course, a fact beyond any doubt.

Napoleon's advent to power was at first welcomed by many of his contemporaries, among them Hegel, Goethe and other European philosophers and cultural figures. A French journalist wrote in 1802 that ideas that were then born in France paved the way for the realization of the Great Project of Henri IV. References to Henri IV were also to be found in a work by H. Vogt, a German historian, published in 1806. Vogt wrote that Napoleon and his main adversary, Russian Tsar Alexander I, might sign a bilateral treaty and thus play the part that Henri IV had laid claim to.

A. Zinzerling, a German lawyer, offered in 1809 to set up a political confederation of European states that would create a sort of allied state – a monarchy with the French Emperor at the head. The project, put forward by Karl Christian Friedrich Krause, a German philosopher, was also widely known. His idea was to set up a world system with the French Emperor as its motive force. Krause held very conservative, mystical religious views, fundamentally different from the humanistic projects of the European Enlightenment. Krause's main work was entitled *A Prototype of Humanity* but in his book *The Alliance of Humanity* (1801) he asserted that it was in France that the process of the regeneration of society had been started which would eventually lead to the unification of all European nations into a single state. Later, Krause even more definitely associated the realization of his ideas with Napoleon and the future 'world state' to be set up by him. He was completely in accord with the Emperor's project and served as its theoretical substantiation.

Thus, the French Emperor's actions and his later statements and recollections, just like works by various philosophers and public leaders, clearly testify that universalist ideas had been regenerated in Europe. In this case they meant a new version of European unity with unification by force and violence.

Meanwhile, the epoch of consolidation of national states had a great impact on the essence and nature of European universalism for the idea of a federal system – a prototype of the United States of Europe – was born, although the federation or confederation was conceived as French dominated. It was inevitable that Napoleon and his associates often recalled the Great Project of Henri IV, based on the idea of French domination in Europe.

Napoleon's plans and policy stood in glaring opposition to the European realities of the seventeenth and eighteenth centuries: a system of national states had been set up in Europe and a certain political balance had been achieved on the international scene. The Napoleonic Wars and French domination had exploded that system, although they were, in a certain sense, a result of the notorious 'European balance'.

The Napoleonic Wars and the imperial practice as a whole pro-voked resistance by the European peoples. National awareness was ever growing in various parts of Europe in opposition to the uni-versalist ideas, and that nascent trend assumed a pronounced anti-

29

French nature in the first decade of the eighteenth century. Experience shows that an attempt at introducing one-nation domination in Europe (that of France) and the idea of Europe's unification on the model and by will of that state lead nowhere.

In the course of the anti-Napoleonic campaign, the designs of the European monarchist reaction to bring to nought the results of the French Revolution and restore the former feudal system were in full accord with the mood of national exclusiveness and superiority that was gaining currency among the bourgeoisie and nobility in a number of European countries – in opposition to the idea of French domination. German philosopher Johann Herder said back in 1792 that the French could not possibly be regarded as a 'chosen people', and in the early nineteenth century, his compatriot, O. Schlegel, wrote quite definitely that Germany was the heart of Europe, a young and powerful nation. The unification of Germany, he believed, had to become a prelude to 'a large continental association'.

Austria regarded the collapse of the Napoleonic Empire as a prerequisite for the restoration of Austrian domination in south-east and southern Europe. It was, however, hardly possible to combine the ideas of nationalism and national feelings with the Austrian Empire, for this patchwork Hapsburg domain, with numerous nationalities incorporated in it, was then being swept by popular movements which were fighting against Austrian oppression.

Napoleon's project met with strong opposition in England and Russia, two of Europe's leading states. France in the revolutionary epoch and Napoleon's rule were viewed as a mortal threat by those countries' ruling circles, as an enemy that threatened the feudal monarchist regimes in Europe. A supreme authority, usurped by Napoleon's Empire, and the enslavement of Europe posed a threat to the position of England. Although Napoleon did not regard England as part of Europe, which was, he believed, confined to the continent, nevertheless, he planned, after having brought Europe to its knees, to limit Britain's influence and power substantially and challenge its position as 'the ruler of the seas'.

As for Russia, Napoleon intended to conquer it and incorporate its territory in his future European Empire. Las Cases in his notes, mentioned above, wrote about the Emperor's idea that a victory at Moscow would have laid the foundations of the system he, Napoleon, had planned to establish.

Thus, it may be said that, according to many parameters and because of various aspects of the European idea, Napoleon's plans and specific actions ran counter to the objective course of Europe's development. Napoleon's 'experiment' and his attempt to establish French domination in Europe only led to the unification of the European states which had varying goals and intentions. On many points, the ambitions of Metternich and Alexander I, the English king and the Prussian monarch hardly differed from the French Emperor's designs. However, while the intentions of the monarchist regimes were diametrically opposed to the liberation goals of the European peoples, all these contradictory factors were joined in a united anti-Napoleonic movement.

Although the French Emperor and his associates spoke about their plans for a European Federation or Confederation, in essence Napoleon's practical deeds hardly resembled the federal projects put forward by many seventeenth- and eighteenth-century thinkers or public leaders. A federation presupposes a certain level of development and independence of the states – its possible members – whereas Napoleon's goal, as we know, was quite different.

The years of Napoleon's imperial rule testify that his version of Europe's unification through prolonged wars ran counter to the interests of European peoples and states. This is why the Empire's collapse was logical and inevitable. The course of history has shown that this method of realizing the European idea was doomed to failure, for it involved aggression, conquest and encroachment on the freedom and sovereignty of countries and peoples, on an all-European scale. However, the idea of the unification of Europe by force and violence was not committed to oblivion, for an attempt at achieving it, as is known, was also made in the twentieth century.

4

EUROPE'S ENLIGHTENMENT

The epoch of Enlightenment and the French Revolution had great import for Russia. While comparing works by French, German, English and Russian writers of the Enlightenment, it should be noted that their views of the issues of war and peace mirrored a wide range of philosophic and socio-political ideas of the European Enlightenment. The epoch of Enlightenment, with its rapidly developing bourgeoisie, the crisis for the feudal system and the growth of popular movements, was an excellent breeding ground for new theories of social development. Public discussion was increasingly focused on the ideas of social treaty, the problems of people's power, democracy and freedom as well as on criticism of religion and church postulates.

The so-called 'peace problématique' was organically close to the wide range of ideas and views of the epoch of Enlightenment. This approach predetermined discussion of the issues of war and peace in the wide socio-historical context, in interconnection with socio-economic, political and ideological problems. Treatises by the Enlighteners of the seventeenth and eighteenth centuries laid down the European tradition for the interpretation of the issues of war and peace which exerted a substantial influence on the subsequent development of theoretical thought and on the nineteenth- and twentieth-century political practice of anti-war movements.

The interconnection between the ideas of Enlightenment and projects of the European idea may be traced in several trends. First, the ideas, specific plans and projects that were put forward were of a clear-cut, pan-European nature. The similarity of subjects and their specific elaboration in various treatises coming from France, Germany, England and Russia was a significant fact in itself. The ideas of Charles Saint-Pierre of France had much in common with those expressed by the Englishman William Penn. Immanuel Kant developed ideas which were in many respects much like the theories of Jean-Jacques Rousseau. The ideas of Russian Enlighteners were in much the same vein as those spread by West European Enlighteners. In other words, we are dealing here with a pan-European process. Naturally, European peace theories had clear-cut national features, attributable to the asynchronous nature of social development and to the special historical traditions and mental make-up of nationalities. Nevertheless, the similarity of the main trends is quite obvious. The ideas of Enlightenment on the issues of war and peace in the seventeenth to nineteenth centuries were a pan-European phenomenon, which revealed the common destinies and traditions of European peoples.

Second, practically almost all treatises and projects of eternal peace included proposals for setting up a pan-European mechanism. The establishment of peace and the provision of guarantees for it were visualized within the framework of pan-European bodies. Some authors only vaguely described such bodies, whereas others gave detailed descriptions of their function and mechanism. Thus, there was obvious interconnection between pan-European postulates and European supranational bodies, on the one hand, and the tasks of the elimination of wars and the establishment of peace in Europe, on the other.

Third, all treatises and plans presupposed the formation of a certain mechanism within the framework of that 'balance' or 'equilibrium' that could be observed in Europe in the seventeenth and eighteenth centuries and, as a rule, set themselves the task of consolidating the alignment of political forces on the continent or changing it in favour of some power or other or a coalition of states. Those treatises and schemes may be interpreted in various ways. Some of them were of a general humanitarian philosophic nature and reflected the desire of their author to put an end to conflict and war, whereas others were of an openly pragmatic nature and included proposals and plans to ensure privileges to some European countries at the expense of others.

Fourth, seventeenth- to eighteenth-century treatises and projects reflected the contradiction between the tendency for the consolidation of national states and the attempts at setting up supranational bodies with various spheres and ranges of power. An analysis of those plans and projects shows that all of them were based on a recognition of the rights and sovereignty of national states. Moreover, many authors laid special stress on the fact that their proposed pan-European bodies were not designed to infringe upon the powers and rights of European states. The dialectic of those contradictory processes and tendencies was typical of Europe even before this; it was also largely typical of the subsequent political development in Europe, including that of the twentieth century.

Fifth, one may assert that the treatises and plans dealing with the issues of war and peace in the seventeenth to nineteenth centuries testify to the existence of various views of the European idea. On the one hand, a humanitarian tradition was formed, which, while taking as its source the projects of Erasmus of Rotterdam and Jan Amos Komenski, eventually led to the radical proposals of Jean-Jacques Rousseau. This trend, which associated pan-European principles and striving for peace with far-reaching social reforms in European countries and on the entire continent, was further developed in the nineteenth century in the views of revolutionary democrats and in the practice of revolutionary and liberation movements. At the same time, however, a liberal-pragmatic trend emerged, which associated European development with an affirmation of the principles of liberalism and liberal democracy. In addition, a process was under way for the elaboration of European norms and principles and a codification of political and international affairs in Europe.

On the other hand, other developments revealed the contradictory nature of the ideology of the Enlightenment as a whole.

VASSILI MALINOVSKY'S EUROPEAN PROJECT

Vassili Malinovsky (1765–1814) was a prominent Russian Enlightener at the turn of the eighteenth century. For a number of years he held the post of director of the Tsarskoye Selo Lyceum, which was Alexander Pushkin's alma mater. Malinovsky's plan, contained in his *A Treatise of War and Peace*, holds a prominent place among those put forward by Russian Enlighteners. Malinovsky wrote it during the 1790s and it was published in St Petersburg in 1803. It provides clear evidence that Malinovsky had a thorough knowledge of Saint-Pierre's work (which had been published in Russia in 1771) and most probably of other similar projects of the period.

In its content, arguments and specific proposals, Malinovsky's work was similar to the treatises of the Enlightenment written in the West. His treatise opens with a section entitled 'The Habit of Waging Wars. Are They Necessary?' The author says that our habits make us look with indifference at things around us, and if we would only try to get rid of this indifference and take a 'realistic view' of war, we would be shocked by the horror and misfortunes it causes. War, the author believes, is a combination of the 'beastly ferocity' and the sophistication of human reason. By robbing people of calm, safety and welfare, war sooner or later leads to their 'complete downfall'. To support this idea, the author cites as examples the fates of Egypt, Greece, Rome, Carthage and many other states and nations which 'met their destruction through war'.

The author states from the outset that his treatise relates to Europe. He attributes this to the fact that Europe had achieved a degree of 'enlightenment and humanism which give it indisputable superiority over the other parts of the world'. In this context, he notes that wars might be justified in an era of barbarism, but they are in glaring contradiction to the era of Enlightenment. War is a great shortcoming to our enlightenment, Malinovsky concludes.

> Enlightenment should spread our views and prove to us that the welfare of each state is inseparable from the welfare of Europe ... Until Europeans, by a general popular decision no longer guarantee all their private advantages, they will always, just as now, make themselves and others unhappy.

Later Malinovsky puts forward a very important idea, saying:

> Europe has long been prepared for peace. The laws, customs and mores, science and trade unite its residents and make it a certain kind of special society. Even the languages, which separated some peoples from others, are not a formidable obstacle in the maintenance of contact by its residents; most of these languages have much in common and some of them may serve as common languages for Europeans ...
>
> Many of the Europeans have the same ancestors and almost all of them represent mixed nationalities. They should be ashamed of regarding one another as enemies ...
>
> It must be hoped that the happy time will come when Europe, as the one Fatherland of all its residents, is no longer tortured by wars. But why should we postpone this bliss? Why should we not put an end to the misfortunes of war now? Haven't we had enough of them? Or perhaps there are still people who regard war as useful?

All these observations serve the author's main goal – to prove that Europe was prepared for peace, for eliminating war from the lives of European peoples. If this were to happen, the name of the Europeans, Malinovsky believes, would evoke respect in all other parts of the world, and Europe would serve as a model for the other continents of our planet.

Malinovsky also discusses the arguments of those who believed that some European powers used wars to their advantage in order to expand their possessions and satisfy their ambitions – a problem which was raised in many writings and treatises. Malinovsky solves it in the spirit of all such works by writing at length about the fact that a state's might does not depend either on its area or on the size of its population. In this context he adduces historical examples, recollecting the times when Sweden belonged to Denmark and Portugal, the Netherlands and part of Italy belonged to Spain, and points out that this had not made them any stronger or more famous, although they possessed these vast territories. 'Acquisition of lands by means of wars is much like adding tall structures to low buildings, for they are out of proportion to the building's foundation. They fall down and the whole building is thus threatened with the danger of destruction.' The strength of the people who live in a given state, Malinovsky believes, is the main and most reliable strength of that state.

Of special interest is the section of the treatise that is devoted to the interdependence between the causes of wars and the specific policies of European states. In this section the author tries to divide wars into aggressive and defensive, and to establish the goals of European states, goals which, he believes, are concealed from the European peoples. While levelling criticism at the policies of monarchs and governments, Malinovsky stamps with ignominy those writers who encourage the people's hostility and protect the sophistry of politics. The author writes in conclusion to this section:

> History raises for us an impenetrable veil concealing its secrets. The main wars of the current century prove that the policy pursued in our day is perilous for the people's welfare, that the European powers have nothing stable in their policies, save for their desire to add to their strength and do harm, and for the bias shown by the peoples and those who govern them, that treaties are violated unashamedly, and that political alliances only contribute to the rapid outbreak of war and involve a great number of peoples in it.

Part 2 of Malinovsky's treatise deals with his proposal for eliminating wars and the establishment of peace in Europe. This part is of great interest, especially when compared with proposals put forward by West European authors. Section 1 of Part 2, entitled 'Nationwide Laws', opens with this sentence: 'Each state is independent, but it borders on another independent state.' Building on this idea, Malinovsky writes that

36

the introduction of nationwide rules or laws, and supervision of their observance, should not be regarded as interference in internal affairs and violation of sovereignty, for this can be done only by mutual agreement, although it should be taken into consideration that if an agreement, emanating from common sense, has been reached, it cannot be renounced for personal reasons.

The author advocates the adoption of general principles, binding on all peoples, regarding them as a guarantee of the non-violation of peace by individual states.

The next section deals with a specific proposal for the establishment of 'a general alliance and council'. Any alliance, Malinovsky notes, is concluded for the personal benefit of two or several nations. 'However, the general alliance of Europe may compensate for the advantages of certain states in that the latter will not be detrimental to the benefit of all.' In another part of the treatise the author again stresses that by setting up a general alliance, European states 'will regard their advantages as indivisible, on the condition that none of the participants should do harm by violating their common decisions'. In his treatise Malinovksy often returns to arguments in support of the importance of 'an alliance by accord'. He says outright that

> the dignity and independence of European powers will not be encroached upon if, after having signed their own laws, they will be responsible for their observance, and each state will retain its rights, at the same time making use of the advantages of others and protecting itself from any harm not only by force of arms but also by force of law.

The author proposes the setting up of a council, which would include the representatives of plenipotentiary allied nations. The council's functions should include the protection of general security and property and the settlement of outstanding issues, on condition that if any state refused to fulfil the decisions of the general council, the culprit would be stripped of all benefits and privileges connected with membership of the council. At the same time Malinovsky stresses the importance of trade – which unites remote nations and lands; to promote trade, he believes, it would be advisable to pass special common laws.

A separate section of the treatise deals with the issue of disarmament. According to the author, all and every kind of armaments and redeployment of troops in general tend to precede wars, so in order to prevent wars it is necessary to introduce restrictions on armaments and redeployment of troops. He even goes so far as to suggest that the intergovernmental council should be warned in advance by its heralds about any steps to accumulate armaments or redeploy troops in order to take restrictive measures, 'if there is no need for it provided for by the law'.

The last part of the treatise is entitled 'A Summary'. Here the author sums up the results of his discussions and also puts forward a number of new ideas. While reiterating his ideas about the role of justice and the significance of common laws, Malinovsky again turns to the idea that keeping each nation within its own borders and a renunciation of their violation creates guarantees of peace and security for the peoples. No less interesting is his idea that 'a reliable and universal peace in Europe may be established exclusively through observance of the truth, for it is the only genuine feature of universal balance'. He is convinced that 'war destroys peace and security', that 'war cannot be legal so long as there are no laws among the nations', that 'if only all governments had their subjects' welfare as their sole goal, they would have a natural alliance among them'.

Malinovsky's treatise was a summary of sorts of the ideas of Russian Enlighteners on the issues of war and peace. However, its distinctive feature was the detailed analysis of the humanistic aspects of peace, its benefits and advantages for the peoples of Russia and the whole of Europe. The author addressed his proposals to the peoples and countries of Europe and looked for ways and means of ensuring peace on the European continent. He did not analyse in detail the various versions and forms of pan-European bodies; he wrote about them in general, without supplying details of their functions and methods of formation. In this respect Malinovsky's project differs fundamentally from those of William Penn and Charles Saint-Pierre.

Naturally, Malinovsky's views should not be idealized. He represented Russian aristocratic circles, and probably for that reason avoided discussing the social aspects of peace in Europe, so his treatise certainly lagged behind Jean-Jacques Rousseau's 'revolutionizing' ideas. However, it was an important document of Russian and European Enlightenment thought at the turn of the nineteenth century.

The ideas of the French Revolution, the principles of freedom, democracy and human rights gained wide currency in the whole of Europe, including Russia. After the defeat of Napoleon's armies, many Russian officers, the best representatives of the Russian nobility, came back home with experience and knowledge of European values. The liberation ideas of the French Revolution, Jean-Jacques Rousseau's treatises and those by other European Enlighteners and Napoleonic reforms were widely discussed in the drawing-rooms of St Petersburg and Moscow. Educated Russian nobility, young officers who had been among the victorious troops in Paris, Vienna and Berlin, had first-hand experience of life in revolutionary France and had familiarized themselves with the liberation ideas of Western Europe. They were ready to carry this experience into Russia by speaking openly against Russian autocracy and serfdom. Progressive Russian thinkers and Russian officers, probably for the first time, felt that they belonged to European history and were part of the European liberation movement.

In the early 1820s Europe seemed to acquire a unity – that of a revolutionary upsurge, connected with uprisings in Piedmont, Greece, Poland and elsewhere. Russia formed an integral part of this process. The uprising of the Decembrists in Senate Square in 1825 (their programme had much in common with the ideas of West European democracy) and the socio-political pronouncements of Pyotr Chaadayev and many others were evidence of Russia's participation in common European processes and its contribution to European social thought.

Confrontation in Russia between those who were orientated towards Western ideals and those who advocated the ideas of Russian exclusiveness dates back to this period.

5

THE HOLY ALLIANCE

FORMATION OF THE HOLY ALLIANCE

The 'Battle of the Nations' at Leipzig (16–19 October 1813) ended with defeat for Napoleon's army. And as the Napoleonic Wars drew to an end, of prime importance on Europe's agenda were the issues of the future government in France, the destiny of the territories captured by Napoleon, and the subsequent power system of Europe as a whole. In accordance with the allies' decisions, adopted in late September 1814, heads of the coalition member-countries arrived in Vienna to attend a congress that was to settle various outstanding political and territorial issues in Europe.

The Congress of Vienna took place under the ideological motto of legitimism, put forward by the French representative, Talleyrand. The principle of legitimism was a substantial feature of the new approach to European affairs and an important element in the formation of a new view of 'the European balance'. On a social plane, this principle was in harmony with the hopes and aspirations of European monarchs to restore the pre-revolutionary state of affairs in Europe. At the same time, the principle of legitimism as a basis for European political settlement was clearly directed against Russia and Prussia, for it presupposed the inviolability of the European borders of the late eighteenth century.

The Vienna Congress revealed profound disagreement among European states. The new 'European balance' was being formed in an atmosphere of sharp dispute. Prussia was clearly planning to grab Saxony, whose king had supported Napoleon. Prussia looked to Russia for support in this matter although at the same time it feared Russia. Metternich engaged in intrigues against both Prussia and Russia, whereas England schemed against all of them by following the tried and tested divide-and-rule method. Alexander I sought to ensure a privileged position for Russia which should, he felt, follow logically from its military victories. In particular, he hoped to receive Poland, or a considerable part of it. The Russian Tsar did not trust the French leaders much and had a strong distrust of Metternich and of Austria's policy. At the same time, Alexander I preferred France to be strong enough to be a counterweight to Prussia.

His position in this respect was much to the advantage of France, which thus had the chance to avoid further humiliation and, more importantly, territorial division. Many foreign historians have attributed the diplomatic success of France at the Vienna Congress to Talleyrand, whereas others have assessed his astute diplomacy more circumspectly, with due account of the part played by the alignment of forces and the powers' positions in enabling France to raise its head at the Vienna Congress.

The sharp disagreements among the participants in the Congress were revealed by the fact that the two victorious countries – England and Austria – settled their accounts with France separately, by signing with it a secret trilateral treaty on 3 January 1815, which was directed against Russia and Prussia, their former allies in the war against Napoleon. The parties to the treaty pledged mutual assistance in case of an attack against one of them.

The last meeting of the Vienna Congress was held on 9 June 1815 (a few days before the Battle of Waterloo). On that day the Congress adopted the Final Act which included 121 articles with 17 supplements.

The trilateral Russian–Austrian–Prussian Treaty on the establishment of a Holy Alliance, signed in Paris on 26 September 1815, served as a logical outcome of the Vienna Congress. Later this alliance was joined by many other states. England, although not joining it officially, declared its approval of the treaty's postulates and principles. Participants in the Holy Alliance undertook 'in any case and anywhere . . . to render mutual aid, assistance and support'. Characteristically, they not only stated their goals and principles but also tried to work out mechanisms for collective action against any revolutionary movements or acts on the continent.

This kind of alliance was unprecedented in Europe's history and by it the European idea was manifested in its reactionary form. Of course, each of its members still acted with due account of its own national needs and interests, by combining crude and primitive tactics with sophisticated and camouflaged ones. The name Holy Alliance was also quite significant: it threw a religious–mystical, protective cloak over it.

The Holy Alliance was by no means a supranational body or organization but was rather a political agreement that set out common

41

intentions and outlined the basis and terms for joint action. The specific form of that political agreement was later manifested in pan-European meetings at the level of ambassadors and foreign ministers and in the congress of the monarchs of the four victorious powers and France. At this turning point in European history the foundation was laid for uniting the forces of European reactionism which represented a version of the realization of the European idea. That version agreed with the universalist ideas, which still existed and which were developing in Europe.

As noted above, universalist ideas were often contradictory and at times diametrically opposed. The eighteenth-century ideas of the Enlightenment reflected the mood in Europe in favour of joining forces for the promotion of eternal peace and social reforms throughout the continent. However, some theorists had tried to justify Napoleon's hegemonistic policy and such ideas and theories persisted in the post-Napoleonic period as well. Their differentiation and polarization was revealed in sharp clashes and social antagonism in Europe.

The trends that had led to the establishment of the Holy Alliance and the idea of joint action against revolution were also manifest in a number of treatises and projects of the 1820s. Universalist theories were used often in accordance with, but sometimes against, their authors' will by the advocates of alliance in Europe's monarchist forces. In 1814, for instance, *Deutsche Zeitschrift* carried Krause's article 'A Project for a European Alliance of States'. Krause was already known as the author of *A Prototype of Humanity*, in which he put forward the idea of a world state, with Napoleon at its head. In the new conditions Krause kept to the same range of problems. This time, however, he pinned his hopes on an alliance against Napoleon. Krause believed that the establishment of such an alliance would lead neither to the elimination of national states or the abrogation of their laws and customs, nor to the limitation of their sovereignty. He also rejected the possibility of religious or dynastic principles being used as a basis for the future alliance, since, he asserted, it should be based on new legal principles and new norms of international law. Constitutions of individual states, he said, should correspond to that new international law, with any violations of or deviations from general legal principles cut short by a system of fines and other penal measures, rather than by coercion or by force of arms.

According to Krause, the members of such an alliance were to be free, equal and sovereign; they should be free to enter or leave it any time they wished. He also suggested setting up a Court of the Peoples for the settlement of controversial issues. Heads of state or their representatives should be appointed to the supreme bodies of the alliance. Any issue should be adopted only by a unanimous vote, proceeding from the one-country-one-vote principle.

An alliance of states, according to Krause, had to declare to all peoples that it regarded itself as the only legal representative of those states, that it renounced the idea of aggressive seizure of land and that it was ready to protect all its members from attack. Of the utmost importance was the principle that alliance members had no right to wage war independently; that right was the exclusive prerogative of the alliance.

As can be seen, Krause's plan was rather controversial. On the one hand, it advocated the sovereignty and independence of individual states and peoples, in line with the spirit of eighteenth-century projects, and on the other, the establishment of an alliance of European states with a definite supranational structure and wide powers, so that it combined the old universalist ideas and legal norms with elements of the new bourgeois law, born at the dawn of the capitalist epoch. Krause was, however, vague about the goals of his proposed alliance, and after the downfall of Napoleon's Empire, such an idea could assume a protective-reactionary nature and might be used as a tool to suppress revolutionary movements.

The schemes and ideas put forward in the post-Napoleonic period reflected European monarchs' fear of revolution, of a possible new outburst of popular discontent. The desire of European reactionary circles to supply theoretical substantiation to and realize various forms of unification for joint action against revolution and liberation movements has been a keynote in European and world policies ever since, especially at the turning points of history. This applies in full measure to the new international political system set up after the Vienna Congress. Under this system the four Great Powers (England, Russia, Austria and Prussia) usurped the right to decide the destiny of Europe and showed a readiness to unite their efforts. However, that system proved to be little more than a new version of 'the European balance'. If we take the diaries and memoirs of European politicians of the first half of the nineteenth century and numerous historical studies, we shall certainly come across the words 'European balance' there. The interpretation of the 'European balance' as a phenomenon with a permanent and universal nature, much used by present-day politicans and historians, is largely based on the structure which was formed in Europe in the early nineteenth century. Having identical goals, of course, did not remove the deep political conflicts between the participants in that system, conflicts that were more, or less, acute at various periods in all spheres of European political affairs, including the issue of the means to be adopted to suppress revolutionary movements.

It is also noteworthy that quite often political considerations were given priority over those of solidarity. In such cases, Russian or English diplomacy, for example, was ready to show a certain liberalism and even to flirt with a revolutionary movement in order to undermine the position of their rivals. The top echelons of power in Europe naturally followed this political game closely, and if they found that a revolutionary movement of European peoples had reached a critical point in its development, considerations of solidarity with the interests of certain social strata took the upper hand.

This sort of pragmatism underlay the essence of the system, the balance that was established in Europe after 1815. Revolutionary events of that period in Italy, Piedmont and Greece (1820–21), in Russia (December 1825), in France (1830) and in Poland (1830–31) and the 1848–49 revolutions had a strong impact on the political system in Europe and on the substance and form of 'European balance'. The social aspect of the European political system was again moved to the foreground in the first half of the nineteenth century and was an omnipresent, though invisible, factor in the solution of all European issues. Another factor worthy of note is a realignment of political forces in Europe, a new European balance.

Acute intra-European conflicts, the true substance of the 'European balance', were revealed during the July 1830 revolution in France. Another series of conflicts was attributable to a sharpening in the 'Eastern issue'. The political situation had become exceedingly unstable, and it was increasingly clear that Russia and England were in the forefront of confrontation in Europe.

Such was the situation in Europe by 1848, a year that proved an important landmark in the development of the European revolutionary movement. The 1848–49 revolutions revealed typical features of the Vienna system. Prussian troops put down an uprising in Southern Germany and Saxony, French troops invaded Italy and the Russian tsarist authorities, in co-operation with Austria, suppressed the revolution in Hungary. Although England never officially sent its troops to suppress any uprising, it was among the leading European monarchist powers. At the same time, the events of 1848–49 revealed in full measure the acute nature of the conflicts and antagonism among the European powers and the instability of the notorious 'European balance' that had been established in 1815.

After the defeat of the 1848–49 revolutions, the situation in Europe was fundamentally different from that of the preceding decades. The great European powers had on the whole retained their positions, although their unity had been thoroughly eroded. Europe was entering into a new era of bitter conflict. The 'European balance' was being replaced by ever-deepening rivalries, fraught with new disputes and armed clashes.

The 'balance' that was established in Europe after 1815 had undergone substantial changes by the mid-nineteenth century. To be more precise, that balance had been tipped. A new Anglo-French alliance, directed against Russia, was being formed; the Austrian monarchy no longer loomed large on the European horizon; Prussia's claims to domination in Germany were more and more insistent, and when those claims were largely realized in the 1860s, it had a major impact on the subsequent policy of France; Italy's unification was completed in the late 1850s. Thus the second half of the nineteenth century saw a realignment of forces on the European scene, both as a result of and causing a new series of conflicts.

On the whole, developments in Europe in the first half of the nineteenth century, just as before, bore testimony to clashing national interests and attempts to establish some form of supranational unification. Consolidation of national statehood in Europe dealt a mortal blow to all sorts of universalist theories and plans which would involve encroaching on national interests. The failure of Napoleon's 'experiment' testified once more to the fruitlessness of any attempt at a 'unification' of Europe or its subjugation to the domination of one state. It was not by chance, therefore, that the idea of the sovereignty of European states still underlay most European theories and projects. The Vienna system and the new version of the 'European balance' were both based on national-state principles.

6

GIUSEPPE MAZZINI AND THE UNIFICATION OF REVOLUTIONARY FORCES: YOUNG EUROPE

The formation of the Holy Alliance and joint action by its participants were manifestations of the consolidation of reactionary forces on a European scale. However, liberation and monarchist movements in Europe showed no less obvious a desire for unity. The process of interaction between, and mutual influence of, revolutionary movements have been fruitfully studied by Soviet historians and their colleagues in other European countries. Only some of the trends and lines of this process will be dealt with here.

The ideas of the French Revolution, as is known, met with a wide response throughout Europe. The liberal circles in Warsaw, St Petersburg, Prague and Berlin discussed the possibility of a revolutionary outburst on the French model in their countries. Clandestine groups, societies and organizations were being formed in many countries. However, the triumph of European reactionaries very soon revealed that the struggle for independence and the overthrow of tyranny called for joint efforts and actions. The Decembrist movement in Russia had wide repercussions in Europe. Even before December 1825, plans for assisting Greek revolutionaries and the Italian Carbonari were discussed animatedly by revolutionary circles in many countries. The events in 1830–31 in Poland had a considerable effect on the mood of the progressive European public.

It was in the 1830s that the first attempt was made in Europe to unite revolutionary efforts in various countries. Of course, not much was achieved at this stage, but the existence of such an attempt is significant in itself. These initiatives were, to a considerable degree, associated with the name of Giuseppe Mazzini, a prominent Italian public leader of the nineteenth century and a true advocate of the European idea.

In his writings Mazzini advocated the idea of the common European cultural and historical heritage and, in this context, laid great stress on the mission of Italy. Mazzini looked for new impulses to promote European unity in a regenerated Italy. He wrote that Italy had been

> awakened on three occasions since the downfall of pagan Rome had cut short the development of ancient civilization and it served as a cradle of modern civilization. First, the call was born in Italy to replace the triumph of physical force with the idea of European spiritual unity. On the second occasion, Italy illuminated the world with the spirit of Enlightenment which was reflected in its art and literature. And, for the third time, Italy will strike a mighty blow at the symbol of unity of the Middle Ages and replace it with social unity. Therefore, it is in Rome alone – and foreigners should be reminded of this – that a third call for unity in our days may be issued.

Purely Italian and Europeanist ideas were closely interlinked in Mazzini's works. At the same time he built on the idea of some 'division of humanity into groups united by common goals which are free in their choice of means to attain those goals'. Utopian and somewhat abstract ideas were imbued with a democratic content in Mazzini's works, and they were developed in the context of the liberation struggle in Europe. That democratic streak and his public activity compensated in part for his abstract constructs and promoted Mazzini to the status of one of the most prominent ideologists and leaders of the European democratic movement in the nineteenth century.

Mazzini made an attempt at setting up a pan-European revolutionary organization through the unification of Young Italy, which was founded by him in 1831, with Young Poland and Young Germany, founded in the early 1830s. On 11–15 April 1834 representatives of these three organizations adopted the Statute of Young Europe and the Act of Fraternity. These documents said that Young Europe represented a prototype for the Europe of the future, where the interests of countries would be harmonized with those of humanity.

Mazzini, the founder of and inspiration behind Young Europe, wrote:

> There is a new European association, set up on a broad basis, that is proving to be the development of the century, that arose from the ruins of the old Carbonari organization. This association

is a federation of peoples, based on the principles of national independence and the freedom of each in internal affairs. They are unanimous in their common faith and in active fraternity on issues of common interest. This is a Holy Alliance of nations, and each nation that will be the first to revolt will promote in every possible way the realization of the common plan determining the activity of the association.

The programme of the proposed association was vague in many respects, although basically it was of a democratic nature. Young Europe was opposed to the reactionary Holy Alliance of the European countries' monarchs and projected a democratic vision of Europe and European unity. Mazzini wrote:

> We have set up Young Europe six days after the Lyons uprising and three weeks after its defeat, at a time when there was no hope left for the movement in France. That was our response to the victory won by the 'republican monarchy' over the people. That was ... a declaration of democracy that it leads a real, collective European existence. (V. Nevler, 'Mazzini and "Young Europe"', *Problems in History*, 1977, No.4.)

Europe's reactionaries launched a campaign of reprisals against Young Italy, Young Switzerland and other such organizations, with the result that they had to cease their activity.

In 1843 Mazzini, on behalf of the leadership of Young Italy, urged the democractic public of Russia to set up a Holy Alliance of peoples opposed to absolutist governments. Soviet scholars have studied the way the organization Young Russia was set up and have found much in common between the aims of its programme and those of Young Italy and Young Europe. True, Young Russia was set up later, in the early 1860s, but the influence of their revolutionary ideas is obvious. The Russian revolutionaries who founded Young Russia, just like their counterparts from Young Italy, staked their hopes on popular action and even discussed the advisability of using the motto of Young Italy, 'Now and Forever'.

While I do not intend to discuss in detail the activities of Young Europe and the national organizations close to it, it is important to stress that the revolutionary forces in Europe did try to combine their efforts and create a counterweight to European reactionism. The liberation process in Europe was certainly complicated and heterogeneous, with each country contributing its own features. However, many basic features of the European revolutionary movement were similar, revealing a general trend in European development. Thus, when we speak about Europe as a definite community it should be remembered that the liberation movement in Europe in the nineteenth century not only developed in many parts of the continent but also assumed common European features.

The humanitarian tradition in the development of European political thought which was associated with the prominent figures of the European Enlightenment was further developed during the nineteenth century. To a considerable extent it was reflected in the writings of Claude-Henri Saint-Simon, an outstanding French utopian socialist. Even in one of his first works, *A Genevan's Letters to Contemporaries* (1802–3), he directed public attention 'to the political situation in the most enlightened part of the globe':

> At present, the actions of European governments are not restrained by any notable counteraction by the subjects; however, judging by the mood in England, Germany and Italy, it would be an easy guess that this calm will not be long-lived if urgent precautionary measures are not adopted, for, gentlemen, we should not indulge in self-deception, we must admit that the current crisis of human reason is typical of all enlightened peoples and that the symptoms that were to be observed in France in the period of the revolutionary outburst there, a sober-minded observer may also observe among the Britons and even Germans.

Saint-Simon suggested that a pan-European assembly should be convened, to be attended by twenty-one 'delegates of humanity', coming from England, France, Germany and Italy. He believed that 'as soon as elections have been held to the Supreme Council and to the councils of individual nations, the scourge of war will be banished from Europe, never to return'. It must be remembered that these lines were written when Europe was being consumed by the flames of war, unleashed by Napoleon in order to implement his plans for conquering Europe.

Of great importance to our subject is Saint-Simon's *A Study of Universal Gravitation*, written in the period of the Napoleonic Wars and first published after the author's death, in 1843, for it deals with his proposals for reforms to be introduced into European society. Its title was not chosen accidentally, since, according to Saint-Simon, 'the idea of universal gravity should serve as a basis for a new philosophical theory, and a new political system in Europe will come as a consequence of new philosophy'. Saint-Simon knew that his idea would certainly not be met with understanding but rather with opposition. As he points out: 'The method offered by me may at first sight look like the philosophical ravings of a madman, much like the proposal for eternal peace put forward by Abbot Saint-Pierre.' He supports his ideas by citing history and proclaims Charlemagne to be the true founder of European society, since he had firmly united various peoples, binding all nationalities by religious links to Rome and making that city independent from any secular power. He states:

> Charlemagne realized that the multi-million population of a whole section of the world, with islands situated close by, which incorporates many nationalities sharply different in their customs and languages, divided by natural obstacles from one another and residing in areas with different climates and consuming different food, cannot be subjects of the same government. He also realized that those various peoples occupying neighbouring territories would inevitably wage wars if not bound together by common ideas and if a special body of the most educated people did not take pains to apply common principles to objects of mutual interest to them. He realized that religion was a moral code common to all European peoples and that an administrative body, including the officials of that religion, should serve that common purpose. Finally, he realized that religion and its top officials should be independent and, consequently, free from direct subordination to any national government. Such were the motives behind his decision to grant the Pope supreme power in Rome and its lands.

Saint-Simon believed that for five hundred years (from the ninth to the fifteenth century) Europe had enjoyed the general benefit of that clever social organization: spiritual power was balanced by the authority of secular power; internecine strife had never taken place. As for the Crusades, Saint-Simon believed that the misfortunes they caused for Europe were outweighed by the great benefits they brought to the European peoples.

The crisis that shook Europe in Saint-Simon's time was attributed by him to the absence of an idea that could unite all European peoples. As soon as a theory that corresponded to the level of education appeared, he says, everything would return to normal and a common system for European peoples would be restored automatically.

In his subsequent works, such as *On Restructuring European Society* and *On Measures Against the 1815 Coalition* (the latter written with August Thierry), Saint-Simon discusses a plan of reforms for Europe. He assesses the events of 1814–15, saying that 'the right cause of civilization united the peoples of Europe against the government of France . . . which had put a military yoke on its neighbours'. He offers to introduce reforms both with the help of national parliaments and pan-European administrative bodies. He speaks in this instance about three kinds of power: national parliaments representing individual countries' interests, a European parliament representing common interests and a special body regulating relations between them.

National parliaments should be elected in accordance with the laws of each country. The European parliament should consist of 240 representatives, divided, on the British model, into a House of Commons and a House of Lords. Deputies to the House of Commons should be elected for a term of ten years by an electorate of all literate persons, whereas members of the House of Lords should be appointed by the king. Saint-Simon felt that deputies standing for election to the lower house should possess at least 25,000 francs, whereas those for the upper house should have a fortune of no less than 1,000,000 francs, and the upper house should also include twenty persons who had won European renown in the spheres of science, commerce, industry or administration. The European parliament would elect a King of Europe whose function would be to regulate power.

Saint-Simon offered to build roads and navigable canals in all European countries, to drain swamps, introduce a uniform system of public education and produce a common moral code throughout the continent. While offering these measures, Saint-Simon called for peace without violence and only peaceful competition among the peoples, stressing that 'people whose purpose is the productive process cherish peace above all, for war hampers production and trade, disrupting all means of communication and barring the way to exchanges'.

Saint-Simon's faith in industrial progress was something new in his project. In a special work, entitled *Industry*, he devoted much space to the problems of industrial development, associating with it changes in the political and moral spheres. 'The Golden Age of humanity', Saint-Simon wrote, 'will not end with us, it will develop in future, too.'

Saint-Simon did not indulge in any illusions about the rapid realization of his projects. Transformation, he wrote, involves great difficulties. It would be necessary to wait for the time when all nations lived under parliamentary regimes. In other words, one of the outstanding philosophers of the nineteenth century expressed an understanding of the fact that the reorganization of the European political system was closely bound up with radical reforms in the domestic affairs of European countries.

There were many utopian elements in Saint-Simon's views and proposals. His ideas were contradictory and rather naive, associated as they were with his faith in some king as a superarbiter of Europe, or with a new Christian faith enriched by the experience of medieval Europe. At the same time, however, his humanistic ideas of moral self-improvement, his denunciation of war and his attempts at presenting the European Federation as a peaceful association of European nations rather than as an ordinary conglomeration of states, and even less as that of hereditary monarchs, expressed a democratic trend in the development of European political thought. Saint-Simon's European schemes represented an antithesis to the reactionary programmes and formations (of the Holy Alliance type); they represented a democratic vision of sorts of prospects for European development.

Other theories and concepts of socialist thought were meanwhile developing at a rapid pace. Socialist organizations and associations were being set up in France, England, Germany and Russia and socialist literature was being published.

Regrettably, the unity of those forces was being undermined by substantial dissensions; the sectarian principles of Marxists and representatives of other trends in socialist thought prevented them from uniting their efforts. However, the important thing was that the socialist idea was manifested in various trends and forms. Socialist thought was elaborating its own approach to European unity in the general course of revolutionary and liberation movements on the continent. Thus, trends were formed which in the late nineteenth and early twentieth centuries led to the formation of various parties and organizations in the working-class movement that both co-operated and were in conflict with one another.

The events of the 1850s–90s, just like subsequent developments, showed that various European socialist organizations had not been able to achieve a European consensus on a common democratic basis, which had a negative effect on the development of the international working-class movement.

7

EUROPEAN PACIFISM AND THE SLOGAN OF A UNITED STATES OF EUROPE

A pacifist movement, which was most vividly manifested at peace congresses held in Europe in the second half of the 1840s and later, proved a substantial element in the Europe of the mid-nineteenth century. The first such peace congress was held in London in June 1843; the second was in Brussels in September 1848; the third in Paris in August 1849; the fourth in Frankfurt in 1850; and the fifth in London in July 1851. These congresses were attended by increasing numbers of delegates: the first congress had 326 delegates, the fifth, 1,200. In later years more peace congresses of this kind were held, but their significance was on the wane.

New European ideas and projects were put forward within the framework of the pacifist movement, which was extremely heterogeneous in its composition, goals and forms of activity. On the one hand, especially at the outset, it was definitely marked by the influence of revolutionary-democratic elements, who set themselves the goal of creating opposition to associations of European reactionaries by rallying around the ideas of peace and freedom in Europe. Revolutionary-democratic circles were represented by Giuseppe Mazzini, Giuseppe Garibaldi, Victor Hugo and Louis Blanc, among others.

However, apart from the revolutionary-democratic wing, the influence of moderate liberal circles was pronounced even at several early congresses. They appealed to general humanistic moods, seeking to find supporters both among the public and European governments. It should be remembered that this movement was born in Europe in the context of the 1848–49 revolutions, when European reactionaries wanted to suppress the mass movement, and bourgeois liberals connived at the policy conducted by Louis Cavaignac and his ilk. In such conditions, pacifist slogans and appeals were seldom in harmony with the daily practice of European development and very often did not meet with wide support.

Typical in this respect is a pronouncement by Alexander Hertzen about events that followed the defeat of the 1848–49 revolutions and symbolized the ruin of all the ideas that had inspired the peoples of Europe:

> And you, Mazzini, Garibaldi, the last of God's servants, the last of the Mohicans, cross your arms and be quiet. You are not needed any longer. You've done what you could. Now you should retreat before madness, brutal bloodshed with the help of which Europe has committed suicide or, rather, reaction has murdered it.

Government circles had also taken up pacifist ideas – which was something new, indeed – and set about formulating so-called official pacifism. Although this phenomenon was in practice rather heterogeneous and contradictory, its essence remained the same, in that it was an attempt by the ruling classes of the European states to make use of the ideas of peace in their policies and in the fierce struggle for European domination.

The divergence between the pacifist movement and 'official pacifism' was to become more pronounced later, but in the 1840s–50s the first signs of this split were quite obvious. However, the emergence on the European political scene of the pacifist movement and the spread of 'peace' ideas proved an important stage in European history. European pacifism had an important role to play in the European movement.

The ideas and practice of the European pacifists provided arguments for the need for eternal peace; they renounced war as a method of settlement of any conflict or problem. Pacifists were often criticized for their abstract ideas and utopianism, for being far removed from reality and for the advocacy of non-violence in opposing evil forces. This may be true, yet it should be conceded that although the pacifist movement was extremely heterogeneous, it nevertheless developed according to humanitarian traditions and contributed to peace-making ideas and activities.

It is not our task here to analyse the motive forces and nature of the pacifist movement. We are interested primarily in its association with Europeanist theories and slogans and the significance of this period in the evolution of the European idea is immense. It was at this time that the liberal vision of Europe emerged and the liberal schemes for European unity which were put forward in many respects influenced the ideas and practice of European liberalism in the twentieth century as well.

After Napoleon's 'experiment' the national liberation movement received a strong impetus for its development throughout Europe – as a reaction to that experiment. That is why in the 1820s–30s many of the European ideas largely had a national tinge.

The European idea French-style was at that time expressed by Jules Michelet: 'What is the least simple, the least natural and most artificial, that is, less lethal but more humane and more free in the world – that is Europe; and the most European of them all is my country, France.' At the same time in Germany, Hegel, developing the idea of the spirit, proclaimed Europe the supreme achievement of the latter, and Germany, the German world, as the essence of Europe.

Finally, it was in the second half of the nineteenth century that many world organizations and alliances, which promoted the development of world universalist ideas, were formed. Meanwhile the European federalist theory, put forward by circles connected with the governments of European states, was canvassed with ever-increasing ardour. The French historian P. Renouvain, who had made a thorough study of the European movement, wrote that people in many countries simultaneously supported the idea of a United States of Europe.

The term 'United States of Europe' was often used by Mazzini, although, according to some sources, it was Mazzini's friend, Carlo Cattaneo, an Italian republican leader, historian and economist, who was the first to use it. It was not accidental, though, for during this period Italy was 'setting the fashion' in Europe in the sphere of European ideas. Cattaneo wrote that the nationalities principle was conducive to the break-up of states in Eastern Europe and to a fragmented federation of free peoples, and that federation was the only form of unity that could be established among those peoples. We can attain peace only when we have the United States of Europe, he asserted. In France this idea was put forward by Henri Faigereid and the lawyer, Veniser. In 1848, the French newspaper *Le Moniteur Universel*, the English *Daily Telegraph* and many other publications wrote about the United States of Europe.

Cattaneo mentioned four symbols of European unity: the unity of power, manifested in imperial power; the unity of law, manifested in Roman law; the unity of faith, manifested in Christianity; and the unity of language, manifested in popular Latin. Ever since its appearance the slogan of the United States of Europe had become an object of bitter political squabbles. It was interpreted in various ways, depending on whose social and political interests it served.

We have already mentioned the first peace congresses. The third peace congress, held in Paris, was the most interesting of them all. It was chaired by the French writer Victor Hugo. In his opening address Hugo declared the following, which has since become widely known:

> The day will come, when, you France, you Russia, you Italy, you England, and you Germany – all of you, all nations of the continent, without losing your distinctive features and your magnificent originality, are merged into a certain superior society to form a European brotherhood, just like Normandy, Brittany, Lorraine and Alsace. All our provinces have been merged into a united France. The day will come when markets, open for trade, and minds, open for ideas are the only battlefield! The day will come when shells and bombs have been replaced by election ballots, universal vote and the wise mediation of the great Supreme Senate, which will become for Europe what Parliament is for England, the Reichstag for Germany, the National Assembly for France. The day will come when guns will be put on display in museums, just as now objects of torture are, and people will be astonished that such barbarism was at all possible. The day will come when we shall witness two giant alliances of states – the United States of America and the United States of Europe, which, facing each other and having exchanged a handshake over the ocean, will exchange their products, their industrial goods, works of art, human genius; we shall see how they will plough virgin lands throughout the world, settle deserts and bring to perfection, under the attentive eye of their Creator, all his creations and combine two immense forces – the people's brotherhood and God's might – for the common weal!

This address by Victor Hugo may serve as an image of democratic Europeanism typical of that epoch.

Participants in subsequent congresses discussed more specific issues of European political affairs. At the Frankfurt Congress, German delegates tried to put the issue of Schleswig-Holstein on the agenda. Debates were also held on disarmament. Bitter disagreements among the participants were immediately apparent and pacifist proclamations of a general nature retreated under the pressure of the particular interests of European states.

In subsequent years the slogan United States of Europe tended to reappear on the European horizon. In the 1850s–60s it was imbued with a democratic and humanistic content for Hugo, Mazzini and Garibaldi who regarded pan-Europeanist ideas and projects as a means of struggle against European reactionism and the policy conducted by the Holy Alliance. The slogan was later used by the League of Peace, set up in Paris in 1867 (in 1872 the League was renamed the Society of Friends of Peace and in 1883 it changed again to the Arbitration Society) and by the International League of Peace and Freedom, founded in Geneva in 1869. The latter was headed by Camille Lemonnier and A. Gögg. The International League's activity was concentrated on political and social issues. In its discussion of international issues it returned to the idea of the United States of Europe. Its periodical, *Les Etats Unis de l'Europe*, served as a good advertisement for the idea and was published in Berne on a monthly basis. The League for a European Alliance, founded in Germany in 1862 by E. Loewenthal, a journalist, also maintained contacts with the League of Peace and Freedom.

The League of Peace and Freedom was heterogeneous in composition. Many European countries, including Russia, were represented in it. Apart from revolutionary democrats such as Giuseppe Garibaldi, Giuseppe Mazzini, Victor Hugo, Louis Blanc, Mikhail Bakunin, John Stuart Mill, Nikolai Ogarev and Lajos Kossuth, the League also included a considerable number of liberals.

Lemonnier wrote that the League's final goal was to establish universal eternal peace by setting up a pan-European republican federation, the so-called United States of Europe. Participants in many of the League's congresses stressed among other things the need to overthrow the old system of administration and put an end to the arms race. At one of the League's congresses (chaired by Victor Hugo), the formula 'Federation of the Peoples of Europe' was used instead of the United States of Europe. However, the League never enjoyed massive support among the general public, its calls for peace were of a declarative nature, and the words 'peace and freedom', part of its name, had little relevance in practice.

The problem of disarmament was viewed by its members on a purely moral plane, for neither real sources of armaments nor ways to attain disarmament were determined. Suffice it to say that one resolution adopted by the League said that it was impossible to solve the problem of disarmament until the United States of Europe was a reality.

The League's federative programme was also quite utopian and abstract. While recognizing the principle of 'the nation's sovereignty', the League put forward at the same time the idea of certain supra-national interests which had to serve as the first step on the road to the formation of a European federation, a republican United States of Europe. League members held that the following political principles should be observed by a country requesting admission to that federa-tion: introduction of universal suffrage, the right to impose and lift taxes, the right to conclude peace and declare war, the right to sign and ratify political treaties and trade agreements, and the right to make amendments to the constitution. The problem of freedom and democracy was interpreted in the same spirit by the most progressive members of the League.

Alexander Hertzen was among those who signed a message of greeting to the League on the occasion of its formation. A prominent representative of the Russian revolutionary movement, he supported energetically the idea of a pan-European democratic organization as a counterweight to the reactionary forces. The sponsors of the League's first congress invited Hertzen to attend it: 'You not only represent a party of peace but also a party based on freedom, a party that believes that peace is unthinkable without freedom, a party that seeks to replace war and oppression by a peaceful republican alliance of the peoples.' However, Hertzen, who sincerely supported the ideals of peace and freedom, did not attend the congress, largely because he disliked the attitude held by many West European leaders towards Russia. As a representative of revolutionary Russia, Hertzen believed that 'Western democrats had no moral right to criticize the Russian people by referring to Russia's despotic system from positions of "the frail freedoms of Western institutions" that were being increasingly trampled underfoot by the military-bureaucratic regimes'.

The results of the first congress of the League held in Geneva, only strengthened Hertzen's negative attitude to Western democracy and its stand on the Russian issue. In view of this, Hertzen and Ogarev decided to publish *Kolokol* (*Bell*) a magazine in French in which the revolutionary events in Russia were reviewed in the context of the European revolutionary movement. Ogarev, who had acted as a vice-chairman at the Geneva Congress, also denounced the campaign of criticism, launched in Western Europe, against Russia, in the course of which the idea was put forward of a preventive war to be proclaimed by Western powers against Russia. Many West European leaders, even some holding liberal views, refused to recog-nize the objective role played by Russia in rendering assistance to the national liberation movement in the Balkans. Hertzen and Ogarev denied the accusations of pan-Slavonic sympathies in their address. At the same time, they criticized Bakunin's position (on the destruction of the state as such in Russia), which he had set out in his address at the Geneva Congress.

Hertzen did not attend the second congress of the League of Peace and Freedom, held in Bern in 1868, because of his stand on pacifism, although he once again stressed the importance of joint action by Russian and West European revolutionaries. Thus, Hertzen's relations with the League testified, on the one hand, to the links between the liberation movement in Russia and Western Europe, and, on the other, they revealed the variety of positions adopted by participants in the European movement, including that of the interdependence of peace and freedom.

The issue of attitudes to the League of Peace and Freedom was the subject of discussion at a sitting of the First International, in particular in connection with Bakunin's idea of the League's joining the International and his proposal that representatives of the International should attend the League's constituent congress. Karl Marx criticized the League 'for its reluctance to study the social aspects of the way to peace, refusal to carry on the active struggle against the reactionary policies pursued by England and France'. He described the League as 'a stillborn baby of bourgeois republican society'. However, taking into account a great number of revolutionary democratic leaders among the League's members and proceeding from the principle that all forms and means of struggle should be made use of, the International, on Marx's initiative, permitted its members to take part in the League's activities on an individual basis.

The overall weakness of pacifist movements and organizations, including one of the most radical of them – the International League of Peace and Freedom, was revealed in the early 1870s. By this time the situation in Europe had changed dramatically. After the Franco-Prussian war of 1870–71 and the defeat of the Paris Commune, the European right went on the offensive in all spheres. Bismarck's policy in a new Germany and the right's offensive in France left no hope for European liberals. In the 1870s and after, the situation was quite auspicious for the formation of new coalitions and the outbreak of new conflicts in Europe. In this context pacifist slogans and proclamations were either senseless or simply served as a screen for the self-interests of various European states.

Some historians state in their studies that the European countries' and peoples' movement for national unity (Italy and Germany) ran counter to pan-European theories. In reality the process was more complicated. New interest in European ideas and the proclamation of

59

the slogan of the United States of Europe from the outset served as the manifestation of a growing liberation movement of European peoples and served as an antithesis of sorts to the Holy Alliance. That is why, initially, the tone of the pan-European movement was set by European democratic leaders such as Garibaldi, Hugo and Mazzini. Among them were many followers of Saint-Simon. All of them drew on the heritage of progressive thinkers of the Enlightenment. The idea of European unity was viewed by them as being closely connected with the struggle against despotism and tyranny for the freedom and independence of the peoples. They rejected the idea of a supra-national Europe and advocated an alliance of free European peoples and a federation of countries which were fighting for republican, democratic forms of government. By carrying on the traditions of the past, the advocates of a European federation associated its realization with the establishment of peace among European countries and peoples.

However, the situation in Europe in the second half of the nineteenth century differed fundamentally from that in the period of the French Revolution in the late-eighteenth century. The bourgeoisie by then tended to renounce any revolutionary ideas. Many liberals preferred Cavaignac's dictatorship and Bismarck's strong rule rather than the democratic slogans proclaimed by Blanc, Garibaldi, Hertzen and Hugo. They no longer showed sympathy for the slogans of the Republican United States of Europe, for the crisis of bourgeois liberalism had predetermined the crisis of liberal European ideas.

The extremely vague nature of the programme proclaimed that left-wing circles should also be taken into account. The absence of a positive programme was among the factors which precipitated the crisis of the League's left-wingers and made many prominent leaders, writers and scientists change their attitude to it. The journal *Les Etats Unis de l'Europe* rapidly lost popularity, and its publication ended in 1885. In its last issue Lemonnier wrote sadly, 'The formation of a federation of the peoples and the institution of international tribunal seemed to me no longer possible in Europe.' Garibaldi, Blanc and Hugo sent messages of greetings to the League's congress held in Lugano in 1872, but they decided soon after not to show even such formal signs of respect for future congresses.

In the late-nineteenth century, Europe entered into a new stage of development. Germany was then rapidly gaining strength in the heart of Europe and very soon threw down the gauntlet to its eastern and western neighbours. A new system of blocs and alliances was being formed in Europe, which were locked in fierce fighting for European domination and for the redivision of colonies and dependencies. The bitter rivalries among the European powers that eventually led to the First World War made nonsense of the ideas and plans for European unity embodied in the slogan the United States of Europe. Moreover, ruling circles in European countries cleverly manipulated the pacifist ideas which had previously been the exclusive privilege of the public organizations. 'Official pacifism' with its mechanisms, specific means, methods and forms was often used as a screen for expansionist schemes and plans. These factors inevitably predetermined the crisis in democratic and liberal European ideas which had fostered such great and widespread enthusiasm among the European masses of the 1840s–60s.

8

RUSSIAN PACIFISM

Russian pacifism has its source in the eighteenth century, when peace-making ideas were put forward in the first works of such Russian Enlighteners as Semyon Desnitsky, Yakov Kozelsky, Alexander Radishchev and Roman Tsebrikov, who associated the ideas of peace with social restructuring. In his treatise, analysed above, Vassili Malinovsky discussed the issue of eternal peace with close reference to the restructuring and unification of Europe.

Just as in Western Europe, pacifist ideas were rapidly developing in Russia in the second half of the nineteenth century. They were put forward by lawyers, philosophers, historians, public figures and diplomats and were discussed along with proposals on disarmament, arbitration, etc. – the same issues as were discussed in Western Europe during these years.

For instance, it is a fact that in 1873 Prince Pyotr of Oldenburg, a grandson of Pavel I, presented to Bismarck a draft international agreement on arbitration. Prominent Russian pacifists were represented by political scientists, lawyers and men of letters such as F. Martens, L. Komarovsky, I. Blokh, Ya. Novikov, V. Tenishev, M. Engelgardt, B. Chicherin and M. Taube, with the magificent figure of Leo Tolstoy towering over them. Books by, among others, Mikhail Engelgardt (such as *Progress as Evolution of Cruelty*, 1899, and *Eternal Peace and Disarmament* 1899), Fyodor Martens, vice-president of the European Institute of International Law (*Modern International Law of Civilized Nations*, 1882), Professor L.A. Komsrovsky of Moscow University (*The Main Aspects of the Idea of Peace in History*, 1895), Prince V.N. Tenishev, a Russian MP, pacifist and philanthropist (*Eternal Peace and International Court of Arbitration*, 1909), and Baron M. Taube (*Principles of Peace and Law in International Conflicts in the Middle Ages*, 1899), served as a sound theoretical foundation for the development of the pacifist idea in Russia. The prominent Russian painter, Vassili Vereshchagin, who incarnated a pacifist vision of war in his paintings, demanded in 1897 that an international congress on disarmament be convened. However, the most well-known became the works that were published in the West by Russian industrialists, I.S. Blokh and Ya. Novikov. In his *Protectionism* (1890), *War and Its False Benefits* and *The Fight of Europe against China* (*The Future of the White Race*), and other works Novikov described war as the degradation of humanity, for he believed economic progress to be the main precondition for the unification of humanity. I.S. Blokh, a prominent pacifist, won world-wide renown for his six-volume study *War of the Future in Its Technical, Economic and Political Aspects*, brought out in 1898, as well as for the foundation at his own expense of the International Museum of War and Peace in Lucerne, Switzerland.

In general, Russian pacifists' concepts of international law drew on European spiritual sources or, to be more precise, on their English and French traditions. The ethical principles of pacifism of Leo Tolstoy and his followers were world-famous. Tolstoy not only raised the problem of a correlaton between politics and morale but also offered a theoretical substantiation of the concept of non-resistance to evil, that is, fighting violence with non-violence, and later in the practice of using non-violent methods of struggle against military force and revolutionary maximalism.

The alternative of non-violence, offered by Tolstoy, as an international method of settling conflicts, based on the general human idea of non-violence, assumed a universal nature. The idea and evolution of a non-violent alternative developed in harmony with the trend for internationalization of socio-economic affairs, where new forms of regulation of people's behaviour were already emerging.

What is the essence of the socio-ethical concept of pacifism, its historical logic? What is the meaning of its universalism? Tolstoy realized that the main contradiction of his time was that 'between the military position of the peoples and the moral principles of Christianity and humanism', that is, between military-political violence and morals, and he offered a non-violent alternative to Russia and humanity.

He justly believed that there were two ways to settle conflicts, that is, to oppose violence with violence or, according to the Christian doctrine, renounce the violent method of opposing violence. Tolstoy believed that non-violence is not passiveness, not acceptance of the situation, not renunciation of active methods of struggle, not keeping aloof from reality. He wrote:

> Non-resistance to evil by violence does not mean not to oppose evil, it only means not to offer violence to oppose it . . . You

63

cannot put down fire with the help of fire, or extinguish water with water, or defeat evil with evil. That has been done since time immemorial with the result that we have found ourselves in the obtaining situation.

Tolstoy regarded universal military service as the highest degree of violence but it was considered necessary for supporting the state and of vital importance to the state's existence: 'It is the stone in the castle's vault that holds up its walls, and if you take it out, the whole building will collapse.' Tolstoy's campaign against universal military service, for the right to abstain from it, and his angry opposition to military budgets and the arms drive were an effective and courageous protest against armed violence.

Tolstoy's alternative of non-violence exerted great influence on the formation of a global peace-making philosophy and on increasing its non-violent potential. The idea of opposing war by abstaining from military service has become a fundamental ethical basic of human rights with respect to military service, when people may refuse to serve in the army as conscientious objectors.

At the same time, the ideas of a religious-humanistic cosmopolitan ethic stimulated the development of the concept of relativity of borders, limitation of state sovereignty and the elaboration of the doctrine of federalism and a world government. Such a revolutionary peace-making philosophy proposed by the great Russian thinker at the turn of the century was naturally strongly opposed by both conservatives and revolutionaries.

The best assessment of this situation was offered by Tolstoy himself.

> The conservatives were indignant at the fact that the doctrine of non-resistance to evil barred the way to violent suppression of revolutionary elements, whereas the revolutionaries were indignant at the fact that the doctrine of non-resistance barred the way to the overthrow of the conservatives. Paradoxically enough, the revolutionaries attacked the principle of non-resistance in spite of the fact that it was the most formidable and dangerous weapon against any kind of despotism, for ever since the world began, all kinds of violence – from the Inquisition to the Schlisselburg Fortress – have been based on a radically different principle, that of the need to resist evil by violence.

In Tolstoy's lifetime and later, until the outbreak of the First World War, the Tolstoyan movement in Russia, represented by a group of his faithful followers and several peasant communes, was only able to make a limited impact, being constantly threatened with reprisals by the government. And although Tolstoy's ideas of non-violence had made a considerably greater impact on the world public, in Russia, both before the First World War and during the war, Tolstoy's supporters, who collected signatures for a protest against the war and refused to serve in the army, were thrown into prison on charges of state treason.

In 1895, peasants of the Dukhobor religious sect, who held views similar to Tolstoy's doctrine, acting in accordance with the programme of 'moral reforms' drawn up by their leader, P.V. Vergin, destroyed their weapons, refused to carry out military service and handed back their military cards to the authorities, with the result that many of them were forced to emigrate in order to avoid state repression. Tolstoy, who had always supported them, took steps to provide them with financial assistance and donated a share of his own literary income for their benefit.

On the whole, the religious pacifist movement in Russia, represented as it was by a small number of people who were subjected to constant persecution, did not exert any significant influence in Russian society, being rather in the nature of an exclusive enclave. However, during the same period, a trend formed in the Russian pacifist movement that was based on the principles of international law and depended on liberal Russian intellectuals for support.

Russian pacifist lawyers could not accept Tolstoy's socio-ethic concept, for he regarded an unjust state 'as an assembly of a group of people who rape other people' and viewed with mistrust Western governments' alleged search for 'such a combination that would restrict their own actions', that is, a Court of Arbitration. Instead, the lawyers put forward a progamme for the settlement of conflicts according to the principles of international law, with an emphasis on World Peace Congresses and the national peace societies, which were founded in the West in the late nineteenth century. Although they regarded Tolstoy as 'a great peace-maker', a master of the human mind and an anti-militarist, they recognized the need for an army capable of ensuring defence.

Russian pacifism was the product of Russian liberalism, and a Peace Society was established in Russia with much difficulty. It was founded by prominent lawyers and intellectuals, who called themselves 'peace-lovers' and 'pacifists' and were members of the Talk Circle, and headed by Count Komarovsky and Prince P.D. Dolgorukov. The statute of the Russian Peace Society was written in the late nineteenth century by its original founders. However, when Prince Dolgorukov asked Foreign Minister Sinyagin for permission to set up the society again, he received the following answer: 'Let's discuss other, more important matters.' In fact, this talk took place soon after the call for peace issued by Tsar Nicolas II, when Russian diplomacy was busy advocating the convocation of The Hague peace conference.

The issue of setting up a Russian Peace Society was raised again in August 1908, when Tolstoy's eightieth birthday was celebrated. After prolonged and tortuous talks at the Department of Societies, permission was finally granted. The Moscow Peace Society, with Prince Dolgorukov and Count Komarovsky at its head, was only set up in December 1909 and by 1911 it had a membership of 300, with branches in Revel and St Petersburg.

The Kiev Peace Society, founded in 1909 by Count M.S. Tyshkevich, O.T. Glinka and O.P. Kosach, had eighty-five members, with politicians, diplomats and top clergy among them. The society operated with considerable help from the Catholic Church and received the blessing of Pope Pius X.

In 1912 publication of *Vestnik mira* (*Bulletin of Peace*), Russia's first pacifist periodical, was started in St Petersburg; it canvassed pacifist ideas and promoted the formation of new pacifist groups. That is why at a meeting in Moscow, held on 27 April 1913 and attended by delegates from St Petersburg, Moscow, Kiev, Novocherkassek, Helsingfors, Warsaw and Revel, an attempt was made at the unification of peace groups and societies. This, however, ended in failure on the eve of the First World War.

A number of women's organizations took part in the Russian pacifist movement. The most important among them was the Russian Committee of the League of Peace, founded in 1899 in St Petersburg, with A.N. Shabanova at its head. The Committee adopted a resolution of Russian women's 'solidarity with peace' and organized a mammoth meeting of women on 4 May 1913. The resolution was signed by 40,000 women. The Russian Society of Mutual Charity, chaired by Shabanova, also advocated pacifist ideas.

The Orthodox clergy were dependent upon and completely under the control of the state during this period so they did not join the pacifist movement – although many Russian pacifists were convinced that the Church, if it were independent and free to act in the spirit of Christian doctrine, would be the most appropriate body to advocate the idea of peace.

Essentially, Russian pacifists were active in three spheres: research into the norms of international law, campaigning for armament cuts and promoting the ideas of the maintenance of peace. The pacifists, especially Count Komarovsky, believed that the idea of peace generally passes through three stages in its development: national unification, interparliamentary unions and peace conferences. A fourth stage, establishment of an international organization, would follow and was described by them as 'an international organization of humanity', 'a legal organization of the nations' whose shoots were visible in the universalist trend in the development of civilization in the early 1900s.

The pacifists attempted to intervene in state affairs such as budget and finance, foreign policy and defence even though they were considered, according to Milyukov, 'risky enough not only from the viewpoint of the broad public's indifference to those issues'. However, the elaboration of the concept of the International Tribunal and the Court of Arbitration was their dominant concern. After the foundation of the Peace Society, the organizations united their efforts to promote the idea of maintenance of peace on the basis of international law. For example, in the spring of 1911, the Russian Parliamentary Group raised the issue of arms limitation at a sitting of the State Duma and moved that it be put on the agenda of the Third Hague Conference. Apart from this, a report was prepared detailing problems in the peacemaking procedure and the International Court. On 6 November 1911, the Moscow Peace Society adopted resolutions on the need to have a Court of Arbitration and urged the Tsarist government to sign agreements on an obligatory procedure of arbitration, at least with allied or friendly states.

After the outbreak of the Balkan wars, Russian pacifists called on Russia and Austria to observe strict neutrality, although most of the society members had previously voted against this resolution and it had not been officially adopted. 'This war', *Vestnik mira* wrote in December 1912, 'testifies more than any other that wars break out because of the selfish and unjust motives of some people and the shortsightedness and negligence of others rather than as a result of the inner logic of events or historical necessity.'

The Europeanist movement of the second half of the nineteenth century was an important stage in the evolution of Europeanism. Building on the ideas and practice of the French Revolution, the movement developed the concepts of human rights and democratic principles. The slogan of a United States of Europe was first put forward and substantiated then, and it was interpreted in the context of the liberation movement and democratic reforms on the continent. The Europeanism of Victor Hugo and Giuseppe Mazzini and their associates in many respects inspired the Europeanist theorists of the twentieth century. Michelet and Chateaubriand, Cattaneo and Gögg have all contributed to the development of Europeanist ideas and desires.

But while the pacifist tradition has firmly established itself in European social thought, a negative and narrow class-ridden approach to the democratic pacifist movement of the nineteenth century and the idea of a United States of Europe has long predominated in Soviet historiography. While admitting the natural and objective distinctions in the positions of revolutionary democrats and bourgeois liberals, Soviet historiography refused to see the progressive aspects of the latter, concentrating its attention on the 'limited' and 'inconsistent' nature of bourgeois liberalism and its contact with the bourgeois 'ruling circles'. This approach reflected Soviet historiography's over-ideologized position and class irreconcilability and also the complete lack of acceptance by Marxism–Leninism of liberal ideas and views.

The renouncement of this narrow approach to history now makes it possible for Russian historians to take a more realistic view of the European liberalism of the 1850s–90s and the contribution made by liberal Europeanist thought to the formation of the concept of European unity.

In analysing the events of the 1850s–90s, it is necessary to consider the ideas of Slavonic identity. The trend for the unification of Slavonic peoples served as a prerequisite for the formulation and development of pan-Slavonic ideas, which provoked sharp controversy among conservative and moderate liberal circles. Revolutionary-democratic thinkers in Russia and other European Slavonic countries also took part in those clashes.

9

NIKOLAI DANILEVSKY'S *RUSSIA AND EUROPE*

Nikolai Danilevsky, a scholar who took an interest in many subjects, including natural sciences, was known as a predecessor of Oswald Spengler and Arnold Toynbee. He was the author of the concept of cultural-historical types (or 'local' civilizations) and a prominent theoretician of pan-Slavism. 'Does Russia belong to Europe?' was the central issue of Danilevsky's book *Russia and Europe* (1864). That question was a focus of attention in Russian social thinking throughout the nineteenth century and Danilevsky contributed to the discussion about Russia and Europe, East and West, that had been started in the mid-nineteenth century by Slavophiles and Westerners in Russia.

Followers of the Slavophile doctrine, whose popularity was on the decline by the 1870s, regarded Danilevsky's book as a catechism for the doctrine. At the same time, however, he introduced some new, for Slavophiles, aspects for the solution of the problem, primarily owing to the fact that the comparison of Europe and Russia seemed to be a logical step in the context of the world historical process. In exploring the subject of Russia–Europe, the author inevitably raised the questions 'What is Europe?' and 'What is Russia?' and introduced the problem of the evolution of the Russian idea in history.

Being a follower of Giovanni Battista Vico and Johann Gottfried Herder, Danilevsky produced a multilinear diagram of the world historical process, taking original national culture in its cyclical development as its basic unit. Danilevsky combined the idea of cyclism with that of the onward movement of history that is based on continuity in the development of various forms of culture and changes in socio-economic relations. Consequently, progress was regarded by Danilevsky as an opportunity 'to criss-cross the whole space, which is the sphere of the historical activity of humanity, in all directions', and not as a linear onward movement. Thus, any culture, Danilevsky believed, promotes progressive development, for it creates its own inimitable version of historical development. Danilevsky's concepts enabled him to counterpose to the widespread idea of Eurocentrism the principle of the equivalent value of cultures, valued by him mostly for their originality.

Danilevsky believed that any people having a language of their own and political independence could form a cultural-historical type and cover a certain cycle of development. Danilevsky, whose views had for some time been developed under the influence of positivism, was among the first Russian historians who sought to present history as an 'organic' process and make history a science bound by the same standards as the natural sciences. It was partly because of the influence of positivism that, according to Danilevsky, culture went through the same stages in its development as a living organism. The initial stage in its development, when the distinctive features of a national culture are formed, was described by Danilevsky as an ethonographic period. This was followed by the process of formation of statehood, which serves as a period of discipline of sorts for a people. As a result, a strong state power emerges; this power is called upon to protect the original chamber of the culture and offers an opportunity for the people to switch from 'the unbridled tribal freedom' to the state of civic freedom. After this begins a stage of prosperity which Danilevsky compared to the period of fruition in vegetation. It is a time of civilizing activity, a realization of all opportunities for the cultural-historical type. Just as in living organisms, this stage is followed by a decline that leads the civilization to catastrophe (Rome) or stagnation (China). Later, the given cultural-historical type may still exist but as a component part of a new type.

Danilevsky looked for confirmation of his concept of world history, picking out the most significant examples that corresponded to his model. However, he believed his most vivid proof was a comparison of Europe and Russia, a central theme of his book. Danilevsky regarded Europe as typifying the Germanic–Romanic cultural-historical type that arose from the ruins of the Roman Empire rather than a traditional part of the world, and he saw Russia as the centre of the Slavonic cultural-historical type which had inherited the traditions of Greek–Byzantine civilization.

Proceeding from his idea of the asynchronous development of cultural-historical types, Danilevsky believed that the Europe and Russia of that period had lived through various stages of development since the sixteenth century, with Europe being in the stage of civilization and Russia in the final period of the formation of statehood. Thus, in Danilevsky's system, European progress was devoid of the unique nature ascribed to it by many nineteenth-century Western historians who regarded Europe as the vehicle of civilizing principles in history. Danilevsky regarded the stage of European prosperity as a logical stage for all cultural-historical types that would inevitably be followed by decline. No one civilization can solve all the tasks facing humanity, none of them can fully realize the 'idea' of history and progress – this is the basic thesis of Danilevsky's book.

In analysing European history, Danilevsky admits the achievements of that civilization in the sphere of culture and politics: 'they have managed to combine the political might of the state with its internal freedom'. At the same time, Danilevsky notes negative aspects and contradictions which, he believes, would inevitably lead Europe to catastrophe. Characteristically and in contrast to Spengler, to whom Danilevsky is often compared, Danilevsky attributes Europe's decline to specific historical reasons, rooted in political and economic relations, rather than to the regularities of a biological cycle. In his forecasts of Europe's future Danilevsky takes a stand similar to that of the Slavophiles, with their utter rejection of the bourgeois relations and revolutionary upheavals that were caused by the process of proletarianization and pauperization of the masses.

The two main factors responsible for the negative results and which affected the special features of European development were, Danilevsky believed, first, the fact that the European cultural-historical type was born at a time when the Roman Empire fell from the blows of Franco-Germanic tribes and, second, the excessive stress placed on the individualistic and 'violent' principles of the vanquished and the victors. The conquest, Danilevsky maintained, had a boomerang effect on the new society, and this factor had contributed to the emergence of an equally effective feudal dependence, which greatly added to the burden of oppression; the ambitious Germanic–Romanic nature was responsible for the split of the Catholic Church and for religious intolerance and, later, led to atheism. The entire history of Europe as seen by Danilevsky was marked by the violent nature of its processes which, inevitably, had to lead to conflict and catastrophe.

In contrast, Russia's history was quite organic and natural. According to Danilevsky's concepts, this could also be attributed to the nature of the formation of statehood, the establishment of feudal relations and the acquisition of new lands. Russia's organic development, which was ascribed by Danilevsky to the mild Slavonic disposition and to the absence of conquest in its history, should,

Danilevsky believed, enable Russia to realize all aspects of civilizing activity and enter into a new stage in the development of cultural-historical types.

Naturally, many of Danilevsky's conclusions are debatable and have not been corroborated by later developments – especially his desire to contrast the destinies of Europe and Russia and exclude the possibility of integration. His assessments of serfdom, of the advantages of the monarchist rule in Russia and of the 'sanity' of socio-economic relations in post-reform Russia were clearly idealized. At the same time, however, his attempt to present Russia and Europe as two different cultural-historical types, each with its own specific historical development and mentality and whose development is in many respects determined by special external factors, is the subject of great interest.

Danilevsky's book summarizes the main dispute engaged in by Russian social thinkers, with the result that he takes the old arguments between Russian Westerners and Slavophiles to a new level. Soviet historiography, as a rule, took a rather one-sided and oversimplified view of the concepts advocated by the Westerners and Slavophiles. While there were various trends common to both, one thing was clear: their disputes reflected different visions of European realities, the future of Europe and Russia's place in it.

In the context of the late nineteenth–early twentieth centuries, the extreme wing of the Slavophiles rejected out of hand, from positions of pan-Slavism, any form of acceptance by Russia of European civilization. Danilevsky analysed the problem of 'Russia–Europe' in a broad scientific-cultural context, attaching to it a civilizing meaning. Through his works, Danilevsky expressed the views of those who in fact excluded Russia from Europe and the European tradition. European values, associated with the Greek–Roman tradition, were regarded by him as alien to the Russian spirit and mentality. Danilevsky's views represented a substantial stage in the evolution of the so-called Russian idea which is interpreted as an antithesis to the European idea, the European spirit and the pan-European cultural-historical tradition.

In addition, after the defeat of the 1848–49 revolutions, disappointment in the European model became increasingly widespread among Russian Westerners, especially among democratically minded intellectuals. As a result, Russian social thought clearly began drifting away from West European traditions; hence, European ideas and moods receded into the background in Russia.

So the tendency that had been so vividly manifested after Napoleon's defeat with the homecoming of Russian officers who had been strongly influenced by the liberal ideas of the French Enlightenment and the theories of Voltaire and Rousseau was clearly declining even though it had been briefly nourished in the mid-nineteenth century by feelings of sympathy for the Italian Carbonari and the Greek revolutonaries. Moreover, new problems had arisen on Russia's political horizon that reflected a growing revolutionary mood, and presaged the emergence of social democracy and Bolshevism and the offensive launched by the Russian reactionaries.

10

THE PROJECT OF MIDDLE EUROPE: NEW INTERPRETATIONS OF THE SLOGAN OF THE UNITED STATES OF EUROPE

The early twentieth century ushered in a radically new stage in world and European development. Mass media, the formation of big monopolies and cartels, as well as blocs and coalitions, stimulated the spread of imperialist and universalist ideas, reflecting mounting centrifugal trends in world development.

On this basis, ideas and plans for European unification, including those under the slogan the United States of Europe, revived. However, in the new historical context that slogan lost its democratic content. Vague and speculative enough as it was in the mid-nineteenth century, in the early twentieth century it was regarded in certain circles as a symbol that merely expressed nostalgia for the past century. The idea of a United States of Europe now betrayed the liberals' fears about the continent's future, at a time when Europe was being split into powerful, hostile blocs and coalitions and when the great powers' rivalries assumed a global scale and were fraught with the danger of a new world war.

Moreover, that slogan was also used by some leaders of international social democracy. They spoke about the United States of Europe in order to counter reactionary alliances and military blocs. In particular, the slogan was an object of hot debate at branch conferences of the Russian Social-Democratic Labour Party (RSDLP) held in Berne in February–March 1915. However, even there the slogan was devoid of any specific ideas.

Guided by their liberal illusions and unmindful of the new stage in European development, bourgeois liberals and certain social-democratic circles still thought in terms of the European realities of

74

the past century. With the sharpening of international imperialist conflicts, those circles sought to prove that the United States of Europe would serve as a cure-all and help find a way out of the crisis. These were of course pipe-dreams – and there were others.

Certain circles regarded the United States of Europe as an obstacle to the advance of the radical-left section of the working-class movement. Various projects for European unification which were revived at the turn of the century were also used by the reactionary circles of imperialist powers to attain their aggressive goals. The Germans sought to win European domination, recarve the already divided world and dreamed of winning new colonies, sources of minerals and markets. Great Britain wanted to preserve its position as a leading world power and spared no effort to retain its colonies and win its contest with Germany for world domination. France was engaged in rivalries with Germany and looked for new allies in Europe and outside it. Tsarist Russia was hatching plans to set up a Slavonic Federation that would enable it, on the one hand, to rebuff German encroachments and, on the other, to buttress its positions in Slavonic countries and in the Balkans.

In a period of internationalization of capital and the formation of monopolies, capitalist countries' rivalries assumed a global scale. European 'unity' was realized in the establishment of a system of military–political blocs and pacts, which was a logical consequence of the notorious 'European balance'. A fierce clash between the two hostile European coalitions, the Entente and the German–Austrian blocs, was inevitable.

Simultaneously, the process of the final division of the world was taking place. European capitalism again manifested its unity in the conquest of what remained of the colonies. France seized Tunisia; Belgium produced new forms of domination in the Congo; France and Great Britain signed an agreement on the division of spheres of influence in Iran; and Germany, Great Britain, France, Tsarist Russia, Italy, Austria and Hungary, jointly with the United States and Japan, brutally suppressed the Boxer Rebellion in China.

A wide range of slogans and doctrines were put forward in a number of projects for Europe in the early twentieth century, which found expression in the opposing positions held by various European powers, social forces and movements.

Let us first analyse the results of the Congress of Political Sciences, held in Paris in 1900, which discussed various European ideas of the turn of the century. The congress was sponsored by the Society of Graduates and Students of the Free School of Political Sciences.

Discussions at the congress were concentrated on the issue of the formation of the United States of Europe. In their reports to the congress, A. Leroi-Bolier and four other delegates dealt with various aspects of the problem and stressed the vital need for a pan-European organization.

The basis of Leroi-Bolier's statement was that no adequate steps had been taken to uphold common European interests. An expedition of Europeans to China in 1900 (which was the euphemism used to denote the action to suppress the Boxer uprising) had revealed that European powers were quite unprepared for joint action. Therefore it would be highly desirable to set up a standing body – a union or an association of European states – to uphold common European interests. This idea, Leroi-Bolier believed, would not only attract the attention of a daydreamer or a philosopher, probably bent on attaining a superhuman ideal of peace and justice on Earth. Such an idea, he said, was also worthy of the attention of a positive mind, of a person who would put material and political considerations above all and who could not fail to see the great damage caused to Europe through rivalries and hostility among its regions in the context of current increases in broad international contacts.

Convinced that strength was the main precondition for the maintenance of peace, Leroi-Bolier expressed his firm belief that the unification of Europe into a single alliance would add new strength to it and ensure peace, as well as eliminating many of the inter-state conflicts. However, the formation of an American-style United States of Europe was hardly acceptable, Leroi-Bolier believed. The European nations had such a glorious and rich past that they would never agree to renounce their historical and national identities. No matter what benefits Europe might receive from unification, it would have lost another, no less important quality – its cultural superiority. A European alliance should restrain the ardour of narrow-minded nationalist circles, but, on the other hand, it should not rob anyone of their motherland. Hence, the German union as it was before 1866 or the Swiss union before 1848 should serve as a model, Leroi-Bolier believed.

However, he excluded Great Britain and Russia from the European alliance of the future, as he saw it, since the interests of the former, because of its imperial possessions, were different from those of the rest of Europe and Russia, he believed, was not a part of historical Europe. The speaker's other arguments served to substantiate the thesis of the non-European nature of Russia and its residents, for, Leroi-Bolier asserted, its traditions and political systems, the public spirit and even nature itself made it different from the West. He tried to prove that Russia was not bound by feelings of Western solidarity, which characterized the German and Romanic peoples, no matter how different they could be in other respects. Leroi-Bolier pointed out that even those Russians who did not share such national prejudices believed that Russia, as the natural leader of the Slavonic and Orthodox world, had its special mission. Even if they did not dare speak about Russia's future domination in the West, they believed that owing to its vast area and rich natural resources it might be spared the trouble of joining a pan-European alliance. However, the speaker said, common political and economic interests would lead to the conclusion of an agreement between Russia and Western Europe, and the Franco-Russian alliance was the first step towards this.

In his report to the congress, A. Fleur pointed out that Europe was more than a geographic notion or a political fiction and that European countries felt an ever greater mutual solidarity and strove for more active joint action in managing Eastern affairs in order to promote the interests of Europe as a whole. Fleur discussed the issue of setting up, on the lower reaches of the Danube, a European Commission charged with ensuring freedom of navigation on the Danube and the neutrality of the Suez Canal, which would be directly against the excessive claims of Great Britain. This Commission, the speaker asserted, would be an embodiment of the idea of a European association to serve common and permanent European interests.

R. Dollo, in his report to the congress, divided common European interests into three groups: political, economic and 'sanitary'. The political interests of Europe as a whole dictated the need to hold international congresses and set up alliances of the Holy Alliance type, as well as to ensure the neutrality of some countries, measures to protect the Mediterranean as a sea used by all European countries, etc. International agreements on rivers, customs duties and forms of international financial control were all manifestly of pan-European economic interest. European 'sanitary' interests were frequently discussed at international conferences and included, among other things, ways to prevent the spread of Asian epidemics to Europe.

The interests of Europe as a spiritual and cultural entity were not restricted to one continent; they were applicable in other parts of the world as well. Their sphere of application in America was contracting rapidly because of European errors, although there was still wide scope for activity in this respect in Africa. Decisions adopted by the 1884–85 Berlin Conference, Dollo asserted, would prove beneficial to Europe and to the indigenous African population. It was also vitally important for Europe, Dollo stressed, that Latin American republics should not yield to US economic and political pressure. Latin America had closer links with southern Europe than with the United States. Dollo expressed regret that Spain and France had taken almost no steps to promote their influence in that region, pointing out that the seizure of the Philippines by the United States had come as a consequence of negligence on the part of Europe. Great Britain had yielded to the United States on the Panama Canal issue, and no one knew how long the former would be able to keep its hold on the West Indies and Canada. If the decisions of the 1889–90 Washington Congress were implemented, all Latin American republics would be entirely dependent on the US in the economic sphere, which, Dollo believed, would do a lot of harm not only to those republics but also to Europe.

G. Isamber's report dealt with a wide range of problems connected with projects for European unification. He pointed out to the Congress that the establishment of peace in Europe had been previously associated with disarmament and the formation of the Court of Arbitration. However, The Hague Conference revealed that the realization of those two objectives was hardly practicable. As far as the Court of Arbitration was concerned, while the states applied to it on a purely voluntary basis, its activity could scarcely be effective. However, to make applications to it obligatory would necessitate setting up a political organization with legislative and executive functions to give the Court's decisions the legal force of those adopted by the International Court. For an alliance of states to be vital and reliable, its members must be united both by identity of interests and by a common civilization.

Taking account of these criteria, Isamber discussed the problem of relations between Europe and the US. He pointed out that, although Europe and the United States had their origins and religion in common and most of the US population had had an education similar to their European counterparts, the United States had its own distinctive economic interests. However, in order to promote universal peace, it would be desirable for the US and Europe to unite in a gigantic political 'syndicate'.

Isamber believed that the unification of all European states would create a force that could exert an influence in all parts of the world; if Spain joined such an organization, the US would not dare to seize its colonies. In discussing the composition of such a European alliance, Isamber opposed the idea of Turkey joining it, for it represented a different civilization. He considered that a confederation would be the best form for the unification of European countries. As distinct from federation members, confederation members remained sovereign states, he said, and since separate states over-zealously uphold their independence, they would hardly agree to a closer alliance.

The confederation, Isamber believed, should be a republic, not a monarchy, for the latter presupposed the principle of subordination which would be unacceptable to free states. Moreover, electing a monarch might well trigger off disturbances and upheavals. Pan-European representative bodies should be based on the principles of equality of separate states and proportional representation, and all states should be represented in the European army in proportion to their population. If one of the allied states did not obey an obligatory decision, the pan-European Executive Council could use that army to enforce that decision.

The ideas put forward by speakers at the Congress of Political Sciences make it possible to draw some general conclusions about the transformation of the slogan the United States of Europe by the beginning of the twentieth century.

First, the slogan was obviously now interpreted in a different way. Clearly the United States of Europe that was discussed at the Congress was different from the association that had been planned to be contraposed to the reactionary Holy Alliance by Mazzini, Hugo and Garibaldi. This time the association of European countries was planned to be a shock force in the struggle for colonies and dependencies. So the former slogan of a United States of Europe, which once united European democrats and liberals, in the new circumstances was being turned into a weapon in the hands of those who strove for domination.

Supporters of the European confederation admitted with regret that, among other things, Europe had lost Latin America and had not realized its opportunities in Africa. In the context of the rivalries between the great powers, they sought to limit the growing influence of the United States of America. Discussions held in 1900 showed that the battle for natural resources and markets was the focus of general attention, thus making it a global problem in the policy of the great powers.

Second, the idea of the United States of Europe, which in the 1840s–60s had been associated with the establishment of global peace, thus revealing the interconnection between Europeanism and pacifism, at the turn of the century was fraught with the threat of new wars and conflicts, on a global scale. Pacifist motifs were gradually ousted by the ideas of domination and schemes of preparations for war. This turn of events not only signified the onset of a new stage in world history but also represented a crisis for pacifism and reflected its inability to prevent conflict and war.

'Official pacifism' was gaining increasingly greater currency. Pacifist phraseology was successfully used in official policy certainly not for peaceful purposes but rather to camouflage the real intentions of European governments. Terms such as 'disarmament', 'arbitration' and 'guarantees' were often used as a screen by those who were making war preparations and represented the force behind the arms drive.

Third, ideas for European unification, both on a continental and regional scale, were used effectively in the powers' rivalries for European domination. This trend in Europeanism had deep roots. For many decades the slogans and theories of European alliances had been put forward by French politicians and statesmen to establish French domination in Europe. In the nineteenth century some Italian politicians and thinkers were dreaming about a revival of the former grandeur of Italy in Europe. The Iron Chancellor Bismarck, who sought to unite the dissociated German states, at that time obviously wished to see a united Germany as the predominant European power. Various ideas and projects for gaining influence in Europe were put forward by the Russian tsarist authorities as well.

Thus in the early twentieth century, such theories and specific projects were once again revived. This time they combined regional and continental, national and international interests and various positions – from openly rightist and aggressive to bourgeois-liberal and social-democratic – were now united in propaganda for the United States of Europe.

The scheme for setting up a so-called Middle Europe can be assessed in a similar way. The prehistory of the ideas of Middle Europe dates from the time of Metternich and Friedrich List, and was revived in connection with the events of 1848 and 1860. Bismarck was fond of talking about the grandeur of the future Middle Europe. The idea of Middle Europe was, as a rule, associated with the destiny of Austro-Hungary. The geographic borders of Middle Europe were the subject of fierce debate, which again stressed the political meaning of the project for central European unity.

The idea of Middle Europe was summarized by the German politician Friedrich Naumann, in his book *Mitteleuropa* which was published in 1916. The author warned from the outset that the formation of Middle Europe was 'a difficult task and that one act or decision would be insufficient for its realization. It will take no less than half a century.' Naumann attempted to prove that Middle Europe had its own history and proclaimed Charlemagne, Rudolf Habsburg,

Maximilian and Charles V to be Middle European personalities. He associated the Napoleonic era with the beginning of a new stage in the history of Middle Europe and sang the praises of Bismarck, whom he regarded as a politician of a later period:

> If Bismarck had been able to rise from the dead in order to conduct peace talks after the war, he would have been greeted enthusiastically not only by all parties of the German Empire but also by all nationalities in Austria and Hungary without any exception, for, in spite of the lost battle of Königsgrad, he would have been regarded by all of us as the father of Middle Europe – from the Northern Sea to the Bosnian border.

Middle Europe, Naumann believed, was the result of Prussian victories, especially those of the spring of 1870.

He then turned to establishing the essence of Middle Europe. Its basis, he believed, would be an alliance between Germany, Austria and Hungary – naturally under the aegis of Germany: 'To have Austria and Prussia merged in a historical alliance would be almost tantamount to combining the eighteenth and nineteenth centuries.'

The main stages on the way to the formation of Middle Europe, Naumann believed, would be the solution of economic and customs issues, the formation of joint armies and shared institutions. 'Now or never', he exclaimed, 'a single entity should be set up between East and West, that is Middle Europe should be formed between Russia and the Western powers.' The description of the economic basis of Middle Europe gives a clue to the vision of the author and his associates. 'The German economic system', he wrote 'should be accepted by the whole of Middle Europe. A military defensive alliance will serve as the basis of internal contacts.'

While justifying Germany's rights in the formation of Middle Europe, Naumann puts forward, in particular, the argument that Middle Europe would occupy an area of 6.5 million square kilometres, that is, smaller than countries such as Russia, China, the United States of America or Brazil.

The issue of Middle Europe's borders, as solved by Naumann, was of immense interest. In one chapter, Naumann mentions the territory situated between the Baltic and the Mediterranean and also the European and Asian parts of Turkey, including a part of Arabia. He does not specify directly the countries and regions that were meant, as he saw it, to be incorporated into Middle Europe, although, according to numerous data cited in the book, one may conclude that Naumann

81

and his supporters intended to unite under the aegis of Germany a vast territory, which, apart from Germany, must include Austro-Hungary and its possessions in the Balkans and the Danube basin.

Naumann points out that some supporters of the Middle Europe project proposed to incorporate Holland, the Scandinavian countries, Romania, Bulgaria and Greece, while others were even ready to include France, Spain, Italy, Switzerland and Belgium, planning to form later the United States of Europe. Naumann, however, believed that such ideas were unrealistic and even harmful. 'We refrain from such vague plans', he states. 'At the current juncture we speak exclusively about the unification of Germany and Austro-Hungary, for those two states should be united before it is at all possible to think about issuing a call to other countries that may yield successful results.'

Naumann seems to be afraid of provoking a showdown by arousing the discontent of Austrians and Hungarians, who 'are concerned exclusively about their own Balkan and Turkish interests which they take closer to heart than ours, and they are embarrassed by the fact that Germany will be willing to pursue its Turkish policy without consulting them'. However, almost in the same breath, Naumann cannot resist the temptation to mention some of the lands that could, with the passage of time, be incorporated in Middle Europe.

> Who can predict in what direction the trench borders of Middle Europe will run? Will it include Romania and Bessarabia? Will those borders run along the Vistula or won't they? Should Bulgaria be incorporated in the sphere of Middle Europe? Shall we be able to ensure that the railway leading to Constantinople remains in the possession of our reliable allies? What's to become of Antwerp? What will be the situation in the Baltic Sea after the war? Thus, hundreds of questions arise. The indisputable thing is that their solution hinges largely on whether or not the German–Austro-Hungarian alliance is a desirable and settled matter. The formation of Middle Europe depends on it.

As you can see, Naumann shared the mood of those who wanted to see the borders of Middle Europe far to the west, south and east of the continent. Anyway, he states unequivocally that 'the area of the world economic region called Middle Europe should be greater than that of Germany, Austria and Hungary'.

In his book Naumann devotes special attention to the problem of the mechanisms of administration in the future united formation.

In this context, Prague is offered as the Middle European centre, Hamburg as its maritime trade centre, Berlin as its stock-exchange centre, and Vienna as its juridical centre. Naumann also analyses military aspects of the future alliance, pointing out that 'the need for a unified military organization is conditional on the notion of an economic world area'. In conclusion, Naumann states that the solution of the issue of Middle Europe would depend on the results of a world war, when each state would certainly consider its future chances and potentialities.

> Hungary probably bears the greatest share of responsibility. This non-German state holds in its hands to a certain extent the future destiny of the German nation, for if Hungary refused to join Middle Europe, its formation would be hardly possible at all ... However, it should be supposed that the idea of Middle Europe would meet with powerful support by the monarchs of the two allied empires; the Austrian and German Emperors together with their peoples are faced with the most important problem that will call for the complete renunciation of many old principles and the comprehension of many new ones. The Nibelung loyalty should serve as the basic principle of the common state system ... After this war we shall never be the same again. We shall return from the front as citizens of Middle Europe.

Such was the project for European restructuring offered by theoreticians of the German Empire in the years of the First World War. Middle Europe was among the first specific proposals for European integration in the twentieth century. It reflected the growing ambitions of Germany's ruling circles who sought to unify a considerable part of Europe under the aegis of Germany.

In fact, this project revived in a new historical context the trend for the unification of the whole of Europe, or a part of it, under the domination of one European power. European unification under the aegis of Germany was opposed by other European countries. In particular, it was during the years of the First World War that the so-called Mediterranean or Latin ideas for the unification of European nations were revived.

In February 1915, a meeting was held in Paris for representatives of the so-called Latin nations, which was chaired by P. Dechanel. The President of the French Republic, Raymond Poincaré, greeted its participants. Representatives of Greece, Portugal, Romania, Spain,

Italy and France were among those who attended it and addressed the audience.

Supporters of 'Latin Europe' appealed to the traditions of antiquity and also used the phraseology of Mazzini and other leaders of the Risorgimento period. They included all Mediterranean countries in the 'Latin-Roman Empire', paying attention above all to moral and cultural-historical factors, without losing sight of political considerations associated with the consolidation of those countries' efforts in the fight against Germany.

This sounded very much like ideological preparation for Italy's entry into the war on the side of the Entente – which happened three months after the Paris meeting. The supporters of Latin Europe sought to conceal the aims pursued by Italy and the Entente in the war and presented the war as a campaign launched by 'democratic' Europe against reactionary Germany and its allies.

The early twentieth century also saw a revival of the 'Slavonic idea', always a stable tradition in Russian public opinion, that was attributable to the desire of some rather heterogeneous strata in Russian society to offer the pan-Slavonic idea in opposition to pan-Germanic projects.

In July 1908, the first pan-Slavonic congress was held in Prague, and the second such congress was held in Sofia in 1910. These congresses were dominated by reactionaries, who manipulated the pan-Slavonic ideas in order to smuggle in the ideas of autocracy, chauvinism and orthodoxy. However, there were many members of the artistic and academic communities in Russia and other Slavonic countries who unequivocally advocated the idea of the Slavonic people's cultural identity and tried to put forward nineteenth-century democratic traditions.

During these years the idea of a Balkan Federation was also put forward, and met with broad support in social-democratic circles; Russian social democrats, led by Lenin, strove to make use of both the Slavonic and Balkan ideas to promote the development of the revolutionary movement in eastern and south-eastern Europe.

In general, in the early twentieth-century pan-German projects, the Latin and Slavonic ideas and the proposal for a Balkan Federation represented various aspects and versions of the developments in the European idea on a regional level. They were also evidence of sharp social and political struggles taking place around the various European ideas, concepts and projects.

Discussions on a United States of Europe by social-democratic circles took place on a continent-wide scale in the early twentieth century and therefore attracted the attention of left-wing circles to European projects. Those circles voiced the interests of the working class, trade unions and democratically minded intellectuals. Although fundamentally different views were expressed by Western social democrats and Bolsheviks, the very fact that joint discussions were held and interest was shown in the ideas of Lenin, Karl Kautsky, Georgy Plekhanov, Friedrich Adler, and others gave these discussions a pan-European dimension, so that they seemed to be a continuation of those held in the mid-nineteenth century.

But, alas, the joint discussions and mutual interest soon ended and the split between Bolsheviks and European social democracy, both ideological and political, rapidly became a reality.

11

LENIN'S CONCEPT OF WORLD
REVOLUTION: OCTOBER 1917 AND
THE DESTINIES OF EUROPE

Lenin's concept of world development and the history of socialism
had a great impact on the situation in the world and Europe. He, without doubt, knew about the various ideas and projects for European
unification. Moreover, the slogan of the United States of Europe was
a subject of hot debate among social-democrats throughout the world
before and during the First World War. This was probably why Lenin
turned to that subject by publishing his article 'On the Slogan of the
United States of Europe'. In it he says:

> If the slogan of the republican United States of Europe, put
> forward after the three most reactionary European monarchies,
> with that of Russia at the head, had been toppled, is absolutely
> invulnerable as a political slogan, then another essential problem
> remains, that of the economic content and meaning of that
> slogan. From the viewpoint of the economic basis of imperialism,
> i.e., the export of capital and the world's division by 'advanced'
> and 'civilized' colonial powers, and under capitalism the United
> States of Europe is either impossible or reactionary . . .

Under capitalism, he went on, the United States of Europe would
be tantamount to an agreement to the division of colonies. However,
under capitalism, any other basis or principle of division than force
was impossible. A billionaire could not share 'the national income' of
a capitalist country with anyone in any other way than in proportion to
his capital. He continues:

> Of course, temporary agreements between capitalists and powers
> are possible. In this sense the United States of Europe is also

possible as an agreement among European capitalists ... but what sort of agreement? Exclusively in order to suppress socialism in Europe by joint efforts and protect the plundered colonies by joint efforts against Japan and America ...

In that historical context, according to Lenin, the slogan of the United States of Europe could hardly serve as a means of attaining peace; that slogan was far from an alternative solution of the problem. The United States of Europe (if it were possible) would be just a temporary version of the system of imperialist blocs.

As can be seen, Lenin puts the problem of the United States of Europe, with his typical spirit, in a revolutionary context and discusses it as part of the concept of world revolution. But what was its essence? Lenin saw its final goal in the inevitable victory of world, and probably European, revolution. With respect to Europe Lenin's position was that it was a matter of unity, solidarity and actual joining of revolutionary efforts.

Germany and Great Britain were regarded by Lenin as the key European countries (after Russia) which had to follow in the footsteps of Russia. He thus put on the agenda the spread of the Soviet model of social development throughout the whole of Europe. In one sense, he viewed European unification in the context of world revolution. Naturally enough, it was not Europeanism as it had been interpreted by European thinkers of the past.

However, this was an idea which served as a continuation of theories that underlay the projects of the period of the French Revolution, when European countries were often described as revolutionary sisters. Lenin wrote at a time when European states might have formed an alliance of revolutionary countries, often referring to Marx's words about 'the great brotherhood' and the unity of world and European proletariat. According to Lenin's concept, Europe should have attained its new revolutionary-type activity, with all attributes and forms of the state system and political practice that were established in Russia in October 1917.

Before the October Revolution that viewpoint was rather speculative – it was a call, slogan or idea – whereas after it the possibility of transferring Russia's example and experience to Europe became a reality, a genuine aim of the state policy of Soviet Russia.

After the formation of the Comintern this aim assumed a world-wide dimension, having become the goal of the world communist movement, and in that particular context, primarily of the European communist movement. The Bolsheviks' European mission was revolution on a European scale, organized on the Bolshevik model. Lenin's concept of world revolution reflected his general vision of world development and the world historical process. Europe's future was viewed by Bolsheviks as the rejection of both bourgeois democracy and bourgeois values, that is, the values that had formed the basis of Europeanism since the French Revolution.

Central to the messianic mission of the October Revolution and Leninism was the fact that the Bolsheviks sought to bring liberation, a new Motherland and a new dimension of history primarily to the working people of Russia, but also to those of Europe and the whole world. That was the position held by most Bolshevik leaders. Added to this was the idea of the withering away of the state as the final goal, and some Bolshevik theoreticians also spoke about plans for a world association and the brotherhood of European and other peoples in a united community.

However, Lenin's concept should not be reduced exclusively to the idea of a world revolution. Russia, with its traditions and a special mission in the world, and Europe held a special place in Lenin's thinking and in his political theories and views. The national idea and commitment to the Russian tradition objectively clashed with Lenin's concept of world revolution. If we borrow the phraseology of the past, Russian nationalism in Soviet practice clashed with the internationalism which followed logically from orientation on world revolution.

This conflict can be traced in Lenin's pre-revolutionary writings and post-revolutionary practice. Hot debates in late 1917 and early 1918 about signing the Brest Peace Treaty with Germany brought to the fore the issues of the interconnection between national and international principles. In Lenin's general concept, this dualism obviously reflected the real picture of the development of Russian socio-political thought between the 1850s and 1900. Bolshevism sought to combine the Western and Slavophile traditions of Russian history, which was by no means accidental, for Bolshevism was both a specific Russian phenomenon and an international trend in social democracy.

In the context of the history of the European idea it may be pointed out that Lenin's doctrine on this issue was an attempt to follow the European Marxist tradition, its task being the triumph of the proletarian revolution primarily in Europe, and also the accumulation of Russian historical experience, combined with carrying on Russian traditions of the past. However, the subject of relations between Soviet Russia and Europe also had a specific historical aspect, associated with the situation in the world and Europe at that period, the policy of Soviet Russia after the victory of the October Revolution and action taken by the Western world.

The October Revolution and the First World War had a great impact on European development. First, Europe had lost its social homogeneity. Along with the states which had considerable experience of capitalist development over a long period of time, a new state had been set up in Europe that proclaimed socialism as its final goal and had implemented radical economic, social, political and cultural reforms. Thus, Russia now stood apart from the system of European states, a political system which had existed for many decades.

Second, the First World War led to a new balance of forces in Europe. The Austro-German bloc, one of the opposing coalitions, was defeated, with Great Britain and France moving to the fore on the European scene.

Apart from the new balance of forces resulting from the First World War, the war had also affected European thinking. Soviet historiography has probably underestimated this factor. Numerous books, works by thinkers and public leaders and memoirs written by diplomats, which appeared soon after the war were full of concern for the destiny of Europe. There was a premonition of imminent disaster in the air, a prevailing mood of decadence and pessimism.

Essentially after the October Revolution and the First World War Europe had entered a new stage in its development. The victorious revolution in Russia culminated in the establishment of a state with universal socialism as its goal: reforms in industry, restructuring of the social fabric and a new political system were specific stages on the way to this. An undeveloped democracy in Russia, with a multi-party system in an embryonic stage, and an open smear campaign unleashed against Social Revolutionaries and Mensheviks were factors behind the victory of the Bolshevik political programme and the Bolsheviks' orientation towards single-party government.

Sharp confrontations of hostile forces, rigid political and social principles and the division of many regions largely led to the tragic and protracted civil war that claimed thousands of lives, created dreadful havoc in the country and brought about economic catastrophe. That this was also partly due to the economic paralysis and political crisis caused in Russia by the world war, even before the October Revolution and the 1917 revolutionary outburst, was attributable to the dogmatic views held by Bolshevik leaders, their reluctance to co-operate with other parties and movements, and their maximalist programmatic principles.

The orientation of the new Russia's leaders on world revolution had far-reaching consequences for European and world development. Realization of the concept of world revolution in specific political practice presupposed support for and stimulation of European revolutionary movements, primarily in Germany, by Russia. The concept of world revolution was naturally closely linked with the Soviet Republic's relations with the rest of the world, particularly with European countries.

The concept of world revolution went through several stages in its development. The first stage (1917–20) was that of revolutionary hopes and aspirations, when the winds of the imminent world revolution were blowing throughout Russia. However, after 1920, when the revolutionary movement was on the ebb and there was almost no hope left for a European revolution, the second stage of the realization of the concept of world revolution set in. Although the concept was by no means renounced by the Soviet leaders and those of the Comintern, their determination for world revolution developed in other directions and assumed other forms. At that time the tasks were to set up communist parties in various European countries which would enjoy massive support and to make preparations for mass action by Europe's working classes.

The Soviet leaders' firm stand on the concept of world revolution gave rise to sharp confrontations and divisions in the world, especially in Europe, as well as to mistrust of the Soviet state. Paradoxically enough, the idea of world revolution fostered the Soviet leaders' imperial aspirations, prodding them to interference in the internal affairs of other countries and peoples.

During the 1920s and 1930s there were ups and downs in the development of the process of world revolution. After the advent of the Nazis to power in Germany, as is known, the situation in Europe changed, and the revolutionary forces were faced with other tasks. However, even in the second half of the 1930s ideas of world revolution were still cherished by the Soviet leaders.

One might cite many examples in European development after 1917 that would serve as evidence of the practical realization of this Soviet policy in internal affairs. For example, the November 1918 revolution in Germany, the 1919 revolutionary events in Austria and Hungary, the formation of the Comintern and communist parties, and the mass demonstrations by the working class and all European working people in the 1920s. All these are evidence of a revolutionary upsurge and the new situation in Europe following the October Revolution in Russia.

It is noteworthy that loyalty to the concept of world revolution was opposed to Western powers' policy. As soon as the Russian Revolution broke out, leading political parties and most prominent leaders in capitalist countries displayed sharply negative attitudes to the Russian social experiment. Non-recognition of the Soviet Republic, trade and economic blockades, foreign intervention and constant attempts to overthrow Soviet power testified to the fact that this trend in Western policy with respect to the USSR assumed a lasting and stable nature. One may quote numerous examples of decisions by the leaders of Great Britain, France and their transatlantic ally, as well as of other countries, directed against revolutionary Russia. The idea of holding down socialism and Bolshevism and preventing them spreading to Europe dominated the ideological and political strategy of the West.

Thus, on the one hand, the concept of world revolution and, on the other, the attitude of the capitalist world inevitably bred hostility and conflict between the new Russia's government and the capitalist world. The deepening split in social-democratic circles contributed to that confrontation. The Bolsheviks' rejection of the social-democratic programme with its reformist orientation, political and organizational clashes between the Bolsheviks and other socialist parties in Russia, and reprisals meted out to Social Revolutionaries and Mensheviks in Soviet Russia added to the tension in relations between the Bolsheviks and international social democracy. The formation of the Comintern and its split from the Socialist International only added to general hostility from Europe.

Thus, so far as the European idea is concerned, it may be said that, on the one hand, the Bolsheviks sought to organize Europe on a Soviet revolutionary model, seeing Europe's future in unification and victory for all revolutionary forces, and thereby increasingly isolating themselves not only from European conservatives but also from liberal and social-democratic circles. On the other hand, the abyss that divided West European left-wing forces was growing ever wider. Ever since the 1920s West European communist and socialist parties have stood in relentless opposition. Their visions of Europe and attitudes to European values and prospects of development were sharply different, which only added to the polarization and deepening of disagreements in European public opinion and its attitude to European realities.

However, the policy of Soviet Russia was not limited to offering support to the ideas of world revolution. The developments during that period were rather contradictory. An analysis of developments in the Soviet Union clearly shows that the trend of promoting world revolution and stimulating the revolutionary movement in other European countries went hand in hand with the idea of establishing normal economic and political relations with the capitalist world. There is currently a trend in historiography, including Soviet historiography, to contrast these two tendencies to prove that Lenin had come to the decision to attempt a peaceful coexistence with capitalism only after the failure of the course orientated on world revolution. However, some historians have concluded that dualism has always been a fixture in Soviet foreign policy, and in Lenin's time was manifested in the obvious contradiction between the policy for world revolution and the policy for peaceful co-existence.

In essence, Lenin's idea was to attempt to combine the two policies. He regarded the establishment of relations with capitalist countries in the context of the world revolution idea, considering them to be a primary respite, a stop-gap stage. But gradually the policy of building links with the West became important in its own right.

In this context a number of Lenin's articles during the First World War should be recalled. In one of them he wrote that after the possible victory of revolution in Russia, other countries would 'for some time retain a bourgeois or a pre-bourgeois system'. This statement may be regarded as implying possible future relations with other states for the Soviet country.

The same dual tendency was present in the Decree of Peace, the first foreign policy document adopted by the Soviet government. On the one hand, it clearly reflected the idea of world, primarily European, revolution and of the support to be offered by the new government to it, whereas, on the other hand, the decree stated that the Soviet government would remain loyal to the good-neighbour and equal treaties signed by Russia with other countries before the revolution.

The tendency was also clearly manifested in 1918, when the Soviet government already had to hand proposals for the promotion of economic and political relations with capitalist countries. It was then that many treaties and agreements were first prepared (such as the Soviet–US programme for trade and economic relations, the Soviet–German economic agreement, and projects for promoting relations with Great Britain and Scandinavian countries). The same was true for the concept of plans for involving foreign capital in the economic restructuring of Soviet Russia.

Similar processes took place in the West. Along with the policy of non-recognition of Soviet Russia and organization of joint actions against it in the West, a considerable section of the public, primarily in Great Britain and Germany, were in favour of establishing *de facto* relations with the Soviet government. That trend was gradually gaining strength, and in 1920 the British Prime Minister Lloyd George said that inasmuch as Russia depended on Britain, Britain in its turn also depended on Russia (he meant largely trade and economic relations). It was also in 1920 that the Soviet People's Commissar for Foreign Affairs Georgy Chicherin first used the term 'peaceful coexistence', meaning Soviet Russia's relations with Western countries.

The trend for peaceful coexistence began to be more vividly manifested in 1921–22. In early 1922, in the course of preparations for the Genoa Conference, Lenin started working with notions such as the interdependence of capitalist and socialist economies. The 1922 Genoa Conference discussed problems of economic rehabilitation in Europe. The fact that a Soviet delegation participated in it and the nature of the Soviet proposals testify to a substantial evolution in the concepts of Lenin and the Bolsheviks.

Changes in the international situation and the special stress in Soviet policy on the search for agreement with the West were caused by the introduction in Soviet Russia of the New Economic Policy (NEP), which was marked not only by changes in internal economic activity but also by emphasis on trade and economic contacts with the capitalist world and the desire to obtain loans and credit.

The Soviet programme in Genoa reflected not only purely specific pragmatic interests but also far-reaching ideas of economic co-operation between European countries and Soviet Russia. Russia was ready and willing to establish links with the European economy. The Soviet delegation had proposals on a general programme for utilization of fuel and power resources, for a single gold monetary unit and for the construction of a transcontinental London–Vladivostok railway to link Russia with Europe. Lenin described this programme as bourgeois-pacifist, thus revealing a volte-face in the Soviet stand on relations with the West in general and on pacifism, which had been severely criticized by Lenin in his works and speeches.

The Genoa Conference served as a turning point in Soviet foreign policy and in the position of the West, for Western Europe and Soviet Russia then started looking for ways to compromise and formulated the rules of the game that would make it possible to reach agreement and find points of contact in the divided Europe. Compromise in this case involved both the economic and political spheres. The Rapallo Treaty, signed by the Soviet Republic and Germany, ushered in a new stage in political co-operation between European countries and Russia.

In 1924 the Soviet Union was recognized by most of the Western countries, including all the leading European states. Great Britain was the first to extend recognition to the Soviet Union, and was followed by Italy, Austria, Norway, Sweden, Denmark and Greece. Finally, in October 1924, France established diplomatic relations with the USSR. Germany had maintained diplomatic relations with the Soviet Republic since 1922. All in all, by the mid-1920s the leading European countries had extended *de facto* and *de jure* recognition to Bolshevist Russia. The French journal *Europe Nouvelle* wrote at that time: 'Like it or lump it, the Soviet system is a reality. You can hardly gain anything by turning a blind eye to the reality.'

Tangible changes were also in evidence in politics. Relevant examples in this respect are the non-aggression pacts the USSR signed with Turkey (December 1925), Germany (April 1926), Lithuania (September 1926), Finland (January 1932), Latvia (February 1932), Estonia (May 1932), Poland (July 1932) and other countries. The Soviet–French non-aggression treaty, signed in 1932, was of special importance.

As the international climate deteriorated, issues of European security and disarmament were coming to the fore on the European scene, and both Western countries and Soviet Russia took part in their solution.

In general, the Soviet stand before and after the Genoa Conference reflected a new orientation in Soviet Russia's European policy. Soviet Russia expressed a readiness to join the process of European development, which was tantamount to a readiness to take the country's former place in the system of European powers. Naturally, this referred largely to the politico-economic sphere, whereas it kept aloof from European social thought in spiritual and ideological spheres because of the Bolsheviks' revolutionary, class and ideological principles.

The questions naturally arise as to why, and to what extent, the leaders of the new Russia were prepared to normalize and promote relations with capitalist countries. There were several reasons for their desire to do so. First, by the early 1920s it had become amply clear that all hopes for the triumph of revolution in other European countries had been dashed, so the Soviet government had no reason to expect any support from the revolutionary movements elsewhere. Thus, there was no alternative but to set about the prime task of 'building socialism in one country' and buttressing the Soviet system as the basis of future world revolution. This involved substantial modification of the original model of the concept of world revolution. In that situation, Soviet leaders took energetic steps to promote interaction and co-operation with the capitalist West.

Second, in conditions of prolonged ideological confrontation and political discord, trade and economic factors were playing an increasingly important role. The NEP and the need for loans and credit called for new priorities in relations with capitalist countries, for economic contacts were unthinkable without a favourable political climate and the settlement of other controversial issues.

Third, a new stand was taken by the West. Alarmed at first by the Bolshevik experiment and the threat of the further spread of the revolutionary epidemic from Russia, capitalist countries were gradually regaining their calm. The ebb in revolutionary activity in Europe helped the West regain its sense of stability. So, in the leading European states, public leaders and business circles showed a readiness to replace their hostile course by recognition of the Bolsheviks' government and co-operation with them.

Fourth, experience had shown that superior common European interests, realities and traditions were much more important than ideological differences. The former included European economic co-operation, long-standing traditional trade and economic relations between Germany, Great Britain, France and other states, on the one hand, and Russia, on the other.

Geopolitical factors contributed in no small degree to this. The European balance was inconceivable without Russia, that is, without its contribution to the European powers' concerted action.

All these factors contributed to the European countries' decisions to normalize relations with the Soviet Union.

The participation of the USSR in European affairs did not affect in any way the Bolshevik leaders' attitude to the European movement and European projects. However, there was no doubt that normalization of relations in the political and economic spheres restored the USSR's position in the European structure and had a certain effect on future development in Europe. But, simultaneously, new troubles and conflicts appeared as the course of the world revolution, dreams about 'socialism's triumph on a world scale' and ideological intolerance towards the West remained the leading tendencies of Soviet Union policy.

12

SETTLEMENT, VERSAILLES-STYLE

The Russian Revolution was not the only reason behind changes in Europe after the First World War. Apart from the formation of the Soviet Union and the areas of dissension mentioned above, the system of relationships among the leading European countries had also changed.

The First World War ushered in, as it were, a new era in European history. In 1918–19 the following situation took shape in Europe. After the October Revolution, Russia, a great European power, left the pre-war international system and took a different road. The Austro-Hungarian monarchy, which had for many decades played a significant role on the European scene, disappeared from the map of Europe. Germany, a leading European power which had laid claim to unlimited domination in Europe, was defeated. France and Great Britain, the two European countries which had emerged victorious from the First World War, now opted for calling the tune in European politics. These two powers were the authors of the Versailles system which they regarded as the foundation for the formation of a 'new' Europe that would serve their own aims.

The gradual involvement of the United States of America in European affairs was something else new on the horizon. The US leaders exerted increasingly greater influence on the course of events in the world, with Europe playing no small role in the calculations of the transatlantic politicians.

Thus, Europe, which had for many decades been dominated by monolithic empires, changed radically. New states had replaced old empires, and nationalism – or the national idea – gained wide currency, especially in Central and Eastern Europe. In that context various pan-European ideas receded into the background, and Europeanism was losing its former popularity and appeal. Europe as one spirit with a unity of goals and actions was, in fact, no more than the wishful thinking of some philosophers.

European nationalism, in combination with a peculiar synthesis of revolutionary messianism and imperial mentality in Russia, proffered many complications and difficulties for Europe. In the spiritual sphere, European intellectuals were overwhelmed by pessimism and felt robbed of their former values, so an atmosphere of despondency and hopelessness prevailed among them. This trend was reflected in literature and the arts. Prospects for European regeneration were rather hazy and no one could say what shape developments would take in the future.

A revival of globalist trends, expressed primarily in the League of Nations, seemed like a glimmer of hope. However, very soon this organization revealed its inability to offer solutions to world and European issues.

I have already mentioned the new involvement of the United States in European affairs, but the Americans tried to solve more general problems as well. In his Fourteen Points, President Wilson made an attempt at offering a new vision of the world, but it proved rather too abstract or, in one case, overpragmatic, when he set the only task as that of the elimination of Bolshevism.

Emphasis on the right of nations to self-determination was probably the most important aspect of the US president's programme. The same idea was effectively used by Lenin and other Bolshevik leaders. The concept of self-determination reflected other European and world trends resulting from the emergence of new states, so, naturally, it did not change the substance of the spirit of European unity.

The European powers' idea was to lay the foundation of a new European system at Versailles, with political (mainly geopolitical) rather than spiritual or purely pan-European factors predominating and pushing into the background the Europeanist traditions, which had been so popular in the second half of the nineteenth century and which had revived interest in Europeanism through discussion of the slogan the United States of Europe in the early twentieth century.

In *L'idée d'Europe dans l'Histoire* (Paris, 1967), French historian J. Duroselle wrote that in 1918–19 Europe was actually non-existent, and noted on another occasion that 'the October Revolution excluded Russia from Europe'. It would, perhaps, be more accurate to say that the old Europe no longer existed and that in those years an entirely new Europe was emerging, which was fundamentally different from what it had been in the past.

The Versailles system reflected the new vision of Europe of the victorious countries and their desire to draw up a long-term, pro-gramme for European development. The Versailles system comprised a series of treaties and agreements signed after the First World War by the victorious countries with the vanquished Germany, as well as other treaties signed by the leading European powers with the smaller European countries.

In essence, it was a notable method of peaceful settlement after a conflict on a global scale. It is not our task to analyse here the various aspects of the Paris Conference or the Versailles Peace Treaty, which was signed in 1919. We are concerned exclusively with pan-European problems in so far as they reveal the stand taken by European powers on the issues of a new version of 'the European balance', their view of Europe and their attempts at shaping a new configuration of Europe. Such factors make it possible for us to assess the modifications in the approach to the European idea which had an impact on European development in the period between the two world wars.

What were the authors of the Versailles system trying to achieve? What sort of alternative were they preparing for Europe in the decades to follow? What was their idea of European unity?

It should first be pointed out that the authors of the Versailles system were not prepared to recognize the Soviet government: there was no room for Russia in the Europe of the future as they saw it, that is; in the future, Europe would be against Russia, they believed. The Russian issue was constantly discussed at the Paris Conference, and at times it dominated all other discussions and decisions. This was only to be expected since the conference was held at the height of the Civil War in Russia and the West was convinced that the Soviet government would soon be toppled.

Recognition of the formation of new European states was another important aspect of the Versailles system. A series of agreements, attached to the Versailles Peace Treaty, defined the state borders of Hungary, Romania, Czechoslovakia, Albania, Yugoslavia and other countries. The authors of the Versailles system merely confirmed on paper what in fact had been attained by the peoples of south-eastern and Central Europe. The actual treaties connected with the Versailles Peace fixed the status quo and independence won by those countries in the course of the liberation movement. The Western politicians' goal was to prevent excessive radicalization of reforms in the newly independent countries.

Settlement of territorial and border issues according to the Versailles model was the reason behind many conflicts and bitter disagreements that arose later. The recarved map of Europe was a source of instability and fraught with new complications.

South-eastern and Central Europe were conflict-prone zones,

where the great powers had room for manoeuvre. The newly emerged, small European countries, including some that had existed before the First World War, were then targets for European development. Settlement Versailles-style presupposed the existence of small states within the sphere of influence of one or other of the European powers – mainly France or Great Britain. At the same time, France and Great Britain viewed the Versailles decisions and the formation of a group of new states through the prism of their own European interests and their own disagreements.

The most important Versailles decision referred to the vanquished Germany. European unity and 'European balance' had undergone changes at the turn of the century during clashes between the two opposing blocs. So in Versailles the Franco-British bloc laid the foundation of a new 'balance'. However, there was not complete agreement between the allies. French and British leaders' stands on European settlement were different.

At first sight it might have seemed that the victors had utterly crushed Germany, relegating it to a second-rate status. However, the humiliation that Germany had been subjected to, and the system of reparations and restrictions imposed on it, were fraught with new controversies.

Germany, a major Central European power, could hardly lose its status of a great power for ever. Of course, it was possible to eliminate its aggressive potential, thus removing the basis of German militarism. However, the authors of the Versailles system refrained from doing so. As a result, the Versailles decision from the outset served as a breeding ground for revanchist ideas, which soon manifested themselves. German reactionary circles received a very convenient rallying cry and an opportunity to appeal to nationalist and chauvinist moods among the broad masses. Plans for a review of the Versailles principles and compensation for the national humiliation served as the basis for the theoretical principles of Nazism. The general atmosphere of uncertainty in Europe and instability in the smaller European countries gave German reactionary circles room to manoeuvre.

However, other developments were of much greater importance than such specific Versailles decisions, for new disputes soon came to the surface, causing bitter clashes on the continent. The treaties signed with smaller European countries had included a large number of controversial territorial issues which, in their totality, gave rise to conflict in Europe. The Balkans and Central Europe had the greatest number of hot spots. Thus, the Versailles system itself, or to be more precise, the Versailles method of settlement after the First World

99

War, gave rise to new complications – which eventually led to a tragic outcome in the 1930s.

Soon after the signing of the Versailles Peace Treaty, therefore, some new elements had emerged on the European scene (the geo-political factor, the loss of the traditional foundation of the European balance, Franco-British rivalries and the increasing involvement of the US in European affairs) which finally led to Germany's return to active participation in international affairs. This trend was first manifested in the 1925 Locarno Pact which was the starting point of Germany's gradual adaptation to the new European system. That process developed apace as time went by. Great Britain sought to make use of Germany to buttress its own position and undermine French domination in Europe, whereas the US sought to promote Germany's advance with the help of the Dawes Plan in order to counterbalance the British–French bloc. Through the Dawes Plan Germany received sizeable US loans and credit, and for reasons of nationalism and chauvinism those investments were concentrated on military prepara-tions. The rehabilitated German economy was developing along militarist lines.

Only five years after the Paris Conference Germany was again to the fore in European affairs. However, Austen Chamberlain and Aristide Briand were sure that they could dictate the tune of the German orchestra, by controlling German development within limits convenient for Great Britain and France. Gradually some of the Versailles restrictions were lifted from Germany; primarily it was permitted – at first 'secretly and illegally' – to produce armaments.

Then the logical questions arise: to what extent was this a conscious policy on the part of the Western powers? Was it an erroneous course, a strategic miscalculation? There are no simple answers to these questions. There were objective and subjective factors which influenced the whole process. However, in general, one might say that the policy that promoted the resurgence of German militarism – intended to be used against the Soviet Union and the Bolshevik threat to Europe in order to promote the great powers' own selfish interests in Europe at the expense of their partners' interests – eventually boomeranged on its own masterminds and the whole of Europe.

The ruling circles of the Weimar Republic cleverly made use of the situation. In the 1920s Germany did not want to be involved in the anti-Soviet schemes of London and Paris. Soviet–German trade and economic relations were developing successfully and political contacts were being maintained at a satisfactory level. However, revanchism was already raising its head. Waves of nationalism and chauvinism swept Germany, and theories of 'Greater Germany', pan-Germanism and German domination in Europe were gaining ever greater currency, along with the idea of revision of the Versailles Treaty and revanchism. In view of this, the situation in Europe was rapidly deteriorating in the early 1930s.

There was also a realignment of forces in the British–French bloc. France was slowly but surely losing its leading position, with Great Britain taking the upper hand in European politics. At the same time, the joint Franco-British policy for Eastern hegemony had led to a shift of emphasis in the stance of influential political forces within the victorious powers. The regeneration of German potential, including its military component, was directed against France rather than Great Britain so that after Nazism came to power in Germany, it was in France that voices were increasingly raised in calling for a rebuff to Nazi encroachments.

In the context of the European situation, one could enumerate clashes of various global interests and tendencies during this period – clashes of national and international interests, as well as the conflict between the desire for interaction and mutual contact in the world, and the determination by some states to seek separatist action. Furthermore, there were stark contrasts between the USSR and the Western world, and between German Nazism, the totalitarian states and bourgeois democracy in Europe which also greatly contributed to the overall complexity of the situation.

All these factors created the conflict-prone situation that prevailed in Europe in the period between the two world wars. It would be an overexaggeration to state that the developments after the First World War were fatally leading to the Second World War. However, it would be undoubtedly correct to conclude that the trends that were in evidence immediately after the end of the First World War and the October Revolution, and special features of the Versailles system and the Locarno agreements, were certainly conducive to conflict in Europe rather than to a stable peace.

One of the historical lessons of the development of international affairs in the twentieth century is that people should realize how dangerous lack of contact among people, countries and nationalities can be, as well as taking a passive attitude in the face of reaction and aggression and the excessive ideologization of international affairs which was predominant in the period between the two world wars. It was extremely difficult to reach agreement and find points of contact in that over-ideologized world, in a Europe that was torn apart by political conflicts.

101

In conclusion, one may say that the human consensus, the common human values that were central to nineteenth-century Europeanism had not been recognized in post-war Europe, so they had not become normative principles which might have united countries and peoples. Common human values were accepted by a narrow circle of European intellectuals, but even among these the values were interpreted in various ways, dependent on the ideological conflicts and sharp social differences that rent Europe in that period.

13

EURASIA AND EURASIANISM

Eurasianism is, of course, largely concerned with Eurasian studies, so it was naturally among the basic traditions of pre-revolutionary Russian historiography. This tradition – the analysis of the original nature of Russian culture – which dates back to the Slavophiles, had been continued in the studies of prominent scholars such as Nikolai Danilevsky, Konstantin Leontyev, Nikolai Berdyayev and Vladimir Solovyov. However, this tradition was not given prominence in Soviet historiography. Now that there is a growing trend for the revival of old traditions and names and the reappraisal of certain theories, the Eurasianists' activities, no doubt, deserve special attention. Since the issue of Russia's true role and identity – whether it belongs to Europe or Asia – has once again become a subject of lively discussion, an extraordinary interest is shown in Eurasianism and Eurasianists.

As long ago as the 1920s–30s, the problems of Russia and Europe, Russia and the East, culture and religion, and the special features of 'the Russian way' were analysed by a group of Russian emigrés. Although all those problems were nothing new – they were, in fact, traditional in Russian science – they became especially topical and had a different content in works by Eurasianists. This was partly attributable to the Eurasianists' historical experience: they regarded the 1917 revolution as a disaster which was followed by the eclipse of Russian culture, making them reappraise the road being traversed by Russia. Many talented researchers, such as P. Savitsky, P. Bicilli, L. Karsavin, G. Florovsky, G. Vernadsky and N. Trubetskoy, took part in the Eurasianist movement.

Why did Trubetskoy, Savitsky and their associates find the term 'Eurasia' more suitable than the habitual one – Russia? The term was borrowed from Alexander Gumboldt who had used it to denote the entire territory of the Old World, which included Europe and Asia. When applied to Russia, this term is indicative of its intermediate position between Europe and Asia, the West and the East. Does this mean that Russian culture combines European and Asian elements? Anticipating such an interpretation, the Eurasianists answered this question in the negative, which was only natural if we take into account the multilinear system of the historical process in the world advocated by them, and their apprehensive attitude towards the influence of alien culture. They viewed Eurasia as a special continent, utterly different from both Europe and Asia. According to some Eurasianists, the very term 'Eurasianism' implies the idea of a continent situated between Europe and Asia, rather than a 'central strip' between them. In that continent Russia's creative mission consists in giving Europe and Asia access to the 'principles of genuine life'. Naturally, this does not mean that the Eurasianists denied the influence of European and Western culture on Russia, although their assessment of that influence was rather complicated.

European influence was acknowledged by them, although exclusively in a negative sense (they rejected its positive aspects), and in this respect, the Eurasianists followed in the footsteps of their predecessors, the advocates of Russia's national originality in the nineteenth and twentieth centuries. While highly praising the gains of European civilization, Eurasianists, nevertheless, recognized only very few positive aspects of European influence. It must be admitted that they reduced the influence as such to the educational-materialist-atheistic line in Russian culture. So, given this narrow interpretation, it followed that the revolution was the sole result of Western influence.

Eurasianists, especially Trubetskoy and Savitsky, simply 'overlooked' the enormous spiritual impact of European ideas, without which the flowering of Russian philosophy and literature in the nineteenth century would have been impossible, and failed to take into account that the trend of 'enlightenment' had developed not only into the nihilism of Raznochintsi, spearheaded against the gentry, but also into the humanism of Turgenev, Tolstoy and Dostoyevsky. True, while discussing Russia's socio-economic pre-revolutionary development in his article 'Two Worlds', Savitsky spoke about Russia's 'involvement' in European civilization. This was reflected, he believed, in the smooth and calm development of Russian capitalism, in the stable forms of lifestyle of certain sections of society that were close to European ones, and in the elevated status of intellectuals. However, it is difficult to say to what extent this 'involvement' was assessed positively by Savitsky, if you take into account the fact that in this article he also wrote about the liberation of original cultural forces which had to take place after Russia's rupture with Europe – which was actually the case in 1917. The authors of other Eurasianist works denied even such very superficial similarity between Russia and Europe.

Quite instructive is also the fact that even Eurasianists who had the chance to have an inside view of Europe did not produce an unbiased, science-based and detailed analysis of that civilization. By rejecting or, to be more precise, even not analysing positive principles, typical of the European way of development, Eurasianists confined themselves merely to the aspects of the subject of 'Europe and Russia' that were put forward by the Slavophiles and their followers in the nineteenth century. The problem of interaction and interpenetration of civilizations was not discussed by Eurasianists in all its complexity, with accounts of positive and negative results. In this respect, Eurasianists were direct followers of the advocates of the special national features of nineteenth-century Russia. They believed that the idea of universality, as a rule, ran counter to that of the preservation of individual features of a culture; they did not compare but opposed Europe to Russia. In any case, it should be noted that in nineteenth-century Western historiography, the multilinear concept did not at once merge with that of universal, world civilization either. So Eurasianists were not original in this respect. Oswald Spengler, their contemporary, offered to regard individual cultures as closed and isolated from one another. Arnold Toynbee held the same view when he started work on *A Study of History* (1934), and it was only in the 1960s that he raised the issue of the inevitability of the merging of local civilizations.

Eurasianists were more inclined to approve of some Eastern influence. It was not accidental that their first collection was entitled *Exodus to the East*. However, irrespective of the somewhat different assessment by Eurasianists of Eastern elements in Russian culture, on the whole, even Eastern influence was only approved of with great reservation. As opponents to a merger with the West, Eurasianists also believed that the influence of the 'restricted spirit of Asia, with its Nirvana and contemplative quietism', was quite dangerous. Russia was opposed to both the 'materialist' culture of the West and the mystical East. Eurasianists stressed that no matter how close it was to the East, Russia was a land of Orthodox faith and its mentality had been shaped on the basis of the Christian system of values. In spite of the fact that Trubetskoy was among the main advocates of the idea of turning eastward, in his article 'Christianity and India's Religions' he denied any similarity between Christianity, on the one hand, and Buddhism, Krishnaism and Vishnaism, on the other. In spite of some superficial similarity, those religions are quite different in substance,

105

so there was no question of their synthesis. Moreover, Trubetskoy described India's religions as 'satanic', since they did not contain the idea of a transcendental God.

The viewpoint of Trubetskoy and Savitsky, according to which Russia was opposed both to the East and West, was certainly not the only one. P. Bicilli expressed a different opinion in his article 'The East and West in Old World History'. He presented the entire Old World as a complicated system of local civilizations which were entirely different, although for many centuries they had been maintaining economic, political and spiritual relations. An integrational approach to the issue of East and West such as Bicilli's made it possible to determine Russia's role, with its synthesis of European and Eastern cultures and with Russia playing the part of a central intermediary between Eastern and Western civilizations.

When, in the nineteenth century, the Slavophiles had been opposed to Europe, they stressed that rationalism, 'materialism' and lack of faith were the leading features of Germanic-Roman civilization. When Ivan Aksakov spoke about 'the vanishing soul', he very aptly described the attitude to Europe taken by all advocates of 'the Russian way'.

The Eurasianists also built on that subject. Thus, while analysing the causes of the 1917 Russian Revolution, Savitsky, who was a theoretician of Europeanism, discussed the spiritual aspects of life in Russia in the nineteenth century in the light of the contest between the two trends. On the one hand, it was the lofty search by Fedor Dostoyevsky, Leo Tolstoy and Vladimir Solovyov and, on the other, it was the nihilistic, materialist trend towards enlightenment which had developed under European influence and was reflected in works by Nikolai Dobrolyubov, Nikolai Chernyshevsky and Dmitri Pisarev. The contest between those two trends, which had produced a split in Russian culture, ended, Savitsky believed, in the triumph of nihilism which eventually led to the revolution. Savitsky was convinced that 1917 was a year of great disaster, comparable to the fall of the Roman Empire, which was followed by an era of Russia's 'barbarization'. Consequently, Russia was involved in the cycle of development of European civilization, and was now living through its premature decline. On the whole, however, Savitsky was inclined to regard the revolution as a grave disaster rather than 'the death' of Russian culture.

Trubetskoy, another theoretician of Eurasianism, also painted a gloomy picture of Russian culture's decline; in its attempt to simulate Europe, he believed, Russia was losing its original features and disrupting the process of its economic development. In his book *Europe and Humanity*, Trubetskoy asserted that cultural development

106

involved the incessant creation of new values, based on the principle of succession, that is, as a result of 'combined imitation'. The logical conclusion, therefore, is that traditionalism is a necessary prerequisite of normal development of culture, otherwise the cultural fund, without which further development of culture is unthinkable, would be irretrievably lost. Infiltration of alien cultural traditions, Trubetskoy felt (just as the Slavophiles before him did), was extremely harmful and destroyed the 'organic' nature of culture. Trubetskoy regarded European culture as the most dangerous of them all in this respect. The rapid expansion of the spiritual values of the Germanic-Roman civilization was regarded by Trubetskoy as the greatest disaster for any original culture. He analysed in detail the mechanism not only of the preservation and development but also of the destruction of the cultural tradition.

So much for the ideas and structures of Eurasianists. Advocates of the Eurasianist ideas, who were, as a rule, Russian émigrés, of course built their concepts taking into account the specific situation in post-revolutionary Russia. However, the general thrust of their argument was directed towards substantiation of the idea of a special type of Eurasian civilization that differed from both Europe and Asia.

In the general historico-cultural context, Eurasianists were looking for some sort of a third way for Russia which would be able to coexist with the ideas of Russian exclusiveness. Eurasianist theories were developed on a realistic basis, whose substance consisted in the realization of the fact that large parts of Russia were to be found both in Europe and Asia and that Christian, Moslem and other religions coexisted on Russian territory. However, a major problem remained; to what extent could those highly varied phenomena contribute to the historico-cultural synthesis and in what way did this affect Russia's relations with Europe?

The subject of 'Russia and Europe' was given a new angle by the Eurasianist interpretation, which gave priority to cultural and intellectual factors. Eurasianism separated Russian social thought from Europe and Europeanism and very often tended to promote old patriarchal traditions and ideas, legitimizing, as it were, Russia's backwardness as compared with the European level of development.

In practice Eurasianism did not gain wide currency; it had a comparatively small following – largely among Russian emigrés of the 1920s. However, while reflecting the realities of world development, the revival of Eurasianist theories in the 1990s turns us back to discussions about Russia and its special approach and mission, and about Russia's place in the system of international relations in Europe and Asia.

14

STALINISM AND EUROPEANISM

While discussing the problem of Russia and Europe in the context of the twentieth century one can hardly overlook the subject of Stalinism. Primarily I have in mind its conceptual aspect, that is, to what extent Stalin's system as an ideology affected the Soviet Union's attitude to Europe and the stand adopted by the European governments and public with respect to the Soviet Union.

In its essence, Stalinism, which sought to combine the old Leninist messianic concepts of world revolution with imperial ambitions, fostered by the traditions of the former Russian Empire, was alien to Europeanism in its political, ideological and spiritual aspects. The system of values imposed on the USSR in the period of Stalin's rule utterly negated liberal-democratic trends in European political thought and practice. The idea of common human values was rejected in the USSR as hostile to genuinely scientific socialism, the 'class consciousness of the working masses'.

The noisy anti-bourgeois campaigns of the 1930s–50s, which reached their climax in the widely publicized drive against bourgeois cosmopolitanism in the late 1940s and early 1950s, widened still further the abyss between the USSR and Europe, as well as that between Soviet and European common human values. Any phenomena that were regarded in the USSR as a retreat from class positions, or what was called holding aloof from politics, were ruthlessly suppressed. Therefore, the principles advocated by theoreticians of Europeanism – human rights, independence of the individual and democratic institutions and so on – were rejected in the USSR.

Stalin and his entourage were inclined to regard the USSR as part of the European political orchestra but, at the same time, proceeded from the idea that there was nothing in common between the USSR and European political thought and traditions. By building on Lenin's tradition and carrying it to the extreme, Soviet ideologists were ready to borrow from the experience of European development and its political and social thought exclusively its revolutionary-democratic traditions, or, to be more precise, its socialist views and utopias. That is why the Soviet public was supposed to be interested only in European personalities such as Maximilien Robespierre, Claude-Henri Saint-Simon and Tommaso Campanella. Not only ultra-conservative treatises but also works by Johann Herder, Johann Fichte, Max Weber and Oswald Spengler, among others, were banned.

Works by famous philosophers were not published in the USSR, and those that were appeared in abridged form with a critical commentary. Certain restrictions were even imposed on Victor Hugo's famous humanistic speeches and articles and, although his novels were (and are) very popular in the USSR, this meant that the broad Soviet public knew nothing about Hugo's brilliant addresses to a peace congress, held in the early 1840s, which can be regarded as the manifesto of nineteenth-century Europeanism. The slogan the United States of Europe was regarded as reactionary, imperialist and anti-Soviet. Coudenhove-Kalergi, its advocate, has until recently been described as a proponent of bourgeois reactionary views and theories. Many more names could be included in this list.

Stalin rejected out of hand the principle of pacifism and pacifist ideology for their abstract and bourgeois nature and narrow class views. Tolstoy's ideas on non-resistance to evil by violence and many other views and projects on the preservation of peace were sharply criticized on the same grounds. Official literature used the specific term 'abstract pacifism' to contrast with the active struggle for peace and against war under the guidance of the Communist Party.

Liberalism was denounced in much the same uncompromising way both as theory and as political practice. Similarly, in theoretical and spiritual respects all kinds of liberal and liberal-democratic views and theories were criticized very harshly. Europeanist ideas and theories put forward by prominent European liberal leaders were dismissed as being in the same group.

This rejection was not only applied to bourgeois liberalism; Stalin would not accept international social democracy either, especially its theoretical thinking. Many works by Karl Kautsky, Victor Adler, Eduard Bernstein, Léon Blum and Filippo Turatti, among others, were either passed over in silence or sharply criticized. Thus, the Stalinist system rejected European political and theoretical thought in the hope of encouraging original socialist thought, codes of behaviour and morals.

In consequence, even the term 'Europeanism' was not used, and if used occasionally, it carried a strictly negative meaning. Neither did

Stalin accept the theories of Russian Eurasians, regarding them as counter-revolutionary emigrants.

On the ideological and theoretical plane, an amalgam had been formed of narrow sectarian socialist ideas, theories of proletarian solidarity and ideas of Russian messianism closely associated with former imperial tendencies and theories. In reality, however, Soviet official policy and the ideological machine rejected even specific European projects that were put forward in the West in the 1920s and 1930s and, later, in the post-war years.

Even if we put aside ideological considerations, it can be stated that European projects of the 1920s and 1930s were regarded in Moscow as anti-Soviet ploys, schemes aimed at the isolation of the USSR and the unification of European countries and peoples on an anti-Soviet basis. This last consideration was hardly ungrounded, for, just as with many European projects, neither the Coudenhove-Kalergi schemes nor the Briand plan, in fact, either presupposed the Soviet Union's participation or were spearheaded against it.

Western, especially European, public opinion largely took a hostile attitude towards the Soviet Union, which was primarily attributable to its criticism of the Stalinist system rather than to a negative attitude to Russia or the USSR. The practice that prevailed in the USSR of reprisals meted out against dissident views, numerous trials, mass repression and anti-bourgeois campaigns made both European intellectuals and the general public view the Soviet Union with antagonism.

All these factors made the confrontation between the Soviet Union and Europe still more pronounced, thus barring the way to co-operation between European peoples and the USSR, with the result that Europe rapidly drifted apart from the USSR. These developments served to consolidate further the negative stand taken by those who denied Russia's European identity and constantly warned about the threat posed by Russia to Europe. Consequently, some Western studies of European history and of the European idea published at that time laid stress on analysis of periods and facts that would confirm the idea of Russia's incompatibility with Europe.

The events of that period added grist to the mill of those who advocated the idea of a particular and classical Europe, confined to the limits of its West European version – 'from Brest to Brest'. The spread of these theories only spurred official Soviet propaganda in its furious anti-bourgeois attacks and supplied new arguments to those who called for more efficient action to combat bourgeois influence and cosmopolitan ideas and theories. As a result, the abyss between

Soviet and Western social and political thought was growing ever wider and deeper.

However, in one sphere Soviet–European co-operation was rapidly developing: the specific policy, pursued in the 1930s in the projects for European security, which objectively involved the Soviet Union in European affairs, was making it an indispensable and important participant in European concerted action. This trend was a tradition of some standing, for Russia had long been a great European power and an indispensable participant in all decisions on European affairs and political struggles. The same situation then prevailed in Western Europe.

While rejecting Stalinism and the socialist system and regarding it as utterly hostile to European tradition and political thought, the European powers not only had to take into account the Soviet position but also to maintain business relations with the USSR, thus effectively involving it in the European political system. The Soviet Union remained a very important factor of and a participant in the concerted action of West European countries. This positive process presupposed the active involvement of the USSR in European affairs (albeit in a very contradictory form), adding new aspects to the general system of relations described as 'Russia and Europe'.

The advent of the Nazis to power in Germany produced radical changes in the European situation. Europeans were now faced with responsibility for the destiny of Europe for European civilization was threatened with mortal danger. Would it be possible to pool European efforts under the banner of anti-fascism? Was it at all possible to produce a pan-European mechanism that might help avoid war, preserve peace and ensure European security? In order to solve these problems, Europe needed the determination to set up a system of European security, which in that situation was a factor of importance to the whole of Europe. In the presence of the Nazi threat it was necessary to reappraise the 'game of contradictions' and to realize the importance of the common responsibility of European states and peoples for the preservation of peace.

The Nazi programme provided for the crushing of socialism in Russia and suppressing the democratic movement, enslaving the whole of Europe and eliminating entire European nations which did not conform to the racial 'theories' of Nazi ideologists. Nazi theoretical constructs and initial practical moves left no doubt that the threat of mortal danger overhung not only the USSR but also all West European democratic countries.

Europe was confronted with the task of counterpoising concerted action and the common security system to the Nazi version of the

European idea, which presupposed the armed conquest of the continent. As time went on, the need for joint action – a system of interaction that would incorporate anti-fascist Europe and the Soviet Union – became increasingly clear. This meant the establishment of a European security system that, for the first time in European history, would assume the features of a pan-European institution, thus becoming a form and a means of manifesting the common responsibility of Europeans for the salvation of European civilization and the prevention of a world holocaust.

For this purpose it was necessary to attain a certain level of political realism, both in political thinking and in the specific practice of international affairs. The Soviet stand was stated in December 1933 when, soon after the seizure of power by Nazis in Germany, the USSR expounded the idea of European collective security. The Soviet message was addressed to all powers not involved in the fascist system, primarily Great Britain and France. Measures suggested by the Soviet Union included an offer to conclude an agreement on mutual defence against aggression with the participation of a considerable number of European states and the Soviet Union's agreement to join the League of Nations on certain terms.

The specific policy of those years gave birth to the idea of an Eastern Pact that would guarantee security for all European countries. participants in the projected pact – the USSR, Germany, Poland, Czechoslovakia, Finland and the Baltic states – were supposed to sign a treaty guaranteeing mutual non-violation of borders and mutual assistance in case of aggression against any of the signatories. According to this plan, the Soviet Union and France were also supposed to sign a treaty of mutual assistance, with France to become a guarantor of the Eastern Pact and the USSR a guarantor of the Locarno Agreements. The plan also provided for mutual consultations by the signatories to the Pact in case of a threat of aggression against any of them. The idea of a regional European pact had to become central to a European security system that might serve as an instrument of preventing aggression in Europe.

Many of the proposals were specified in the course of talks. However, the ideas of all participants' equality and universalism formed the basis of the projected system. Universalism in this case meant the incorporation into the system of all states in the region, without exception.

In May 1935, Soviet–French and Soviet–Czechoslovakian treaties of mutual assistance were signed, and in 1934 the USSR was admitted to the League of Nations.

Ideas of disarmament were of special importance in the deteriorating European situation. Disarmament talks were held under the auspices of the League of Nations (in the Preparatory Commission and at the general conference on reduction and restriction of armaments in 1932–35). After discussions held over a number of years, the disarmament issue was as yet outstanding. The arms race went on just as before and war preparations were in progress in Nazi Germany, in the heart of Europe.

British statesman David Lloyd-George gave an apt description of those disarmament talks, saying that it was a comedy, where disarmament and the security system contended for priority and attracted full audiences to the Geneva theatre. Endless debates, he said, were carried on, with 'elegant', 'brilliant' and 'state' speeches following in swift succession, and disarmament was chasing security and security hunting for disarmament, although they never caught up with each other.

Contributing to the efforts to establish the collective security system were French Minister Louis Barthou, Soviet People's Commissar for Foreign Affairs Maxim Livinov, King Alexander of Yugoslavia and many politicians and public leaders of various European countries. Numerous conferences and meetings were held for the purpose.

According to recent studies by Russian scholars, it has become increasingly clear that Stalin was hardly enthusiastic about the idea of collective security; it was, in fact, Litvinov who was the advocate of that idea and owing to the efforts of Litvinov and his colleagues the European collective security system then took shape.

Very soon, however, that system met with great difficulties. Slowly but surely the notorious policy of appeasement of the Nazi aggressor superseded that of collective security in the West. The idea behind the policy of appeasement was to make the Nazis look eastward.

After the assassination of Louis Barthou there was a sharp turn in French foreign policy. The Soviet–French treaty had not been supplemented with a military convention, and appeasement of Germany became central to French policy. Realistically minded statesmen had been ousted by those whose hostility to the USSR outweighed considerations of political expediency. In fact, France involved the destinies of small European countries which were in the sphere of its influence, in the orbit of its policy, by turning a blind eye to Germany's inroads into traditional French spheres.

British policy had a strong negative effect both on the situation in France and in the whole of Europe; at that time Britain appeared to be the mastermind behind the appeasement policy. Britain had little stake in an integrated Europe. European tendencies and moods had always received considerably less attention in Britain than in Europe and the guidelines of British policy did not change even after Germany had switched from words to deeds. British ruling circles were ready to sacrifice both Austria and Czechoslovakia, as well as some other countries, if necessary, in order to divert Germany's attention eastwards. However, the turn of events meant that Britain was increasingly more involved in European affairs than its politicians had ever expected, for they had declined initiatives aimed at the establishment of a collective security system.

The 1938 Munich Agreement came as a climax to the appeasement policy. Great Britain and France had thus sanctioned Germany's seizure of Czechoslovakia. The then British and French leaders actually tacitly agreed to the expansion of the fascist regime in Europe, turning a blind eye to the *Anschluss* of Austria and Nazi Germany's penetration into the Balkans, the Mediterranean and many south-eastern and Central European countries.

After the Munich Agreement there was still a chance of setting up an anti-fascist coalition when, in the summer of 1939, Soviet–British–French tripartite political and military talks were opened in Moscow. However, there was an about-turn in Soviet foreign policy at that time. Even in March 1939, at the 18th Communist Party Congress, Stalin had hinted that it would be desirable to improve Soviet–German relations. After Vyacheslav Molotov had replaced Litvinov as People's Commissar for Foreign Affairs, this policy began to take shape.

The dramatic events of the summer of 1939 culminated in the notorious Soviet–German Pact, signed on 23 August 1939, with the USSR confidently embarking on a course of co-operation with the aggressor. In violation of all norms of international law, codes of behaviour and morals, the Soviet Union, jointly with Nazi Germany, took part in deciding the destinies of other European states and peoples by dividing them into spheres of their influence. This was an example of Stalin's system whereby all legal and moral principles were trampled underfoot. A strong blow was dealt to the European security system and by signing this pact with Germany the USSR had strongly compromised its image in European public opinion.

In summing up the results of world development in the 1930s and West European, USSR and US policies, one cannot but draw the conclusion that all proposed participants in the future anti-fascist coalition had given priority to their narrow, selfish, national interests and had not united their efforts to give a rebuff to fascism. They had certainly underestimated the fascist threat to the whole of Europe, with common human values and interests pushed into the background.

In such a perilous situation, the leaders of Western democratic countries and the USSR demonstrated their inability to see what humanity really needed. Neither did they realize the need to unite their efforts to stave off fascist aggression. They saw the light only after the German attack on the USSR.

The concept of European security was only an abstract theoretical formula, a lesson of sorts for the future. An over-ideologized vision of the world then eclipsed both world and European realities and interests.

However, the 1930s in Europe were also marked by attempts at achieving unity not only by governments but also by the European people in their struggle against fascism and the threat of war. As pan-European ideas were receding into the background and losing their popularity, the anti-fascist movement was gaining in strength. Various strata of the European general public combined their efforts in the face of the fascist threat. They took an active part in world anti-fascist congresses and fora. In the early 1930s the plan for a world anti-fascist congress had gained support in many European countries. It was preceded by many meetings and fora held on a national scale. French participants in the anti-war movement made a significant contribution to this campaign. Initially, Geneva was planned as the venue of the future world congress, but the Swiss authorities would not grant permission for it, and it was finally decided to hold it in Amsterdam. The committee of its sponsors included Henri Barbusse, Romain Rolland, Heinrich Mann, Maxim Gorky, Albert Einstein, Paul Langevin, Theodore Dreiser and Upton Sinclair.

The congress opened in Amsterdam on 27 August 1932. It was attended by over 2,000 delegates largely from European countries, although there were also delegates from the US, China and India among those present. The Soviet delegation, however, was denied entry visas by the Dutch authorities, so they were unable to attend the congress. Prominent members of Europe's artistic and academic communities were among the delegates, such as Henri Barbusse, Romain Rolland and Martin Andersen Nexö.

In his opening address Barbusse said that it was the world's first anti-war congress to represent a wide range of social strata. The Amsterdam Congress, he went on, had risen on the ruins of con-ferences devoted to issues of peace and disarmament and, in contrast

115

to them, it wished to become a truly international institution that would be capable of active and effective action, not just another manifestation.

Einstein, H. Mann and Rolland, who were unable to attend, sent messages of greetings to the congress.

> In our campaign, [ran one of those messages] whose aim is quite clear: 'Declare war on war!', we do not set much store on labels. We value exclusively our allies' sincerity, their fearlessness and loyalty to the great cause which unites us all. And we shall follow only those who will be the most energetic fighters, who will be ready for the most selfless sacrifices in order to crush the common enemy, no matter who those allies may be. (Z. Belousova, *France and European Security*, Moscow, 1976)

It should be noted that many speakers at the congress closely associated the anti-war movement with the 'class struggle' of the workers and all toiling people. The final manifesto, adopted by the participants in the congress, expressed the same idea, which clearly narrowed the sphere of activity of the movement, isolating it from the broad European strata. Both the congress and the movement as a whole had the narrow sectarian image associated with the communist movement and the extreme left groups in Europe.

At the same time, many intellectuals sought to broaden the sphere of the movement's activity by laying stress on general humanistic ideas. Albert Einstein, for instance, wrote in his message to the congress: 'All advocates of progress irrespective of their political and economic views, should not spare their efforts to make the right to the peaceful settlement of conflicts triumph over brutal force and the unbridled desire for profit.'

A World Anti-war Committee was set up at the congress, including more than 130 representatives from various countries, with Rolland, Barbusse and Langevin elected as members. An International Bureau and other bodies were also formed.

Many meetings were held in various countries after the congress, to discuss its results and plan specific action to step up the anti-war movement. There was also a marked trend for unity of action by representatives of various political parties, trade unions and other public organizations. Major actions by peace fighters were staged within the framework of a campaign launched by the World Anti-war Committee.

It should be stressed that the Amsterdam Congress and many

subsequent actions were held before the advent of the fascists to power. The anti-war movement had been launched in protest to military expenditure and preparations and as a response to increased activity by rightist forces. In January 1933 the situation changed radically: from then on, all mass-scale actions and the anti-war movement took on an increasingly anti-fascist nature, which formed a basis for a new unity of anti-fascist forces.

At the same time, the Labour and Socialist International issued an address to the workers throughout the world, warning them about the dangerous consequences of the advent to power of fascists. Several trade union organizations and representatives of other social forces called for the convocation of a European anti-fascist congress, which was finally held in Playel Hall in Paris in June 1933. A broad discussion was held by its participants about the sphere and form of action to be taken by anti-fascist forces. Participants in the Amsterdam–Playel movement held lively discussions every day. Many of those who advocated the principles of class struggle took a sectarian stand and refused to maintain close contact or act in co-operation with the pacifists. In a new situation, however, some European communist parties took the course of overcoming sectarianism and division in the working-class movement and of turning the united-front tactic into a mighty factor in the struggle against the fascist onslaught.

The Seventh Comintern Congress, held in July–August 1935, was an important landmark in this process. The congress put forward a programme of unification of all anti-fascist forces and movements both within specific countries and on a global scale. The congress formulated new guidelines for the policy to be pursued by communist parties, stating that the Communists were ready to protect 'every inch of bourgeois-democratic freedoms encroached upon by fascism and bourgeois reaction for this is dictated by the interests of the proletarian class struggle'. But in practice many communist parties continued to maintain narrow sectarian positions.

Congresses of European writers, held in the dramatic atmosphere of the growing fascist threat in those years, played an important role in the development of the anti-fascist movement. The most outstanding representatives of European culture attended those congresses and ardent calls were issued for united action to rebuff the fascist on-slaught. The meetings revealed the concern of writers regarding the continent's destiny; they stressed that the age-long traditions of European cultural and historical unity might serve as a unifying factor for joint action by European cultural figures.

The historical experience of the 1930s proved beyond any doubt not only the need for but also the real possibility of the unification of European peoples in the face of the fascist threat, on the basis of their common responsibility for the destiny of the continent. But while the anti-war movement involved a number of intellectuals, the broad mass of the population largely remained aloof from it. Moreover, there was little unity among these intellectuals. The sectarian principles of the Bolsheviks and the Comintern, directed against social democracy, served as a formidable obstacle to the unity of the anti-fascist forces. It was those principles which had acted as a brake on the anti-fascist struggle in the years preceding Hitler's advent to power.

Stalin's formulas of 'abstract' pacifism and humanism, indicative of his reluctance to maintain close contacts with the broad pacifist movement, were a no less formidable obstacle to unity. Western intellectuals followed with concern the campaign of massive reprisals that had been launched in the USSR in the second half of the 1930s.

History has shown that a broad unification of social forces is possible solely on the basis of common human interests, protection of world civilization and renunciation of selfish interests and ideological confrontation. European interests demanded such unity in the 1930s when Europe stood on the threshold of the Second World War. Regrettably, the European anti-fascist forces did not achieve such unity to rebuff fascism and avert a world war.

15

PAN-EUROPEAN IDEAS AND THE MOVEMENT DURING THE 1920s AND 1930s

In the period between the two world wars various schemes for European unification became popular in Europe. Scores of books were published by authors from all walks of life – members of the artistic community, writers, journalists, statesmen and diplomats – who discussed various aspects of European unity, as well as its past and future prospects.

Naturally, they often referred to projects of past epochs and quoted passages from the respective works – by Jean-Jacques Rosseau, Immanuel Kant, and others – reviving public interest in the slogan the United States of Europe and other federative proposals. In their analysis of the European structure in the 1920s–30s, these authors dealt with political, economic and moral aspects of the European problem, and some of them put forward new versions of European unification.

It is sufficient to cast a glance at the titles of books published during that period in various parts of Europe to gain an idea of the wide range of concepts discussed in them. No matter how different they were, most were rather pessimistic as to Europe's prospects for the future. Naturally, their authors' pessimism was largely prompted by their personal experience; nevertheless, the general dark mood was quite obvious.

This mood must have been originally caused by the aftermath of the First World War, which had claimed such a great toll of life and dashed many of the former illusions and aspirations fostered by Europeanist ideas. In the 1920s, the situation in post-Versailles Europe only added to the prevailing pessimistic mood. Curiously enough, the optimistic proclamations by political leaders, who were engaged in shaping a new European structure, were totally out of step with the public mood, for, on the whole, official optimism could deceive no one. In that context, eighteenth- and nineteenth-century projects seemed to be a cure-all that would offer a way to a new Europe.

However, there were also social reasons for the revival of pan-European ideas. With the growing Soviet might, on the one hand, and political instability and disintegration in Europe and mounting economic difficulties there, on the other, pan-European ideas seemed to offer a good way out. Coudenhove-Kalergi, a leading authority in the pan-European movement, affirmed that 'the whole of Europe should recognize the real nature of the Russian danger and realize that European security could be ensured exclusively through the establishment of the United States of Europe' (*Pan-Europe, 1922–1966*, Vienna-Munich, 1966). He meant not only the possibility of realizing specific political projects but also the political and moral climate in Europe. Many advocates of pan-Europist ideas regarded the spiritual unity of the West as an indisputable prerequisite for the unification of Europe.

Of course, many members of the intellectual and academic community were looking for ways to achieve European unity in order to solve common European social problems, overcome chauvinist and nationalist sentiments and remove the threat of rightist extremism and fascism. The economic factor and the objective trend of internationalization of economic affairs were also of substantial importance.

However, the wide range of European concepts had more specific features in common: they were not based on any serious principles and, most important, they did not enjoy mass support in Europe. In fact, the concepts met with response from a comparatively small circle of bourgeois intellectuals.

European nations were witnessing the runaway arms drive and were worried by the decline in living standards and the growing rightist danger. In that context, the speculative theories and slogans of the advocates of pan-Europeanism and the inadequacy of extremely ephemeral pan-European moral principles very often appeared merely a manifestation of nostalgia, experienced by European bourgeois liberal circles, for the mid-nineteenth-century European liberalism of Victor Hugo and Giuseppe Mazzini, which had little relevance to the hard realities of their own epoch. It was on this basis that diverse European projects and ideas were born.

Europeanist problems enjoyed great popularity in the 1920s–30s among prominent political and public leaders such as Edouard Herriot (his book, entitled *L'Europe*, was published in 1930), Tomaš

Masaryk, Eduard Beneš, Walter Rathenau and Gustav Stresemann. Many economists, politicians, financiers and industrialists were engaged in working out ideas for a new European economic system and Europeanist ideas, including that of a European customs union, were also winning popularity in Britain: A. Salter of Britain was among the initiators of the European Free Trade Association (EFTA).

Just as in the early twentieth century, the Europeanist movement again attracted the attention of workers movements and of international social democracy. In 1924 Edo Fimmon of the Netherlands, who later held the post of secretary-general of the International Federation of Transport Workers, published a study devoted to the United States of Europe. Also in 1924, German Social-Democrat Hermann Kran published a booklet entitled *The United States of Europe: The Only Task of Proletarian Policy*; in the same year a workers' publishing house brought out W. Woitinsky's *The United States of Europe*.

Athough all these authors were activists of the Socialist International, their writings did not reflect the general stand taken by that international organization. They expressed the views of their national organizations, but their contribution was not forgotten.

We have already discussed Lenin's attitude to the slogan of the United States of Europe. On 30 June 1923, *Pravda* carried Leon Trotsky's article, 'The Slogan of the United States of Europe is Topical Today', which was his contribution to the disputes on the problem. Trotsky analysed it in the context of relations between Europe and America. It was economic co-operation among European countries alone, he believed, that could save the continent from disintegration and enslavement by the Americans. Trotsky therefore put forward the idea of the United States of European Workers. Just like Coudenhove-Kalergi (who expressed his views later), Trotsky spoke about the participation of the USSR and Britain in such a union.

For Trotsky Soviet participation was unquestionable, but as the British worker movement's evolution towards Marxism seemed to him much slower than that in other European countries, he was rather sceptical as to British workers' possible participation in the process. He did not specify any particular form of European structure or movement – he discussed the issue in principle.

However, in general, just as before, both the Bolsheviks and the communist parties in European countries regarded the slogan of the United States of Europe as a means to promote the concept of world revolution and as a form of possible unification of the revolutionary forces on the European continent.

Various attitudes to pan-European ideas were revealed in the split of the international worker movement. The Bolsheviks continued to think in terms of world revolution, whereas the social democrats had no definite position. Neither the Socialist International nor the Comintern made public their attitude to the revival of pan-European ideas and movements.

However, all searches on this topic in the European record of the period between the two world wars would have probably been unfruitful had it not been for two realistic projects which provoked broad discussion and reflected features that were typical of previous projects in this field. The two projects in question differed from all others because they became an object of political discussion; one was put forward by a public leader and the other by a prominent statesman, on behalf of his government.

The idea for unification of Europe of Austrian Count Coudenhove-Kalergi was put forward in his book, *Pan-Europa*, which appeared in 1923. In June 1924 he sent an open letter to French MPs in which he explained his view of the situation in Europe and suggested some pan-European ideas to remedy it. Like many other advocates of the European idea, he stated that Europe was rent by anarchy and faced the imminent threat of a political, economic and cultural catastrophe.

Coudenhove-Kalergi was without doubt a prominent figure in the pan-European movement: his works and articles made a notable contribution to the development of Europeanist ideas in the twentieth century and to the ideas and projects which served as the basis for West European integration in the post-war years. *Pan-Europa* may be justly regarded as a manifesto of twentieth-century Europeanism.

Count Coudenhove-Kalergi's genealogical tree had its roots in Czechia, Austria, Japan, Poland and Russia and even as a youth he had been keenly aware of his European identity. He begins his book with a reminder that the trend for European unity has deep roots, although it had always been just an idea, without any practical basis. In the nineteenth century, he continues, Europe had dominated the world via its six great powers: the United Kingdom, Russia, Germany, Austro-Hungary, France and Italy. However, the early twentieth century saw the end of Europe's undivided domination, with the rise of the mighty Russian Empire (with its new internal structure), the expansion of the national liberation movement in Asia and the rapid development of America. All these contributed to the eclipse of Europe.

Technical progress, revolution produced by the use of steam and electricity and exploitation of rail and air travel opened broad vistas for humanity. Great European powers were gradually turned into world powers. Europe, the author believed, had to realize that differentiation without complete integration would ruin it and that it should supplement its analytic policy with political synthesis. He suggested that Europe should be unified not only as an alliance of nations but also as a pan-European federation, otherwise (he hinted even then) Europe would be conquered by Russia. He also discussed the problem of European borders, although not from a geographical viewpoint; he attached value primarily to historical borders and the historical evolution of Europe.

While analysing Europe's type of civilization, he singled out America and the Eurasian civilization. He regarded Russia as a synthesis of European and Asian civilizations. The Tatar invasion forced Russia into an Asian orientation in its development, although in the last two centuries it had again given priority to a European orientation by adopting a form of European civilization that was somewhat superficial. Bolshevism had renounced European civilization by disrupting Russia's contacts with democratic and Christian Europe and promoting the development of a new kind of civilization, based on European principles and Asiatic ways and methods.

In general, the author's attitude to Russia is rather contradictory. His book reveals that he recognized Russia's European identity without denying the interdependence between Russia and Asia. He regarded Russia, to some extent, as a synthesis of European and Asian civilizations. In political respects, Coudenhove-Kalergi believed that the concepts of world revolution and Bolshevism, which predominated in post-revolutionary Russia, held great danger for Europe. In today's context, the author's statement that without Russia and Britain Europe could hardly be described as pan-Europe or full Europe is quite understandable. Nevertheless, in the context of the 1920s, he envisioned pan-Europe as the territory between Britain and Africa, on the one hand, and Russia, on the other.

The author viewed the formation of pan-Europe as the only way to avoid war, devoting a whole chapter to the subject. He believed that the threat of war in Europe was very real: war could break out because of some external danger or internal anarchy. In either case, the author believed, the way to salvation lay in the unification of Europe. Thus, organization had to replace anarchy, with arbitration as an alternative to war, disarmament instead of the arms race, mutual guarantees instead of self-defence and co-operation instead of rivalries.

Coudenhove-Kalergi's pan-European project was a political document rather than an appeal to European spiritual values or a manifesto for a universal and just peace (as in the period of European

Enlightenment). However, even in this case, the author could hardly renounce Europe's heritage or the spiritual values of each European nation. For him Dante symbolized Italy; Luther – Germany; Hus and Masaryk – Czechia; Cornelle, Racine, Voltaire, Rousseau, Bonaparte and Hugo – France; Kant, Nietzsche, Goethe, Schiller, Wagner and Bismarck – Germany; Mussolini – modern Italy; and Lenin – Russia. Of course, his choice of names seems somewhat arbitrary: for him great humanists and political leaders equally symbolized the national spirit and grandeur of their states and nations.

Having discussed the historial and political prerequisites for a European Federation, the author offered ways and methods of establishing pan-Europe. First, he suggested convening a pan-European conference as an initial stage in the pan-European evolution. His idea was that the conference should set up commissions for considering the problems of arbitration, guarantees, disarmament, finance, means of communication, debt and cultural issues. Next, he believed, they should sign a treaty of arbitration and mandatory guarantees, set up a pan-European customs union as a step on the way to a homogeneous economic alliance, and, finally, draft and adopt a pan-European constitution.

Coudenhove-Kalergi proposed setting up the United States of Europe on the model of the United States of America, with maximum freedom within it. The pan-European alliance should have two chambers of government: the People's Chamber of 300 representatives (one deputy representing one million people) and the Federal Chamber, with 20 deputies from each of the 26 European states. He recognized the equality of all languages and school education but suggested that knowledge of English should be obligatory for all. So far as colonies were concerned, he suggested that all European states should have free access to Africa.

Defence of democracy in Europe as a whole and in each individual country was to become one of the main tasks of the future Federation. Coudenhove-Kalergi was equally opposed to extreme left and rightist views, for the advocates of the former sought to establish Soviet dictatorship, and those of the latter dreamed of military dictatorship. As a result, Europe was being pushed towards war through the efforts of both.

Let us review the formation process of the pan-European movement and its activities in the 1920s–30s before assessing the merits of Coudenhove-Kalergi's European project. His *pan-Europa* was published in Vienna in October 1923, just as national pan-European groups were being set up and the formation process for a pan-European alliance was started. The magazine *Pan-Europa* was launched in 1924 and its special issues were *L'Europe nouvelle*, published in Paris, Berlin and Vienna, and *L'Europe jeune*, in Berne.

Special columns, with headlines such as 'The United States of Europe' or 'Pan-Europe', were carried by many popular magazines. National pan-European groups were headed by prominent political and public leaders who took an active part in preparations for a pan-European congress and in drafting the programme of the alliance.

The First Pan-European Congress was opened in Vienna on 4 October 1926. It was attended by more than 2,000 delegates, with political leaders, ex-ministers, writers and scientists, as well as members of the artistic community known for their humanistic and pacifist views, among them. Sculptured portaits of prominent advocates of pan-European ideas of past centuries were displayed in the congress hall, among them those of Kant, Napoleon Bonaparte, Nietzsche, Komensky, Abbé Saint-Pierre, Mazzini and Hugo.

Representatives of various European countries, as well as those of America and the League of Nations, took part in the discussions held at the congress. Many speakers stressed the need to establish cordial relations with Russia and America (an American delegate was among those who addressed the congress). The congress was also addressed by Alexander Kerensky, former head of the Russian Provisional Government, a fact which accounted for the complications that arose in relations between the Pan-European Alliance and the Soviet Union. On the one hand, the advocates of the alliance spoke about the Russian (that is, Bolshevik) danger that was threatening Europe, and, on the other, about the impossibility of excluding Russia from the alliance.

The Soviet government from the outset had identified pan-Europeanism with a 'hostile capitalist encirclement that was out to destroy the USSR'. Europeanist ideas were alien to the Bolshevik leaders whose goal was world revolution and the unification of communist forces. Soviet leaders viewed with great hostility and suspicion both European liberalism and pacifism, which were central to the pan-European movement in the initial stage of its development. Finally, Kerensky's participation in the congress only reaffirmed their conviction that they had taken the right course. As a result, the pan-European alliance was being formed without Russia and in an atmosphere of bitter confrontation and hostility on both sides.

Both pan-European and Soviet leaders seemed to have reached a tacit agreement that Russia did not belong in Europe (naturally, it would have been inconceivable for the USSR, for various ideological and political reasons, to identify itself with bourgeois, liberal Europe; on the other hand, Bolshevism was equally unacceptable to the West).

The congress devoted much attention to economic issues: a special committee on economic issues was set up with its headquarters in Brussels.

Coudenhove-Kalergi was elected president of the Pan-European Alliance. He took it for granted that the issue of Pan-Europe had been settled once and for all, so the only remaining problem was when and how the project would be realized.

At its initial stage, the pan-European movement met with broad support in Europe, including official circles. It was hailed enthusiastically by Masaryk and Beneš in Czechoslovakia and Stresemann in Germany, and it was widely supported in France. Soon after, French Foreign Minister Aristide Briand was elected honorary president of the Pan-European Alliance and Jouvenelle, Lucher and Painlevé became active participants.

On 29 Janaury 1925 Edouard Herriot, in his new capacity as Prime Minister of France, called for the unification of Europe: 'My most cherished desire is to witness the realization of the idea of the United States of Europe. I have always supported the idea of the League of Nations, for I regarded it as a draft model of the United States of Europe.' In contrast to Coudenhove-Kalergi, Herriot attached great importance to the League of Nations: he believed that the process of unification in Europe should be started within its framework.

He stressed the importance of adopting laws which would stimulate the development of the European economy and protect the European market. Herriot also pointed out that he took account of the fact that Great Britain might have a stake in European and world affairs.

While supporting the idea of pan-Europe, he offered to take the Pan-European Alliance as a model, including its methods and procedure, which provided for regular convocation of conferences and a permanent secretariat. He called for caution, patience and flexibility, and believed that arbitration, disarmament and security would be guidelines for European political affairs in future. Later, in 1930, Herriot published a book, entitled *L'Europe*, in which he analysed Briand's project and expressed his support for it.

At various stages of the pan-European movement, primarily at its initial stage, prominent European politicans and personalities took part in it, among them Léon Blum, Edouard Daladier and P. Boncourt of France, J. Schacht and K. Wirt of Germany, Philip Noel-Baker of Britain, German writers Thomas and Heinrich Mann, French poet Paul Valéry, Spanish philosopher José Ortega y Gasset, and scientists

Einstein and Freud. The idea of a pan-European alliance also met with a positive response in some industrial circles, especially among French businessmen who sought to set up a strong European alliance as a counterweight to the growing might of Germany.

Building on his ideas, in 1930 Coudenhove-Kalergi offered a more detailed plan for a European Federation, in which he raised the issues of European citizenship, the Federal European Court and the Treasury.

Meanwhile, the Second Pan-European Congress was held in Berlin in May 1930, which was followed by a third congress in Basel in 1932. The second congress was held in an atmosphere of growing chauvinist and militarist moods, a process which culminated in Hitler's advent to power. In the same period, Coudenhove-Kalergi made a statement in which he in fact recognized Germany's right to rearmament – and this led to a split in the pan-European movement at the Third Pan-European Congress.

In the mid-1930s the movement was still active, although it was clear that the euphoria of its first congress was a thing of the past. Advocates of pan-Europeanism tried to breathe new life into the movement at its fourth congress, held in Vienna in 1935; they put forward ideas for a European Confederation, a single European currency, a European customs union, a European Court and a police force.

A British committee in support of pan-Europe was set up in 1939, which was a reaction to the sharply deteriorating international situation. The British public became increasingly aware of the danger of Britain's isolation from the European movement which was regarded as one of the main means of opposing Germany.

After Germany's annexation of Austria, the centre of the pan-European movement was transferred to Berne, while Coudenhove-Kalergi moved to the USA, where he set up the Committee for a Free and United Europe.

However, these were only private initiatives and, overall, the pan-European movement, which had been launched by Coudenhove-Kalergi, lost many of its advocates and its popularity waned.

Apart from Coudenhove-Kalergi, Heerfordt of Denmark also published a book (*New Europe*, 1924) devoted to pan-European problems. Heerfordt has often been described as second in importance as a founder of pan-Europe. An ardent supporter of the League of Nations, he focused on the analysis of its Statute, membership and activities.

Heerfordt suggested setting up a league of European governments. Effective solutions to the tasks confronting Europe, he believed, might be ensured through the establishment of 'The United States of Europe' or 'The European Community'. He tackled the questions of the removal of all customs and the economic barriers between future member-countries, and the introduction of a single currency and administrative system. He attached great importance to the effective operation of the proposed League and was primarily concerned with the problem of preventing wars between member-countries. Each member-country would largely retain the responsibility to promote the development of its own industry, culture and public health system. In this way he intended to preclude the possibility of any country attaining superiority over the others. Relations among the League's member-countries would be similar to those that existed among the citizens in any modern civilized country.

Heerfordt expressed the hope that all controversial issues, such as the Black Sea straits – the Bosporus and the Dardanelles – the Ruhr basin and reparations, would be settled in a peaceful way. The main goal, he believed, was to guarantee the security of France and other countries against possible hostile sorties by Germany.

He also discussed another important issue: how the national development of each European state could be ensured in a united Europe. Heerfordt's stance was perfectly clear – he advocated strong European statehood. While willing to transfer part of the state functions in the spheres of foreign policy and defence to confederate bodies, he believed that they should always be used primarily to ensure peace, prevent military conflicts and promote friendly relations among the nations.

It was probably because of his Scandinavian roots that Heerfordt laid special stress on the importance of European unity for small states. Renunciation of their rivalries by the great powers, he pointed out, would prove beneficial to small states, which would no longer be involved in the great powers' games.

The author thoroughly analysed the experience of the United States of America (with an account of its historical evolution) in his search for analogies and models for the future European Federation. He also cited the examples of the British colonial federations (Canada, Australia and South Africa), the United States of Brazil, the 1871 German Empire, the 1867 German Federation and Switzerland. Thus, Heerfordt's project possessed a sound historical basis.

He was also aware of the difficulties the implementation of his project would involve. The main obstacles, he believed, would lie in his departure from the old traditions, strong national opposition and the unfavourable effect on industry through the lifting of customs tariffs.

Heerfordt believed that there were two ways to lay the groundwork for a European Federation. It could be achieved through active participation of the public (intellectuals, businessmen and journalists) in the process, which should later be supported by the governments and, finally, a pan-European conference should be convened. Another method consisted in each country setting up a national committee to establish the number of supporters of the idea of the Federation. Later those committees might be transformed into national divisions of the European organization. In conclusion, he stated that he regarded his initiative as the major impulse to the whole movement.

Heerfordt was first active in Denmark and later in Sweden and Norway. In general, he went even further than his predecessors, regarding the United States of Europe as a step on the way to World Federation.

In the context of sharp clashes between nationalist and international trends, Heerfordt's project reflected European intellectuals' apprehension in the face of the spread of nationalist and chauvinist ideas. Heerfordt's plan was discussed at sittings and in the lobbies of the League of Nations and by advocates of pan-Europeanism, although in fact it had little practical effect.

The projects of Coudenhove-Kalergi and Heerfordt were the first broad and specific twentieth-century plans for a European Federation, with the system and rights of national European states preserved intact. These pan-European projects were offered on a public level, and they drew on numerous similar projects of the eighteenth and nineteenth centuries. However, with the mounting tension and sharpening conflict in Europe, plans for its unification were obviously unrealistic. They are of interest to us as they show the evolution of the European idea and the attempt to tone down the growing hostility and rivalries in bourgeois Europe, overcome the crisis and prevent 'the eclipse' of Europe, which was the subject of lively discussion in those years.

Clashes between various ideas and phenomena, the spread of nationalism and chauvinism in Germany and of rightist extremism in European capitalist countries, the economic crisis that was gripping the Western world in the late 1920s and early 1930s and the obvious unpopularity of pacifist ideas – all these gave rise to scepticism and despondency among European intellectuals and, in fact, made it difficult to find any stimulus for unification, which undermined the principles of the pan-European movement in these years.

At the same time, pan-European ideas promoted a mental climate that stimulated initiative in political circles and among official leaders.

Characteristically, congresses and meetings held under the banner of the Pan-European Alliance were attended not only by public leaders and prominent personalities but also by government officials. Thus, the public was led to believe that some sort of initiative was to follow on a government level.

In that situation in the late 1920s, the French Foreign Minister Aristide Briand, who was an honorary president of the Pan-European Alliance, put forward an official project of European unification. The situation in Europe and France clearly affected Briand's stance. In the decade that had followed the First World War France largely lost its leading position in Europe. The failure of the Locarno Pact system was revealed in full measure in the 1930s, although in the late 1920s its shortcomings were already obvious. Germany was building up its might, which could not but revive the apprehensions of the French. Slowly but surely France yielded its leadership in Europe to Great Britain. French hopes to make use of the small European states to promote its plans were only partly justified. Moreover, Great Britain and Italy, and also Germany in the late 1920s–early 1930s, were increasingly infiltrating the traditional spheres of French influence. Therefore, French politicians looked for new spheres of activity and for ways to restore French domination in Europe.

During these years Briand, Boncourt and Barthou stood, successively, at the helm in France and were charged with decision-making in foreign policy. As broad-minded statesmen, they were known to maintain contacts with liberal Europeanist circles.

French diplomacy decided to stake everything on the European card, taking into account the ever-growing popularity of pan-European feelings in Europe, the interest of prominent members of the artistic and academic community, and the fact that there had been several pan-European congresses and meetings. This was why Briand's plan was conceived. He was known as a supporter of the ideas of Saint-Pierre, Voltaire and Rousseau, and he often quoted eighteenth-century European liberals in his speeches and articles. However, Briand was primarily a politician, so his actions and projects were prompted by and reflected the pragmatic interests of French ruling circles and French diplomacy, and he made clever use of the Europeanist support in various European countries.

I have already mentioned that the pan-European illusions of bourgeois intellectuals had not met with much favour in Europe. Therefore, the stake on broad public support of the Briand plan proved unrealistic. Consequently, Briand and French diplomacy could only hope for success on an inter-state level. Actually, Briand could hardly have believed in the success of his project himself, but he must have calculated that the discussion of such projects would boost France's image in diplomatic circles and add to its authority in Europe.

Briand described some of the points of his plan in a speech in Geneva in September 1929:

> I believe that the nations which may be described as European nations geographically should be bound together by certain feudal contacts. Those nations should at any moment have an opportunity to contact each other, discuss their interests, adopt mutual decisions and promote a spirit of solidarity in their relations which would be helpful in any emergency. Such association should obviously be predominant in the sphere of economy, but I am sure that, without encroaching on each nation's sovereignty, a federal alliance might be very beneficial from the political and social viewpoint. (A. Tchoubarian, 'Briand's Europe', in *Metamorphoses of Europe*, Moscow, 1993)

Building on this idea, on 1 May 1930 Briand made a specific offer to European member-states of the League of Nations to set up a federative alliance in Europe. Each state that had received Briand's proposal had to send a written reply within a few months. However, even before this Briand had contacted Czechoslovakia's President, Tomaš Masaryk, who had shown interest in European ideas and projects. The 1929–30 economic crisis had a substantial effect on Briand's project plan as a whole and Briand laid special stress on economic factors.

Western scholars pay special attention to the fact that in his speeches Briand incorporated notions and terms such as 'Common Market' and 'European Community', regarding them as corresponding to the modern West European realities. However, apart from purely terminological coincidence, Briand's very amorphous project had little in common with the guiding principles of the advocates of West European integration as it was promulgated after the Second World War. Briand's plan was based on the idea of the full independence and sovereignty of all nations in the proposed Federative Alliance.

He suggested that the structure of the future Federative Alliance should be built on the model of the League of Nations, that 'European conferences' should be held with the participation of all European member-states of the League, and that a 'Political Committee', which was to include a definite number of members, and 'a Secretariat' should be set up. Briand specified neither the goals and substance of the activities to be carried out by the Federative European bodies nor methods for solving the economic and customs problems.

His plan largely dealt with the political aspects of European development and the actual correlation of forces and interests on the European continent. Recourse to the model of the League of Nations accentuated the aspects of international relations, thus revealing the real essence of Briand's plan – his desire to buttress France's position on the European scene. More importantly, Briand's plan, in fact, excluded the USSR from a future European alliance.

The European states' response to the French initiative is of great interest. Briand's plan was actually rejected by the overwhelming majority of European countries – for a variety of reasons. Some countries criticized the attempt to exclude the USSR from the proposed alliance, deeming it necessary to include both the Soviet Union and Turkey. This was the stand taken by Estonia, Lithuania, Germany, Bulgaria and a number of other countries. However, quite predictably, Briand's plan was also opposed for other reasons: Britain rejected such a scheme because its government certainly did not favour the idea of increased French influence in Europe. Neither was it supported by Germany, where the rightist forces were openly striving for power. In addition, it was opposed by Italy.

The plan did receive support from several small states: Bulgaria and Yugoslavia approved it unreservedly, while Norway, Greece and Czechoslovakia accepted it with some reservations.

Thus, official European circles rejected the French Foreign Minister's pan-European plan not only because it was out of step with the European realities of the period but also because of the deep rivalries among the leading European powers.

The Briand Plan was largely directed at restoring France's leadership in Europe. When it is remembered that the Briand–Kellog Peace Pact (authored by Briand in co-operation with the US Secretary of State Frank Kellog) was signed in Paris in August 1928, it is clear that the French ruling circles did not act single-handedly.

In general pan-European ideas, which attracted the attention of a certain section of Europe's liberal intellectuals, did not gain wide currency in the period between the two world wars, for the proposed ideas were impracticable in view of the prevailing situation: the European continent was rent by diverse needs and aims which ruled out the possibility of realizing any federalist project of European unification.

In assessing the pan-European movement of the 1920s–30s in the context of the evolution of the European idea, it should be pointed out

132

that although the movement has made no tangible contribution either to developments on the international scene or to the maintenance of peace, it has left a notable trace in the development of Europeanism. A great number of books and articles were devoted to the subject and many Europeanist periodicals were launched. Apart from the projects discussed here, a great number of models and versions of European unification were put forward in these publications and in the course of discussions held on the subject.

In subsequent years, such pan-European and federalist ideas seemed to lose popularity, but the experience obtained in this sphere was widely applied in the post-war years, when the ideas for a European federation became more realistic.

16

FASCISM AND EUROPEANISM

Fascist ideologists operated widely using Europeanist theories and slogans. Born in Italy in the years of the First World War, fascism seemed initially to concentrate on nationalist goals, although very soon Italian fascists resorted to universalist doctrines, in particular to Europeanist slogans which dated back to the mid-nineteenth century, that is, to the Risorgimento period, including Giuseppe Mazzini's calls for 'Italy's renaissance', and the formation of 'a Latin Europe'. (Incidentally, it has happened many times, in various epochs, that the extreme rightist circles advocating reactionary theories have exploited left liberal and sometimes left radical phraseology.)

The Europeanism of Mussolini's supporters was primarily an ideological slogan rather than a political practice, for Italian fascists could not possibly raise the issue of Europe's unification under their own domination. In 1927 Mussolini declared that 'there are those who are on the rise and those who are on the downard trend in Europe. Italians are among those who increasingly loom large on the European horizon'. He obviously pinned his hopes on the triumph of fascist ideas throughout Europe, which would make it possible, he hoped, for Italy and Rome to become the centre of a new development trend, that is the fascist movement. 'The needs of fascism have already been sown in France, Britain and Germany which already have their own fascists. There, the Italian word is imbued with an international meaning, and it wins the people's hearts' (B. Lopukov, 'The Fascist and Antifascist Variants of "Europeanism" in Italy', in *The Mediterranean and Europe*, Moscow, 1966).

In their attempts to attach universalist features to Italian fascism Mussolini and his associates made use of Europeanist ideas. However, the Italian fascists did not confine themselves to ideological doctrine; they also tried to unite fascists on a European scale. Gravelli, a leading fascist, started publishing the journal *Anti-Europa*, thus opposing the new fascist movement to old liberal Europe. Gravelli wrote that Italian fascists 'are making haste to attain real unity in Europe', 'a Europe guided by Rome'.

In 1932 a world congress was held in Rome under the aegis of Italian fascists. Its sponsors calculated, on the one hand, that it would counteract Briand's pan-European plans and, on the other, that it would rally the European public around Italian-style fascist ideas. Advocates of fascism from various countries attended the congress, and Germany was represented by Goering, Rosenberg, and Schacht.

The participants' speeches were keynoted by a justification for fascism combined with anti-Sovietism, and many of them openly pointed to the need for Europe's unification on the 'basis of anti-Bolshevism'. However, attempts at rallying European fascists under the Italian banner failed, primarily because of Nazi Germany's increasing role in European affairs, with its programme of 'world domination'.

For that reason Germany refused to attend the next world fascist congress, held in Montreux in Switzerland in December 1934. Italian delegates pointed out in their speeches at the congress that Italian fascists did not strive for European domination, that each nation should follow its own road and that the idea of supranationality should be 'harmonized with the national idea'.

However, by the mid-1930s Italy was obviously playing second fiddle in the fascist movement. The 1936 Rome–Berlin agreement, referred to as an 'axis' by Mussolini, which was supposed to serve as a centre of attraction for other European countries, was a confirmation of sorts by Italy that Germany was to play the role of leader, with Italy in second place to its mighty ally. Consequently, attempts at reanimating European ideas on the basis of Italian fascism lost their importance.

Hitler's programme for a new 'world order' and the ideas for enslaving European nations were never concealed by Nazi propaganda. By proclaiming many European nationalities as 'inferior' and the superiority of the 'Aryan race', the Nazis set themselves the task of the physical extermination of whole countries and peoples and the conquest of Europe. They made no secret of the anti-Soviet edge of their programme.

By attacking Poland in 1939 Germany unleashed the Second World War in Europe. Nazi leaders were quite outspoken about their global designs, and initially they showed little interest in European ideas and theories, which is why before 1941 Nazis almost never alluded to any theories or plans for European unification.

After Nazi Germany's invasion of the USSR the situation changed.

Inspired by their initially successful offensive on the Eastern Front, the Nazis started animatedly discussing various plans for European unification. At first they believed that all countries and peoples conquered by them would easily 'adapt' themselves to German domination. However, as a result of heroic resistance and popular partisan warfare in temporarily occupied Soviet territory and the mounting Resistance movement in Western and Eastern Europe, the Nazis had to resort to various plans for 'economic' and 'political' 'development' of the occupied Soviet territory.

Back in May 1941, before the Nazi invasion of the USSR, the economic organization Ost stated in its instructions on the prospects for utilization of Soviet agriculture:

> In future Southern Russia should gravitate towards Europe. Surplus food products produced there may be paid for exclusively, if the south of Russia received the German, i.e., European, consumer goods it needs. Russian competition which may come from the forest areas should be eliminated. No steps should be taken there to combat hunger. Some ten million people will prove redundant there and will die or will have to move to Siberia.
>
> Our minimum goal is to relieve Germany of its obligation to send supplies to the *Wehrmacht*, when the war is in its third year.

In his instructions to 'the civil administration of occupied eastern lands', issued in September 1941, Rosenberg, the Nazi regime's 'ideologist', described the administrative system for the Germanization of the eastern lands:

> War against the USSR is an undertaking of great political importance . . . After the Red Army's defeat, the USSR should be fragmentized according to the ethnic principle, and the lands adjacent to Germany in the east and populated by non-Russian peoples should maintain close political contacts with the Reich.

Forms and methods of Europe's Germanization were analysed in detail in a memorandum of 8 November 1941 which dealt with the main results of a discussion on the issues of economic policy and organization of economic order in occupied eastern regions. Those subjects were also discussed at many other sittings of various organizations of the Third Reich. German Minister of Trade Fank started using the term 'European Economic Community' in his addresses in 1942.

In an address to SS leaders and the police in September 1942 Himmler declared:

> This year we again managed to acquire in our possession considerable areas of that country, and in the next few months we shall conquer even more lands ... in the next year we shall certainly conquer the whole of European Russia.
>
> ... One should study not only English theory but also the practice of the Britons' time in India ... In the next two decades we shall have to settle what are today Germany's eastern provinces – from Eastern Russia to Upper Silesia; we must Germanize and settle Byelorussia, Estonia, Latvia, Lithuania, Ingermanland and the Crimea. In other regions we shall found, just as we are already doing here, small towns with a population of 15,000–20,000 Germans, with German villages scattered within a radius of 10 kilometres around them for all of them to maintain permanent contacts with the centre of German life ... We intend to set up such population centres in the territory stretching away to the Volga, the Don and, I hope, to the Urals.

In June 1943, Oberlander Hauptmann of the 2nd Section of the *Abwehr* wrote in his 'study' on the subject 'Alliance or Exploitation':

> What is it that unites Europe? Little Europe without its liberated eastern lands plays the part of a peninsula in the struggle of the great global vital areas, with its political potential equal to that of Ancient Greece within the framework of the Roman world.
>
> The liberated eastern lands have not yet made their choice between Europe and the USSR. Their identification with Europe and, as a consequence, considerable strengthening of this continent is possible exclusively through free choice of citizenship for the liberated peoples. This choice may also be described as trust in Germany.
>
> It is impossible to win the war in the East by purely military means. The latter should be supplemented and supported by political measures.

This 'study' appeared primarily as a result of the radical change in the course of the Second World War after the *Wehrmacht*'s major setbacks at the Eastern Front, and above all, after the Nazi army's defeat in the Battle of Stalingrad. It was due to this that the Nazi leaders were forced to look for 'new' forms of 'developing' occupied lands.

After the defeat at Stalingrad, the Nazi ideologists started attempting to modify their strategic and tactical concepts in order to discover new methods of asserting their influence on occupied lands. A number of new plans for subjugating the USSR to German fascism were put forward in late 1942 and 1943. In late 1942–early 1943 new 'proposals on Russia' were put forward by the German Ministry of Foreign Affairs, which offered modified 'methods' to deal with the difficulties in the USSR, and in the summer of 1943 a plan for 'the United State of Europe' was drafted. In September 1943 a document from the German Ministry of Foreign Affairs stated that 'the developments call for new decisions' in German foreign policy. Another document in the same series recommended the adoption of more flexible political steps which had to be more than simply declarative. It said, in particular, that winning the struggle against the USSR 'is the most important goal for a united Europe', and so 'an anti-Comintern pact should incorporate all members of the European alliance of states'.

A draft European Charter was even produced, which stated that not a single European nation, whether big or small, could possibly uphold its freedom, independence and productive forces single-handed. That was possible, it said, exclusively within the framework of the European Economic Community.

In the same period Gauleiter Hommer, who actively contributed to drafting the plan for the establishment of a 'united Europe', wrote: 'The USSR was and is our adversary, with whom from the outset any possibility of signing a peace treaty has been excluded and with whom we are carrying on a life-and-death struggle.' At this time German ruling factions were trying to modify to some degree their plans for administration in the occupied countries of Western and Central Europe.

All the documents testify that, faced with the setbacks at the Soviet–German front and the mounting Resistance movement in Europe, certain Nazi leaders tried to save the situation by resorting to Europeanist theories and projects, preparing the Nazi version of the 'unification' of Europe by force of arms, with Nazi goals and designs sold under the label of Europeanist slogans.

Curiously enough, the Nazis actively manipulated the old idea of excluding the USSR from the European community. The aim of their new plans was to whip up the anti-Soviet campaign in the new situation. Documents of the period testify that many participants in the

1944 anti-Hitler plot were also in favour of establishing contacts with the Western powers in order to combine their efforts in the fight against Bolshevism. Even in the autumn of 1943, L. Beck and K. Herdeler, who were to be among the leaders of the 1944 plot, had pointed out in their memorandum that 'Europe needs guaranteed protection from the Russian superpower' and that Europe could ensure its security exclusively with the assistance of Great Britain and Germany.

In fact, Hitler was not concerned about European development, for he was totally devoted to the nationalist ideology of pan-Germanism. However, in many of his speeches, especially at the closing stage of the war, he stressed the historic mission of Germany and national socialism which, as he saw it, was to protect Western civilization or Europe from 'Bolshevism' and 'Jewish domination'. Henri Brugmans, a prominent historian of Europeanism, quotes in his book *L'idée europ-éenne, 1918–1945* (Bruges, 1966) with reference to German author O. Abetza, Pierre Laval's words addressed to Hitler: 'You intend to win a victory in order to organize Europe; but it would be necessary to create Europe in order to emerge victorious in this war.'

In referring to Nazi Germany's Europeanism, I do not mean any definite programme of European development, but rather their conquest of Europe, that is, a forcible unification of Europe by Germany. The Nazi use of Europeanist slogans only goes to show that the slogans of European unity were extremely versatile, amorphous and contradictory. They were also cunningly and actively applied in the everyday practice of European fascism, first, to promote the designs of Mussolini and his associates and later, in Hitler's schemes for the subjugation and physical extermination of millions of Europeans.

Some collaborationists also resorted to Europeanist ideas. In his book, mentioned above, Henri Brugmans wrote about De Mans, a Belgian socialist who envisioned a Europe that was to be united by force of arms. In 1942, Pierre Doyer, another Belgian, published *L'Europe pour les européens*, in which he expressed hope that it would be Hitler's Germany that would ensure economic co-operation without borders on the basis of anti-Bolshevism and the elimination of British influence.

Henri Brugmans draws the conclusion that the European idea was cultivated by both the Nazis and their adversaries in the countries occupied by Hitler's troops.

17

THE RESISTANCE MOVEMENT IN EUROPE

European ideas were also popular among participants in the Resistance movement in the years of the Second World War. They were also discussed and written about by members of the anti-Hitler coalition. These ideas were primarily opposed to Hitler's project of 'a new world order' and served as unifying principles for participants in the anti-fascist Resistance movement. At the same time there was a certain nostalgic tinge in the latter's view of European ideas – a degree of regret for the lost opportunities in European development. Finally, advocates of European ideas among the Resistance fighters sought to visualize the outlines of a post-war Europe. It was not accidental that European ideas became especially widespread after the Battle of Stalingrad in 1943, when it became obvious that Nazi Germany's débâcle was soon to follow. As a rule, European ideas were put forward by moderate liberal segments, whereas the Communists, who represented an important force in the Resistance movement, showed little interest in such ideas and projects.

At the same time, it can hardly be denied that the new interest in common European concerns reflected the prevailing trend to co-ordinate patriotic action in various parts of Europe – in Italy, France, Poland, Yugloslavia, Czechoslovakia, Greece and Norway, etc. In this context, one may describe the Resistance movement as a pan-European phenomenon. The anti-fascist partisan movement on the temporarily occupied territory of the Soviet Union and the struggle of German anti-fascists in the Third Reich were part of the same fight against fascism. Patriots throughout Europe were united by identical goals and the mutual desire to contribute to the victory over Nazism.

L. Valliani, a prominent Italian historian, wrote the following in this connection: 'The Resistance movement varied in each country in its composition, motives and the rhythm of struggle, as well as in social and political goals.' At the same time, 'Resistance' was inspired by the desire to see co-operation among the nations and universal brotherhood established on the ruins of Nazism. In Resistance fighters patriotism was combined with internationalist solidarity. English, American, Polish, French and other soldiers fought shoulder to shoulder in Italy against the Nazi army. The hard-won Soviet victories were of crucial importance for Italy. There were Britons, Americans, Soviet people, Poles, Yugoslavs, Czechs, Slovaks and French among the participants in the Italian Resistance movement. Italian guerrillas also took part in the Resistance movement in France, Yugoslavia and Greece.

The Resistance movement had no single centre, although its participants were inspired by common liberation ideas and goals. In other words, the European idea was then manifested in the joint struggle of the democratic European circles against fascism and Nazism, and in the Europeans' common responsibility for the salvation of Europe and European civilization from the threat of enslavement and destruction.

However, new Europeanist trends developed in the European 'underground', trends that were closely associated with the problem of the post-war European structure. These trends originated in Italy. Altiero Spinelli and Ernesto Rossi, active participants in the Italian Resistance movement who had been sentenced to a prison term on Ventonen Island, wrote a manifesto that was later entitled 'The Ventonen Manifesto'. The Italian historian M. Ferrara wrote that the manifesto had been inspired by certain Risorgimento ideas, primarily by the Mazzini ideal of the United States of Europe.

In his address to the 1983 world conference 'Resistance Movement in Europe', Spinelli explained his view of European unity by citing the events of the Second World War. In comparing the map of Europe on the eve of the Second World War with that of the period before 1914, Spinelli (in L. Valliani, G. Vaccarino and J. Spinelli, *La Resistenza a l'Europe*, 1984) pointed out that 'the idea of a nation-state has been realized almost throughout Europe, except for Switzerland, which exists as a small but multinational federal state'. While pointing to the positive result of the establishment of nation-states that had become 'an important instrument of civic progress', for national unity promoted integration and, later, 'economic, cultural, social and political solidarity of members of a nation', Spinelli noted the presence in the nation's sovereignty of 'conflict-prone elements', which, he believed, were to be found in all states without exception, irrespective of their social system. Those elements, he believed, were expressed in the 'absolute value' of the nation's interest, for the sake of which 'citizens should be ready to make any sacrifices, up to sacrificing their own lives. Thus, for the sake of asserting the priority of one's own national interest over other citizens' interests, people tended to justify the use of force against other nations'.

In developing his ideas, Spinelli states that patriotism inevitably degenerates into nationalism and wars among sovereign states become 'an organic phenomenon, and the opportunity to mobilize feelings, will and resources of nation-states makes wars among them especially brutal'. He believes that the war of 1914–18 was the first global outburst of nationalism which proved that the 'old supranational empires have collapsed, but where the military effort was supported by a politically united nation the state has proved its effectiveness'. Spinelli then illustrates this idea by describing how first in Italy, where there was much discontent with the domestic situation and the country's position on the international scene, and later in Germany, which had been shaken by a series of crises, nationalism and fascism were born, opposed as they were by 'the communist movement that was born by the Red Revolution and that had raised the banner of internationalism'. That movement was passive enough while fascists were at the helm in Italy alone, but it gained strength as soon as German Nazis had come to power. Anti-fascists of all countries united after Franco had unleashed civil war in Spain and Germany had occupied almost the whole of Europe, with the result that all nations were then involved in 'one giant tragedy, caused by the existence of the European system of sovereign nation-states'.

The Resistance movement in European countries is regarded by Spinelli as evidence of the excellence of federalist trends, which had developed during the closing stage of the First World War and in the period between the two world wars. These ideas were later developed in Italy by Luigi Einaudi, Francesco Nitti and Rosselli. Noting that the idea of the United States of Europe had deep historical roots, Spinelli affirms that in the years of the Second World War that idea was further developed as a realization 'of the need to break away from the ideological prison of a sovereign national state'. In a situation where the interests of individual states clashed with those of Europe as a whole, Spinelli gave priority to the latter. He accused individual peoples and countries of nationalism and egoism, while idealizing supranational European bodies.

Spinelli obviously underestimated the strength of European statehood, automatically transferring the illusions and dreams of nineteenth-century European liberals onto the reality of the 1940s and 1950s.

This is why the 'salvation' of Europe during the Second World War depended on the desire for unity and a sense of common responsibility among European countries and peoples for the earliest defeat of fascism and the prevention of a future war, rather than on the replacement of European statehood by supranational bodies.

However, hot debates were to be held between the opponents of European statehood and the so-called nationalists in Western Europe only in the post-war period, whereas in 1943, at the height of wartime battles, the 'Ventonen Manifesto' marked a definite stage in the development of European federalist ideas.

We have analysed Spinelli's views in detail because in the post-war period, too, he was a leading ideologist of West European integration and the author of many books dealing with the history of European unity. Spinelli energetically supported the Marshall Plan; from 1952 to 1970 he held the post of chairman of the Union of European Federalists, and later he was a member of an EEC commission.

While working on the 'Ventonen Manifesto', Spinelli and Rossi made wise use of the ideas put forward by Benedetto Croce:

> New mentality and a new nationality (for . . . nationalities have not been produced by Nature, but they are a form of mentality and formed by history) are now in embryo in all parts of Europe. When 20 years ago, a citizen of the old Kingdom of Naples or a subject of Piedmont, a sub-Alpine state, became Italians, without casting aside their former existence, they elevated it to and diluted it in their new reality. The French, Germans, Italians and all others will be elevated to the status of Europeans and will be thinking in terms of Europe, their hearts will be beating for it, just as before they beat for their smaller fatherlands, which will not be forgotten either. (A. Tchoubarian, *European Almanac, 1990*, Russian edn, Moscow, 1990)

In the same period, the Dutch economist, Dr H.D. Salinger, who also took part in clandestine Resistance activities, wrote a study, under an alias of Hades, devoted to his Europeanist project, entitled 'Die Wiedergeburt von Europe' and distributed illegally. The author wrote about the regeneration of Europe and mentioned a European Federation in this context.

It would also be appropriate here to recall the project by Paul Henri Spaak who in 1942 suggested an idea for an economic alliance among the three Benelux countries in north-eastern Europe.

During the Second World War the idea of the United States of Europe was also put forward by the Italian liberal economist Luigi Einaudi, who later lived in exile in Switzerland, where he wrote a series of articles under the general title 'The United States of Europe', in which he suggested adopting the Swiss federal system as a model for the future European structure.

In 1943, E. Colombo, an Italian, founded the European Movement of Federalists jointly with a group of Frenchmen. In August 1943 a special convention was held in Milan where Spinelli, Rossi and others put forward the plan for a European Federation which presupposed the introduction of European citizenship and other measures.

In 1944, a special conference was held in Geneva which adopted the Manifesto of European Resistance that called for putting an end to the anarchy in Europe resulting from the existence of 30 sovereign states, and establishing a federal alliance of European nations. The conference was attended by delegates from nine countries, among them K. Herdeler, who represented Germany and who, as mentioned above, had already spoken out in favour of the idea of European federation, with the participation of Germany and Western countries and directed against the 'Bolshevik threat'. The Manifesto said:

> It is the Federal Alliance alone that would offer an opportunity to the German people to take part in European affairs without threatening other peoples. It is the Federal Alliance alone that would offer an opportunity to settle border issues in areas with mixed population, which would at last no longer be objects of absurd nationalist designs and would be turned into issues of elementary territorial delimitation within the sphere of purely administrative competence. It is the Federal Alliance alone that would offer an opportunity to preserve democratic institutions so that countries that have not yet attained a certain degree of political maturity would not be able to imperil it. It is the Federal Alliance alone that would offer an opportunity to introduce economic reforms on the continent by eliminating national monopolies and autarchy. It is the Federal Alliance alone that would be able to offer a logical and natural solution to the problem of providing access to sea ports for countries situated far away from the sea shore; of regional utilization of rivers flowing through the territories of several countries; of control over straits and many other problems that have complicated relations among European states in the past few years. (Brugmans, op.cit.)

144

Herdeler, an ex-Bürgermeister of Leipzig who was later executed for participating in an attempt upon Hitler's life, also wrote about the future of Europe. In early 1944 he issued a memorandum which said in part: 'The only goal that could help resolve the current crisis is the formation of a united and active Europe.' In August 1944, shortly before his arrest, he said: 'This war must lead to close integration among European nations, and then the sacrifices will be justified' (Brugmans, op.cit.).

Discussion of European ideas and projects at the closing stage of the Second World War clearly revealed the fierce struggles between the various political forces in the Resistance movement. Europeanism in the Resistance movement, on the one hand, reflected the contradictory nature of European ideas and, on the other, served as a prelude to the fiery discussions to be held by social and political forces about the future of Europe soon after the Second World War.

However, the European idea was not only developed within the Resistance movement. The leaders of the anti-Hitler coalition also spoke and thought about the present and future of Europe on an official level. Issues of the future European structure were included in the 1942 Soviet–British treaty and in the decisions taken at the conferences of the Big Three – Russia, Britain and the US. Of special importance in this connection was the Declaration of Liberated Europe, which was adopted by the heads of the three powers. Of course, these could not be described as specific projects of European unification, but they were attempts to create a new international system in Europe for the future by producing a common formula for post-war European settlement.

However, Europeanist ideas were also current among the people in the countries of the anti-Hitler coalition. We have already mentioned Paul Henri Spaak in this context. Moreover, we may recall that Clement Attlee, a prominent British statesman and future Prime Minister, said in 1939 in his address to the Labour Party that if Europe did not become a federation, it would perish. In wartime, too, he reiterated the same ideas.

18

MODELS OF TOTALITARIAN SOCIALISM AND INTEGRATION IN EASTERN EUROPE

Radical changes were taking place in Eastern and south-eastern Europe after the Second World War. Major socio-economic and political reforms were introduced in many countries in these regions, with the result that they proclaimed their determination to take a socialist orientation in their development. All these countries then chose to copy the Soviet model, which, on the one hand, was associated with many Stalinist distortions of socialism and, on the other, ran counter to the states' historical experience, with their multi-party systems and bourgeois-democractic institutions. In consequence, since the 1950s political tensions have regularly come to a head in these countries, often leading to violent conflicts.

In the post-war period these countries left the capitalist orbit to join the socialist camp, led by the Soviet Union, with all its special features and contradictions. The emergence of the socialist system changed the situation in Europe and strongly affected the attitude to European unity. Confrontation between the two social systems on the continent further complicated the realization of European unity; it served to deepen the divisions in Europe.

At the same time, Stalin felt, probably for the first time during his rule, that there was a chance to spread socialism beyond the limits of one country. Therefore he steered the development of socialist European countries with an iron hand, insisting on the Soviet model and guiding them into the orbit of a joint political course.

As a result, Europe was steadily drifting away from its previous experience of development, with many old dreams and European projects, some of which had originated in Poland and Czechoslovakia, dismissed as unachievable. Europeanism, hardly ever a popular trend in East European countries, was now seen there through the prism of the new ideology and class and social confrontation. A new type of internationalism, associated with loyalty to the Soviet Union and the principles of Marxism–Leninism and socialism, was being formed in East European countries, amid the traditional clashes of the concepts of nationalism and internationalism.

This situation, in combination with reprisals against bourgeois and social-democratic parties and suppression of dissidents among the Communists, contributed to the inexorable process of unification and created an illusion of stablity, but at the same time all this formed a sound and stable basis for antagonism and nationalism. As has often happened in world history, unity attained by force and violence finally proved fragile and gave rise to discontent and centripetal trends fraught with upheavals and conflicts.

In the post-war period Eastern Europe kept aloof from pan-European processes and political and social thought. It was only in the late 1970s–early1980s that publications appeared in Poland, Czecho-slovakia, Bulgaria and the German Democratic Republic which dis-cussed European experience, although this was done rather cautiously. In that period vigorous co-operation was established between the academic community and the general public in those countries and their counterparts in the West, with traditional Polish–French, Bulgarian–French and Czechoslovak–German contacts restored. Regrettably in the initial post-war years the situation was quite different. In parallel with its policy in Eastern Europe, the USSR sought to exert as much influence as it could on Western European affairs.

The increased influence of the forces of the left and the wide popularity of communist parties, primarily in France and Italy, with communists elected to government posts in a number of Western countries, reaffirmed Moscow's belief in the possibility of changes in the social development of Western Europe. Soviet leaders, of course, realized that they could exert only limited influence on those pro-cesses, but the idea of the possibility of a new revolutionary upsurge in Europe gained wide currency in the USSR in that period. Develop-ments in Western Europe were regarded in the USSR with a view to a possible strengthening of the positions of socialism. At the same time Western European communist parties also regarded the USSR as the main guarantor of their positions.

Thus, there was a steady transition – now at a different historical stage – towards the concept of world and European revolution, although this time it was envisioned as the transfer of Eastern

147

influence in Western Europe rather than as a direct revolutionary outburst. It was a new kind of 'Europeanism', associated with the spread and strengthening of socialism (Soviet-style) on the European continent.

At that time the domestic situation in the Soviet Union was extremely complicated. After the victory over Nazism, with the Soviet army units still stationed in Eastern European countries and East Germany, the prevailing mood among the Soviet leaders was a determination to spread socialism to as many European countries as possible. The Soviet model was being consistently and energetically introduced in Bulgaria, Poland, Hungary, Czechoslovakia, Romania, Yugoslavia and Albania, and every effort was made to stimulate the development of left forces in France, Italy and other Western European countries.

This 'socio-class' aspect reflected a new Soviet approach to the idea of world revolution. At the outset of this process the Soviet Union concentrated its attention on Europe, whereas later it started showing greater interest in the Third World.

However, this was not a pure and simple return to the idea of world and European revolution – even in a modified form: these ideas were developed in close interconnection with growing imperial tendencies. Internationalism thus went hand in glove with nationalism. The resurgence of imperial inclinations was largely attributable to the Soviet troops' presence in Europe and a desire to realize old Russian ideas with respect to Poland, the Black Sea straits, etc.

Restoration of national-patriotic traditions in wartime paved the way to the revival of old Russian ideas, although in a new situation they presented a peculiar combination of old ideas and modified views of world revolution and new internationalism, thus forming a certain synthesis, reflected in Soviet policies and strategy, a sort of crossbreed between internationalist ideas and old imperial mentality.

However, the picture would be incomplete if we omitted the campaign against cosmopolitanism, launched in the USSR in the late 1940s–early 1950s. Although it was carried out on a domestic scale, it no doubt reflected far broader problems.

While analysing the domestic situation in the USSR in the post-war period, one should take note of the extensive Western influence in Soviet society at that time. Just as after the First Patriotic War, waged by Russia against Napoleon's army in the early nineteenth century, Russian officers again had an opportunity to familiarize themselves with the European way of life by visiting Germany, Poland, Czechoslovakia and Hungary. Moreover, close co-operation with the Allies in the anti-Hitler coalition, including in the military sphere, promoted personal and other contacts between Soviet officers and men and the Western public.

Stalin and his entourage felt that all this boded nothing good and made a volte face by launching a campaign of criticism of the Western way of life and Western ideology, at the same time meting out reprisals against Soviet intellectuals who, Soviet ideologists believed, admired the Western model and had submitted to Western influences. The campaign against cosmopolitanism was in line with the nationalist and imperial ideas. All this deepened still more the abyss that divided the Soviet Union, with its traditional mentality, ideas and political realities, from Europe and from European social and political thought.

As applied to the history of the European idea, one may say that the developments in the USSR only whipped up anti-European moods and increased opposition to Europeanist theories and projects there. On the ideological plane, Europeanism was assessed as a bourgeois-cosmopolitan trend, hostile to socialism and the Marxist–Leninist ideology. It was probably during the first post-war years that the sharply critical attitude to Europeanist thought, which was to be predominant in the Soviet Union until the second half of the 1980s, was formed.

Authors of books and articles, published in the 1950s–60s, took an extremely negative and hostile attitude to various projects of European unification of the past and especially of the twentieth century. Criticism of bourgeois liberalism, social reformism and social democracy was of the same nature – and it was these trends, as is known, that have largely nourished Europeanist ideas and views.

Sharp criticism of bourgeois ideology in general reached its peak in the 1940s–50s. Outstanding European politicians and thinkers such as Briand, Coudenhove-Kalergi, Mazzini, Toynbee, Michelen and Proudhon also received their share of devastating criticism. Old disputes in Russia between the Westerners and Slavophiles as to Russia's place in Europe and its European identity had persisted and were now revived at this new stage of development in the form of sharp denunciations of 'Western ideas' and influence.

In this context, the new form of Europeanism, which was reflected in the socio-political development of Western European countries and in the development of a new Europe, was negatively assessed in the Soviet Union. So it was logical to expect that Soviet leaders and ideologists would deny the USSR's European identity – and, indeed, they confirmed that the USSR did not belong in 'the Europe of capitalists, bankers, bourgeois liberals, cosmopolitans and revisionist reformers'.

The Soviet political and ideological leaders demanded that Eastern and south-eastern European countries adopt the same attitude, although for them this process was far more complicated owing to their old traditions and historical experience and their close contact with European countries in the past. However, in those years the USSR and its new allies made an attempt at forming a new community (economic, political, military and ideological), which was designed to serve as a foundation for a new European regional unity, with common social and ideological principles. This unity was generated by the establishment of the Council for Mutual Economic Assistance (Comecon) in 1949.

In the process of evolution and in the history of the European idea this community may be regarded as a version of its realization, on a regional level and on a certain social and ideological basis. By solving the problems of the co-ordination of economic development and co-operation among the USSR and a number of East and south-east European countries (later also some Asian and American states), the Comecon strove for the establishment of a system of collaboration and co-operation between countries, and for the establishment of the main principles of an economic scheme to put into practice the ideas of tough state planning, a strong administrative system and a centralized economy. Formed as a counterweight to Western European unification, the Comecon was orientated on autarchy and isolation from the West. Its aim was to replace the traditional contacts between Eastern European countries and the West with their new pro-Soviet orientation.

The leaders of the USSR and Eastern European countries counted on the Comecon in their desire to solve post-war economic problems and at the same time to lay the material and economic foundations for a political and ideological unification of member-countries of the new bloc. The split in the world, brought about by the 1917 Russian Revolution, was now even more obvious, and even more so in Europe's division, which was probably most vividly illustrated by the division of Germany, which had held a central place in various Europeanist theories, especially since the 1850s.

It should be recalled that since Immanuel Kant's time European unity had been closely associated with the development of the German states. In the post-Napoleonic era, first Prussia and later other German lands effectively contributed to the solution of European problems. German political and social thinkers had made a substantial contribution to the development of Europeanist thought. After Germany's unification Bismarck sought to establish a new European order. In the early twentieth century the project of Middle Europe was born in Germany. In the period between the two world wars German intellectuals took an active part in discussions of the Coudenhove-Kalergi project. Gustav Stresemann jointly with Aristide Briand and Austen Chamberlain strove to set up a new European system. Germany was also the birthplace of the Nazi version of European unification. But at the time when Europe was prepared to enter a new stage in its development, Germany was divided.

Nowadays there is a lot of guesswork about what came first: that the Cold War gave birth to Germany's division or vice versa – that German division gave rise to the Cold War. Either way, Germany's division had a great impact on the destiny of Europe. It symbolized the break-up of the European tradition, for the border between the conflicting sides ran through Germany.

In the ideological and political context the Soviet leaders' anti-capitalist mood met with the greatest support in East Germany, where dogmatic interpretation of Marxist–Leninist ideas was carried to the extreme. However, at the same time, East Germany was the weakest link in the chain of the faltering European tradition and in the separation of Eastern Europe and the USSR from Europe.

The socio-class and ideological confrontation was constantly eroded, primarily by the national tradition. If prolonged separation was possible, say, between Poland and Czechoslovakia, on the one hand, and Europe, on the other, it was hardly possible that one group of Germans could be separated from the rest for ever. Moreover, they had their common German history behind them, with a common cultural heritage and traditions.

Subsequent history has shown that the two parts of Germany really could not have been separated for a long period, and though the formula of two German states and two German traditions was invented in the GDR, it was obvious that it would hardly prove a success in the long run.

The Soviet campaign against Western influence met with no response even in East Germany. The combined effect of Soviet socio-class and ideological principles and imperial national traditions contributed to the USSR's drifting apart from Europe, whereas the German national aspect produced the opposite effect, eliminating ideological prejudices and bringing East and West Germany closer together, thus inspiring East Germans with Europeanist ideas.

There was one more important factor. After the defeat of Nazism the Germans were motivated by the desire to restore the system of the Weimar Republic, so the rigid totalitarian system, established by the

GDR leadership, was doomed to clash sooner or later with the age-old tradition of German history, the multi-party system and a desire to ensure a worthy status for Germany in Europe. On the other hand, a different effect was produced by these same factors. A considerable number of Germans could not help but feel a certain nostalgia for Germany's former grandeur and superiority in Europe, so for them, too, restoration of Germany's glory was associated with its unification, not its division.

Thus, it was the sum of various factors that slowly but surely eroded the idea of Germany's prolonged separation, undermining the foundations of the GDR's regime. Moreover, the realities of development in West Germany, its rapid economic advance and prosperity, which led to a great difference in the living standards in Germany's West and East, only added fervour to opposition moods in the GDR and the disaffection of its population. It is true that this was an intellectual and economic aspect of the problem of the interconnection between the German problem and the European idea. However, there were also purely political aspects, associated with developments in post-war relations on the international scene, primarily connected with the theory and practice of the Cold War.

19

THE COLD WAR AND EUROPE

What was the situation European countries and peoples found themselves in after the war? After Nazism had been crushed and Hitler's plans of conquering Europe by force of arms had fallen through, Europe was faced with the problem of its post-war organization. The Nazis' débâcle also led to the bankruptcy both of Europeanist theories and of the practice of Hitlerite Nazism and Italian fascism. It was amply clear that a blatantly aggressive method of realizing European ideas would not work.

European nations had paid dearly for their freedom and independence and for the European civilization, with innumerable sacrifices and great destruction. The Second World War gave ample evidence of the Soviet Union's contribution to the European peoples' struggle: the powerful forces of Hitler's military machine were crushed on the Soviet–German front.

After the war all the democratic forces of capitalist Europe gained considerable strength. The Resistance movement in many West, East and south-east European countries worked out a democratic alternative for Europe. Their goal was to ensure radical socio-economic and political reforms in order to introduce new democratic, political and social institutions in the old traditional system.

The war exposed the unrealistic nature of all kinds of plans to replace European statehood and the established system of national states by various versions of national and supranational domination. European nations that were prepared to join their efforts on a free democratic basis for the triumph of social justice and national liberation, progress of European civilization and the establishment of eternal and just peace, foiled fascist attempts at enslaving European countries and peoples and setting up a regime of extreme reaction and social demagogy that threatened destruction to the great achievements of European civilization.

In wartime great opportunities were revealed and the foundation was laid for political co-operation among the anti-Hitler coalition countries, irrespective of their social system. The collective security system was realized in the various practices of the anti-Hitler coalition, primarily in the actions of the Big Three – the USSR, the United States and Great Britain. The important aspect was not only the joint action to ensure the Nazis' defeat but also the elaboration of the principles of the post-war military settlement, that is, the establishment in Europe of a new system of relations among states that would allow the principles of peace, security and mutual understanding to be affirmed.

The Allies began discussing Europe's post-war structure even in the early stages of the war. In July 1941, in the course of talks on signing the Soviet–British agreement which served as the cornerstone of the anti-Hitler coalition, Soviet representatives spoke about the need to ensure long-term bilateral co-operation. Part Two of the Soviet–British Treaty, signed on 25 May 1942, was devoted to post-war co-operation in order to promote peace and prevent the repetition of aggression. The Soviet–French Treaty, signed in Moscow on 10 December 1944, also included a clause on the need for bilateral co-operation 'in order to ensure international security for effective maintenance of universal peace'. This was also the subject of the Soviet–Polish and the Soviet–Yugoslav treaties signed in 1945.

Problems of the post-war settlement were most thoroughly discussed at the Allied conferences held in Moscow, Teheran, Yalta and Potsdam. For instance, a European Consultative Commission to co-ordinate measures to be taken with respect to Germany after its defeat was set up by the Moscow Conference of Soviet, US and British foreign ministers held in October 1943. Participants in the Moscow Conference also discussed the British project for a federation of the smaller European countries – including Poland, Czechoslovakia, Yugoslavia, Greece, Austria and Hungary. In view of the Soviet Union's firm refusal to approve these plans and the negative stance taken by the United States, the British projects were renounced.

The main problems of a peaceful settlement in post-war Europe were those of Germany's future, the signing of peace treaties with Germany's former allies and, at the same time, settlement of many political, economic and territorial issues as well as the establishment of the United Nations Organization for the promotion of peace and international security. In the course of numerous discussions the Allies drafted a co-ordinated programme for Germany's future democratic development and for ensuring peace and security in the heart of Europe.

Peace treaties with former allies of Germany on a just, democratic basis were an important achievement in the post-war European peaceful settlement. These treaties served the aim of eliminating the vestiges of fascism in those countries and repairing the damage inflicted by the Nazis to other states and peoples. The treaties were called upon to offer those countries every right and opportunity to develop as sovereign and free nations.

The terms of the treaties were thrashed out in the course of fierce debates. There were Soviet, US and British disagreements on a wide range of economic and territorial issues and on the composition of governments in the countries of south-eastern Europe. After prolonged discussions, treaties with Germany's former allies were signed on a democratic basis. It was agreed that Bulgaria, Hungary, Romania, Italy and Finland would guarantee human rights and fundamental freedoms to all their citizens; fascist organizations were banned.

Settlement of territorial issues presupposed the elimination of the consequences of the arbitrary decisions in this sphere adopted by Hitler and his allies in their attempts to redraw the map of Europe. European states' pre-war borders were restored, taking into account changes that had already been fixed in a number of treaties. The post-war settlement of territorial issues was based on historical experience and the political realities of post-war Europe.

In general, these peace treaties opened broad vistas for the independent development of Eastern European countries. All of them were signed on the basis of co-ordinated decisions, adopted by the member-countries of the anti-Hitler coalition, and of the principles of the peaceful coexistence of states with different social systems. The treaties were a tangible contribution to the general normalization of the situation in Europe and a stable peace.

The Declaration of Liberated Europe, adopted at the Yalta Conference, was of immense importance. It said that the leaders of the three Great Powers intended to co-ordinate their policy in the liberated European states and assist in the process of eliminating the vestiges of Nazism and fascism and in the establishment of democratic institutions there. The leaders of the Great Powers reaffirmed their determination to establish an international order, based on legal principles, that would promote peace, security, freedom and the universal welfare of humanity. The establishment of order in Europe, the Declaration pointed out, and the restructuring of national economic affairs should be ensured to make it possible for the liberated nations to stamp out the last vestiges of Nazism and fascism and set up democratic institutions of their own free choice.

Although the co-ordinated programme of European peaceful post-war settlement was worked out in an atmosphere of struggle and clashes between the USSR, on the one hand, and the United States and Britain, on the other, it opened new vistas for the promotion of peace and security on the European continent and gave grounds for hope that the anti-Hitler coalition countries would continue their co-operation in future as well. However, those hopes were not to be justified; for soon after an atmosphere of tension was generated in Europe and throughout the world, ushering in the Cold War era.

The Cold War had a negative effect on the development of the European continent. It led to Europe's division into hostile blocs that stood in tense military opposition to each other in an atmosphere of mutual distrust and suspicion. Every effort was made by both sides to project an alien image of its opponent, with a runaway arms race charged with the threat of armed conflict.

The US nuclear monopoly, its reliance on military strength and economic might, the realization of the Truman Doctrine and, as a consequence, the establishment of American military bases, the policy of rearmament of West Germany and, finally, the formation of NATO – all these moves by the Western states were obvious forerunners of the Cold War.

The Soviet Union, in its turn, was strengthening its armed forces, concentrating a great number of its troops in GDR territory and Eastern Europe. Any manifestations of sovereignty or the desire for independent development in the countries of the 'socialist camp' met with a resolute rebuff by the Soviet Union which never hesitated to use military force (in Hungary in 1956 and in Czechoslovakia in 1968), thus, of course, further exacerbating the international situation.

In the 1940s–50s, virtually all talks among the former wartime Allies were frozen out. Nowadays, historians widely discuss the origin of the Cold War, the essence and meaning of this term, especially how it could have happened that the anti-Hitler coalition countries so rapidly switched from co-operation to confrontation, with the result that the international climate radically changed.

First, it should be noted that in the war years both the USSR and the United States fell into the habit of acting from positions of strength. That was not only the usual practice but also the final argument in the settlement of political issues. The strength syndrome had become part and parcel of the mentality of both countries' politicians and ideologists, who could not change their ways even in peacetime. They could not help yielding to the temptation of resorting to force in order to promote their political goals. The US had the advantage of its atomic weapons and economic might, whereas the USSR had its considerable military presence in Eastern Europe and Germany.

Another factor was associated with the decisions of the 1945 Yalta Conference. The idea of the division of the world into spheres of influence, realized in Yalta, stimulated the division of Europe. Even in the first post-war years the Soviet Union sought to gain a foothold and promote its dominant position in the countries of East, south-east and Central Europe and East Germany.

The post-war world political system was strongly affected by the Yalta syndrome, which was certainly behind the trend for the formation of a bipolar political structure in the world. Any bipolar alignment of forces tends to breed sharp rivalries and leads to total confrontation, which was exactly the case in Soviet–US relations at the closing stage of the war. The USSR sought to involve into its orbit Eastern and south-east European countries, and the United States had consolidated its position as the leader of the Western world.

Closely interrelated in the relations of the two blocs were political, military, social and ideological factors. In principle, the USSR regarded this confrontation from the position of its social and class interests by proclaiming that in this case one could speak about a clash between two types of social relations and ideologies. Thus, this division was only natural, if viewed from the concept of world revolution in combination with the Soviet imperial goals and ideas produced by the Stalinist system.

The United States and its Western European allies, for their part, sought to consolidate the bloc of Western countries to ensure their loyalty to the capitalist system and Western values and to prevent the spread of unlimited Soviet influence in Eastern Europe.

These were the reasons behind the global confrontation which involved almost all European countries. Even before this one could hardly speak about any identical interests and goals for all European states; now, the split in Europe was still more obvious. This process was clearly accelerated by the formation of military-political blocs and organizations.

In this context I would first like to mention the effect of the realization of the Truman Doctrine, which presupposed the involvement of Greece and Turkey in the orbit of US policy, thus excluding the possibility of Soviet influence there. Also, in the military-political sphere, the establishment of the North Atlantic Treaty Organization (NATO) was of crucial importance, unifying as it did the United

States and Canada with Western European countries. The Warsaw Treaty Organization, set up in 1955 as a counterweight to NATO, was also a military-political alliance, uniting under the Soviet aegis a group of East, south-east and Central European countries. Thus, the schism in Europe was formalized for many years to come.

One additional grouping was that of Britain, France, Belgium, Holland and Luxembourg in the Western Alliance, a military-political organization designed to promote the interests of West European leaders. Its participants undertook mutual obligations if any were threatened with some danger. The Defence Committee of the Western Alliance and its military headquarters were set up. Later, after the establishment of NATO, the Western Alliance largely lost its importance, although it was not disbanded.

All these moves were in line with Cold War logic and further stimulated the process of polarization and confrontation, with ideological factors making no small contribution to it. Hostility was growing on both sides with every passing year. Widespread anti-Western campaigns, launched in the Soviet Union, generated a specific ideological atmosphere to justify the Cold War policy, although at the same time those campaigns were a manifestation of the Soviet leaders' desire to keep the USSR isolated from Europe and the US behind the Iron Curtain. On the other hand, anti-Soviet propaganda was also at work in the West, with the USSR described as a source of permanent danger. In this way Cold War myths were spread far and wide.

Discussions about the Marshall Plan provided some of the most open demonstrations of the Cold War and the splitting of Europe. The plan's main goal was to give a new lease of life to European capitalism by supplying a mighty impetus to the economic revival of Western Europe and its technical modernization. However, Eastern European countries and the Soviet Union were also involved in these discussions, expressing hopes for their possible participation in the implementation of the plan's programmes. From the outset American officials spoke about the possible inclusion of the USSR and other Eastern European countries in the programme of American aid. No one knows whether or not that talk was totally sincere. Many American political scientists, historians and diplomats believe, not without reason, that the US Congress would never have approved the Marshall Plan had it provided for aid to the Soviet Union, for the Soviet–US confrontation was becoming central to the US foreign policy of the period, although it is a fact that such formal offers were then really made.

According to Soviet archive materials, Soviet leaders actively discussed the problem of Soviet participation in the programme of economic revival in Europe. However, for Stalin, of decisive importance was the undesirable possibility of the USSR losing its grip on East European countries if they were to become involved in the Marshall Plan, for then they might be steered in the direction of their pre-war economic development.

An analysis of Polish, Czechoslovak, Bulgarian, Hungarian and other archive materials tells us of heated discussions about involvement in the Marshall Plan programmes. All indications are that this issue was then of particular importance for Czechoslovakia. In 1947–48, Czechoslovakia's future development, its system and orientation were at stake, so its stance on the Marshall Plan assumed an essentially political rather than economic importance – it was a matter of the alignment of forces in the country. Newly accessible archive materials reveal that practically all Czechoslovak political forces came out in favour of acceptance of the Marshall Plan. But several days before the opening of the Paris conference Czech leaders were called to Moscow and were ordered not to participate in the plan.

Soviet leaders feared that Eastern European countries joining the Marshall Plan would establish new contacts with the West, which would rapidly turn them back to their practices of the 1920s–30s and impede the Soviet model from strengthening in those countries. However, a number of Eastern Europe's communist leaders were guided by much the same considerations, for they believed that their power resided in the removal of the old multi-party system, limited contacts with the West and pro-Soviet orientation.

The attitude to the Marshall Plan also reflected the vested interests of the USSR in its domestic development. Documents at the disposal of Soviet historians testify that Soviet leaders had varying views on the Marshall Plan issue. Of considerable interest in this respect is a memorandum written by a prominent Soviet academician, who was an economist and who argued – in line with the ideas prevalent at the time – that if the USSR agreed to accept US aid under the Marshall Plan, this would help US imperialism to overcome its own crisis by supplying it with 'new markets'.

Stereotyped, over-ideologized thinking must also have been behind the USSR's negative stance on the Marshall Plan. Ideological prejudices, reflecting the essence of the Stalinist system, took the upper hand in the USSR. Moreover, at about that time major campaigns against cosmopolitanism began in the USSR. To satisfy these demands, the purely economic problems of a war-ravaged country in need of loans, credits and technical assistance were dismissed.

In the end, the Soviet Union, Albania, Bulgaria, Hungary, Poland, Czechoslovakia, Yugoslavia and Finland all refused to participate in the Marshall Plan. In general, subsequent developments testified that the Marshall Plan, despite all its difficulties, proved very effective in the economic rehabilitation of Europe and its gradual transformation into a substantial factor of world development.

Thus, political, diplomatic and economic development in the post-war period led to the splitting of Europe into two hostile blocs, whose confrontation grew in intensity in the late 1940s–50s, with the result that Europe, and the whole world for that matter, became immersed in a tense conflict situation. At that time, naturally, there was no question of any ideas of, or plans for, European unity, or of a European community.

An attempt was made in Eastern Europe to set up a new formation in the nature of a regional European community. We are justified in referring to it because the leaders of the USSR and 'People's Democracies' mentioned in this connection a common social base, an identity of ideological principles, and the working out of common guidelines in the political, economic and military spheres.

Just like certain politicians, theoreticians of 'socialist integration' did not, as a rule, draw on European historical experience: they referred exclusively to the experiences of proletarian internationalism, to 'the working people's solidarity in the struggle for social progress and national liberation'. Nevertheless, if we are considering the European idea and its evolution as a broad and profound concept and phenomenon, manifested in a wide range of attempts at formulating and setting up European communities, then, in this context, 'socialist integration', too, must go down in history as an attempt at unifying part of Europe on the basis of the Soviet socialist model.

The classic version of Europeanism was formed exclusively in the West. In West European countries European ideas were increasingly interpreted in line with the Western version; numerous publications dealing with Europeanism and the European idea discussed this problem exclusively in the context of Western Europe, putting the Soviet Union and a number of East European countries outside the sphere of 'classical' Europe. Every effort was made to nurture the image of Russia's and the Soviet Union's eternal hostility towards Europe, of genuine Europe stretching exclusively 'from Brest to Brest'. This interpretation of Europeanism was designed not only to reflect the realities of the divided Europe and the state of total confrontation

160

in which Europe found itself in the late 1940s but also to offer theoretical substantiation of the incipient process of West European integration, regarded by its ideologists as the materialization of the plans for European unification that had been put forward by the most outstanding European thinkers in the eighteenth and nineteenth centuries.

20

THE HELSINKI PROCESS

A great number of ideas and plans for setting up a European security system have been put forward in the twentieth century, although not a single one of them has yielded successful results and post-war developments in a divided Europe led to increased confrontation. The 1970s, however, will go down in history as the very first experience of pan-European co-operation as a part of the process of *détente*. European *détente* was the first breakthrough in the world political system of Cold War, giving rise to realistic hopes and aspirations. Moreover, the significance of the Helsinki process was not limited to the abatement of the Cold War and changes in the international climate: it was a substantial contribution to European unity.

Talks on holding a European conference were started in the second half of the 1960s. It took several years to define the structure of the future conference and outline the spheres and form of European co-operation. As we know, the Helsinki formula was produced as a result of preliminary talks, and these made it possible to stimulate new processes and set up new all-European institutions.

The Helsinki process, naturally, inspired millions of Europeans with hopes of the relaxation of tensions and, probably, termination of the Cold War, but at the same time it proved to be a new stage in the evolution of the European idea. Before the 1970s, Europeanism had been conceived exclusively in the experience of Western European integration, although in Eastern Europe an integrated community had been set up in order to promote the consolidation of socialist states in Eastern and south-eastern Europe. At this time, however, the first attempt was made to work out certain common rules of the game, setting up a pan-European system of political, economic and diplomatic co-operation between all European countries.

The very fact of holding the European Conference and the signing of the European Peace Charter by heads of European states was of great political importance. A system of security and co-operation on the continent was virtually established. Certain identical interests of the ideologically opposed blocs of European powers (as well as the US and Canada) were defined in order to ensure peace and security on the continent, and every opportunity was offered to promote broad economic co-operation among all European states.

The Helsinki process also ushered in a new stage of development in the humanitarian sphere for it was also during this period that representatives of the European socialist states had to agree that paragraphs on human rights, freedom of migration, etc. be included in European agreements. As might be expected, the socialist countries' leaders only conceded to this in exchange for compromises they wanted in the political and economic spheres. Moreover, they hoped that they would be able to keep the process within certain limits and under their ideological control. It was these humanitarian aspects of the Helsinki process that were to become a major bone of contention at future East–West political talks.

In the context of the European idea the humanitarian sphere was of special importance, for the problems of human rights and freedom of the individual were central to Europeanism and European ideas. Yet, for the first time since the October Revolution, leaders of socialist Russia agreed to hold a joint discussion with Western 'capitalists' whose views were totally alien to Marxist–Leninist concepts.

Ideologists and politicians of the USSR and other countries of the Eastern bloc regarded the concept of human rights essentially as an 'imperialist' attempt at eroding socialism and the socialist community on their own ground. People in socialist countries were brainwashed into believing this, which only added to the hostile attitude of the Eastern European states to the theories of and plans for a European integration based on the principles of human and civil rights and on democratic principles and guidelines.

After those principles had been fixed in the Helsinki documents signed by Western and Eastern European leaders, life was never the same in Europe. Although any tangible consequences and results were still a long way off, the process had been started.

Groups to assist in the realization of the Helsinki agreements were set up in many Western European countries; similar groups were formed in the Soviet Union and in practically all the countries of the Eastern European bloc.

The Helsinki agreements were signed in 1975, and the decade that followed was marked by tense and acrimonious discussions of the main problems and forms of All-European co-operation.

After the conference in Helsinki, meetings and conferences were held in Madrid, Stockholm, Vienna and Paris, and within the framework of the general process, political and economic trends took shape, with talks on military issues representing a special sphere. Just as before, treatment of humanitarian issues as a separate sphere largely depended on internal processes in the USSR and the other countries of the socialist bloc.

The situation in Europe in humanitarian matters after the signing of the Helsinki agreements was extremely complicated. Realization of signed European agreements was not a uniform process, and far more rapid progress was made in the political sphere: new political structures were formed, mainly to work out mechanisms for the prevention of military conflicts, reduction in the level of military threats and the setting up of a European security system.

Considerable progress was also made in talks on economic co-operation among participants in the Helsinki process. Scores of bilateral and multilateral treaties and agreements on trade and economic co-operation were signed and many joint economic ventures and projects were set up. These new trends reflected both the realities of the process of *détente* and common features of life and traditions in Europe. Just as in the past, economic factors promoted the unification of European countries and peoples. For the first time in the post-war period the economic effect of the Helsinki agreements served the purpose of drawing the nations closer together and overcoming economic separatism in Europe. Of course, the process was as yet embryonic; moreover, economic co-operation was limited by the existence of the Common Market and the Comecon, both of which, just as before, stood in opposition to each other.

For the first time in the post-war period new trends were manifested in culture. Broad co-operation in the sphere of culture was provided for by the Helsinki agreements as part of the All-European development process. Cultural co-operation and the common roots of European civilization were among the main elements of the European identity. For this reason, active cultural co-operation, nurtured among European countries in the second half of the 1970s, also ushered in a new stage in the evolution of the European idea. Naturally, these were only first moves in the complicated process of East European peoples' reunion with Europe and their new interest in common European values. To achieve this harmony they had to renounce their stereotyped ideological views and put an end to the ideological confrontation between socialism and capitalism. For this reason, although in the 1970s–80s substantial progress was made in the promotion of East–West contacts, their real significance and degree of realization were somewhat limited. Like no other sphere, culture was closely associated with ideological issues and constant confrontation between the two systems. So the prospects for co-operation in the cultural sphere were fraught with great difficulties and obstacles.

These complications tended to increase in the late 1970s and early 1980s due to economic stagnation and a new campaign of reprisals against dissenters in the USSR and other countries of the socialist bloc. Although several new political and military agreements were signed in the period, the development of the Helsinki process was clearly slowing down. The situation called for new original decisions, which, however, hinged on developments in the Soviet Union and the countries of the 'socialist community'.

The Helsinki agreements were of crucial importance for European development: they touched off a radically new process on the continent. After the split of Europe in 1917 and the bitter East–West confrontation of the post-war period, there was at least a glimmer of hope for some kind of new unity in the cultural and humanitarian spheres. High on the agenda were the establishment of a security system, economic and trade co-operation and a reduction of the level of military confrontation between the two blocs.

Efforts in these areas certainly contributed to a reduction in the level of political and military confrontation and had a substantial effect on the fields of culture and ideology. Although proclamations of European cultural identity were then in the nature of good intentions rather than a reality, the fact that they existed was of great importance as a precursor of future changes.

The Helsinki process was also marked by another feature, associated with the role of the United States in European history and civilization. The involvement of the United States in the process revealed not only the political and military influence of the US as a superpower, and the fact that a European settlement was unthinkable without the US, but also stressed the importance of the US contribution to European history and civilization. Thus, the intrinsic unity of the two civilizations, their mutual interdependence and interpenetration were confirmed. Moreover, the United States became one of the guarantors of European democracy and the human rights that were central to Europeanist ideas, concepts and plans.

Détente and the Helsinki process brought new leaders into prominence in Europe, who offered a new interpretation of Europeanism. The new European realities were most vividly displayed in the words and deeds of the French president, General Charles de Gaulle, and the

165

FRG Chancellor, Willy Brandt. We shall not analyse now those leaders' views of West European integration, for they largely continued the policies formulated by their predecessors. However, de Gaulle and Brandt have gone down in history as the authors of a new policy with respect to Eastern Europe.

De Gaulle first set out his position in the 1960s when he put forward the idea of a united Europe 'from the Atlantic to the Urals'. It is noteworthy that de Gaulle's views were inspired by the specific policy of the late 1960s rather than by pragmatic interests of the moment. The French president took a broader view of the situation: he regarded Europe, stretching from the Atlantic to the Urals, as a definite historical and political unity rather than a purely geographical notion.

In the light of European problems, it is important to stress de Gaulle's frequent references to the fact that he believed Russia to be an inalienable, organic part of Europe. He cited many historical proofs, mentioning Russia's permanent contacts with East and West European nations and interpreted the notions of European culture and civilization broadly enough to include the contribution made by Eastern European countries and Russia. At a press conference, held on 4 February 1965, he explained:

> What I mean is that Europe, the birthplace of modern civilization, should be formed on the basis of accord and co-operation from the Atlantic to the Urals in order to develop its vast resources for it to play jointly with America, its daughter, a worthy role in the progressive development of two billion people, who badly need it.

The national grandeur of France for de Gaulle was not only a result of upholding its own interests but also of the place it held and the role it played in Europe. De Gaulle's Europeanism had a French and European tinge. He carried on, as it were, the old nineteenth-century tradition, when France dictated trends throughout Europe. De Gaulle's initiative broke away from the traditional West European view of the Soviet Union and its allies in the 1950s, when Russia was excluded from classical Europe because of the revival of the old tradition of 'the Russian threat' to Europe. The formula 'from Brest to Brest', produced by political scientists, had served as a justification of sorts and a confirmation of the specific political practice that had prevailed in West European countries since the late 1940s.

De Gaulle not only proclaimed his new vision of Europe but also started to take steps to make it happen. In 1966 he paid a visit to the Soviet Union and made it clear that with Soviet participation he intended to build a new Europe. It should be stressed that de Gaulle associated his Soviet policy with changes in French foreign policy in the framework of the Western alliance. However, his pragmatic goals also possessed a different aspect which extended Europeanist views and concepts. Europeanism, interpreted in the previous few years exclusively in its Western version, assumed, as it were, a fresh dimension, which could not but affect the general theoretical aspect of the topic. New discussions were started about Europe and Russia's place in it; the old and eternal problems were revived, mostly in Western Europe, although they inevitably had repercussions in the Soviet Union as well.

A few years later, a similar impetus came from West Germany when Chancellor Willy Brandt proclaimed his new Eastern policy, which indicated the search for an agreement with Moscow and the involvement of the Soviet Union in a new European structure. He was largely guided by opinions inside Germany, primarily those from the GDR. Thus, West Germany started its prolonged and laborious campaign for the reunification of the German people, with Brandt being fully aware that he could attain this historic goal exclusively via Moscow.

However, the West German Chancellor also operated within broader concepts. Brandt used to say that Europe from the Atlantic to the Urals was primarily a historical rather than a geographical notion. He formulated his later concept when, in the 1980s, he spoke of a new Europeanism of the nuclear-missile era. He now took into account Germany's geopolitical position and the lethal danger it might be faced with in case of conflict. Thus, apart from specific purely domestic interests, his interpretation of Europeanism reflected his apprehension about the threat of a nuclear apocalypse. He often referred to the danger of nuclear warfare, and in view of this he deemed it necessary that the Soviet Union and Eastern European countries should be involved in the European settlement. Consequently, Brandt was among the initiators of the 1971 Soviet–German Treaty, as well as the FRG–Polish, the FRG–Czechoslovak and the FRG–GDR treaties.

The new Eastern policy pursued by the FRG by no means presupposed erosion of the world political system set up after the Second World War, but it served as a basis for a new vision of Europe, for a new European structure. There was a certain correlation of forces in the traditional Russia–Germany–France triangle. As a rule, France and Germany sought to make use of Russia as a counterbalance in their rivalries. For this reason, and apart from more general considerations, after the French initiative, one might have anticipated the sharp turn in FRG policy which came in the mid-1960s.

Thus, in the late 1960s–early 1970s major changes were introduced in the interpretation of the European political situation. The positions of France and the FRG and, later, the European Conference served as the basis of a new view of Europeanism. At that time Europeanist principles and its humanitarian foundation remained intact, although the world political aspects underwent serious changes. In spite of all disagreements and deviations in *détente* and the developments of the second half of the 1970s and the early 1980s (both in the West and the East), there was an identity of views with respect to the goals and tasks of all European states for ensuring peace and security in Europe and the need to work out new principles for the European collective security system.

21

THE EUROPEAN COMMUNITY OR 'LITTLE EUROPE'

The formation and evolution of West European integration – the 'European Community' – was a distinctive feature of post-war development in Western Europe. A ramified system of economic and, later, political bodies and institutions were set up, and the member-countries maintained co-operation in political, economic and social spheres.

Many Western historians and political scientists describe the European Community as a practical realization of various plans and projects offered in the course of European development. These authors (especially in the initial stage of the community's existence) did not spare the superlatives in their assessment of the integration that was in process.

We should first analyse the objective and subjective factors that proved crucial for the unification process in Western Europe and contributed to its realization. The trend for internationalization in industry and public affairs was not only stimulated but also manifested in a radically new form. This trend was associated, on the one hand, with a new upsurge in interdependence in the world as a whole and, on the other, with major changes in the capitalist system, especially in Europe.

Scientific and technological progress and the formation of powerful transnationals paved the way for the establishment of international production and technological complexes in Western Europe which incorporated the capital and industrial resources of many countries. Even in the late 1940s–50s transnationals were firmly entrenched in many Western European countries.

Economic integrational processes, which have eventually led to the establishment of West European economic associations, started operating according to new economic principles soon after the war. Integrational processes in Western European countries were prompted by the desire to unite their efforts for the rehabilitation of the war-ravaged economy and the provision of new incentives for economic growth.

The following important conclusion was drawn in *West European Integration: The Political Aspects* (Moscow, 1985), a study by Soviet experts:

> The growing mutual contacts of national economies in Western Europe, promoted and accelerated by scientific and technical progress, development of major transnational corporations, as well as other economic factors, had led by the late 1950s–early 1960s to a considerably high degree of those economies' inter-dependence. True, in various areas of the region under consideration such interdependence was of varying intensity. It was relatively less obvious in the periphery zones – on the Pyrenean Peninsula, in the south (Greece, Turkey, Malta) and the extreme north (Iceland, Greenland) – which are comparatively less industrialized areas of Western Europe, whereas this tendency was more manifest in areas situated closer to the centre of the subcontinent, the seat of the most industrialized countries. By that time the real process of regional integration had practically started here in the real sense of this notion, when the interaction of national economies is transformed into mutual interpenetration of the national processes of social production.

The Western European countries' economies had been largely rehabilitated by the end of the 1940s, with the United States firmly established as the leader of the capitalist world in the economic sphere. In 1948 the United States accounted for 62.6 per cent of the aggregate product turned out by the industrialized countries, 50 per cent of the total capital investments and for almost 80 per cent of the capitalist world's gold reserves. In 1950 the United States accounted for 76 per cent of the world output of cars, 47 per cent of steel, etc.

At that time none of the 'great' European powers could even think of challenging their transatlantic partner. The Italian magazine *Il Tempo* wrote in 1950:

> Now is the most appropriate time for old Europe to set up the national economy. It is only through unity that Europe can achieve salvation and restore its prestige, won by the old traditions of civilization. Only if it continues following the chosen road [i.e. integration] can Europe be transformed into a force,

170

no matter if it is third or fourth in importance. If there is no unity in Europe, it will certainly be reduced to vassalage in economic and political spheres.

Thus, economic factors and interests, as well as rivalries with the United States, played an important part in the integrational processes that were under way in capitalist Europe. This accounted for a new emphasis in the European movement, with special stress laid on economic aspects, which was practically unprecedented at all previous stages in the development of European ideas and projects. The economic factor was reflected in scores of works, published in this period and in later years, which dealt with the theory of unification of capitalist Europe.

However, economic factors were closely associated with social and political aspects. Western European unification processes developed amid fierce rivalries between East and West and at the beginning of the Cold War. The United States and Western European countries sought to rally the capitalist world's forces in order to 'roll down' communism and retain Eastern European countries within the orbit of the Western world.

The initial post-war years were marked by a sharp rise in the activity of West European Left forces. The democratic alternative of the left wing of the European Resistance movement opened up prospects for radical socio-economic and political reform in Western European countries. Industrial action was on the increase. Influential and powerful trade union centres and federations were formed.

In this situation the traditional West European parties and movements sought to combine their efforts in order to offer resistance to communist influence. So this factor, too, prompted unification tendencies within the framework of European capitalism.

Developments in Asia, Africa and Latin America were also of considerable importance. Because of the collapse of the colonial system and the emergence of scores of independent states, European capitalism was forced to look for common measures and unified approaches in their relations with newly free countries, which were once the colonial dependencies of European powers. The events of the 1950s–70s offer many examples of capitalist countries' joint actions with respect to their former colonies.

Finally, it should be borne in mind that the alignment of forces in the West had changed by this time: Germany and Italy had been defeated, and the power of France had been undermined. Therefore, the United States surged far ahead in the first post-war years. In the atmosphere of strong US pressure and predominant influence that prevailed in the post-war period, Western European countries sought to unite their efforts with their American partner and ally. However in this instance the centrifugal and centripetal tendencies clashed. In spite of the dominant US position – and for many countries because of it – the European political élite was looking for ways and means of retaining their positions in the capitalist world.

Thus the close interweaving of a great variety of factors accounted for the emergence of objective and subjective prerequisites for West European integration. It should be stressed that realization of European ideas was planned exclusively for Western Europe and that this unification was to be implemented separately from Eastern Europe and the USSR.

As I have said, these processes took place in Western Europe, with Eastern European countries and the USSR kept in isolation from traditional European contacts and structures. With totalitarian Soviet-style regimes installed in those countries, democratic institutions were being eliminated there, their multi-party systems were turned into fiction, rights and freedoms were violated, and a punitive apparatus was put into operation. The result was that Eastern Europe was increasingly drifting apart from the West. This in turn, stimulated an urge by West European politicans and intellectuals for unification in order to uphold Western values and principles.

The confrontation between Russia and Europe, which had been the most prominent feature of European development since the 1917 October Revolution, was less pronounced or completely nullified in wartime. However, in the post-war period it was there again, and fiercer than ever.

Inspired by their victory, Stalin and other Soviet leaders did their best to whip up imperial moods and to spread socialism not only eastward but also westward. Many Western leaders, for their part, not only desired to uphold Western values but were also hatching plans to undermine Soviet power thoroughly. This gave rise to an active movement in the West for both political and military unification.

It is only fair to point out, however, that West European unification tendencies had been revived during wartime, and directly after the war they became central to the economic and political development of Western Europe.

Before the implementation of the projects of Western European integration they were widely discussed by the West European élite. In their press statements, reports and lectures advocates of European unification came out in favour of the unification processes, citing

172

examples from the experience and traditions of the past and various nineteenth- and twentieth-century projects for European unification. Participants in the resistance movement also energetically contributed to this process, for they had put forward ideas for European unification during the war.

Political, economic, purely pragmatic and general historico-cultural factors were represented even in the initial post-war years of European development. Europeanism was seen as both a European tradition and a specific political and economic practice.

When Charles de Gaulle visited Brussels in September 1945, he spoke in favour of European unification, and on 19 September 1946 the former British Prime Minister Winston Churchill gave a lecture at Zürich University devoted to the European future. In it he discussed the subjects of European philosophy, ethics and science and referred to Coudenhove-Kalergi, Briand and the experience of the League of Nations.

Churchill pointed to the importance of international blocs and organizations and adduced the example of the British Commonwealth. He was clearly in favour of European unification and the 'European family' and described the French–German partnership as the first step in that direction; Europe's revival was unthinkable without a strong France and a strong Germany. He also mentioned the United States of Europe to which big and small nations could make their important contributions.

Churchill called for the formation of a European family as the United States of Europe, with the establishment of the Council of Europe as the first move. He pointed out that the people of all countries and races should be delivered from the threat of war and oppression, and this must rest on a sound basis when people would rather die than submit to tyranny. France and Germany, he said, should join their efforts in undertaking this task. Great Britain and the British Commonwealth, probably America and, he hoped, Soviet Russia should maintain friendly contacts, and act as sponsors of a new Europe and its right to life and prosperity.

Curiously enough, at this early stage, Churchill still regarded Soviet Russia as a full member of the United States of Europe, apparently putting faith in the experience of the three Great Powers' wartime co-operation.

A year later, various alliances and blocs started to form in Western Europe. In December 1946 Henri Brugmans of Switzerland founded the European Union of Federalists, and two months later, in February 1946, the establishment was announced in London of a committee for studies associated with the formation of the United States of Socialist Europe. In March 1947, Churchill set up the United Europe Committee, which included representatives of the Conservatives, Liberals and a few Labourites. At the same time, a French council for a united Europe was also set up.

As if reviving the traditions and experiences of the pan-European projects of the 1920s–30s, the first European congress of the new European movement was held in The Hague on 7–10 May 1948. Its proclaimed aim was to demonstrate a broad public movement in support of European unity which was active in all Western European democratic countries, and to stimulate a world-wide movement for European unity.

The congress, described as the Congress of Europe, was attended by 800 delegates, with ministers, diplomats, public leaders, MPs, clergymen, writers, scholars and businessmen among them. The opening address was given by Churchill; political, economic and cultural commissions were formed.

In October 1948 the European Movement, with national committees in each country, was founded, in accordance with the congress's decisions. The movement was headed by its four presidents: Winston Churchill, Léon Blum, Paul-Henri Spaak and Alcide de Gasperi. On 25–28 February 1949 the second congress was held in Brussels, and in April 1949 a special conference on economic issues was convened in Westminster, and a conference on cultural issues was held in Lausanne in December 1949. In this way the process of European unification developed on a public level.

At the same time, an active process was under way to set up pan-European bodies on an official level. The Council of Europe, based in Strasbourg, was formed after a long series of discussions and talks. Economic bodies and associations were formed especially rapidly, the first being the Economic Commission for Europe (1946). The establishment of the Organization of European Economic Co-operation in 1948 (to help implement the Marshall Plan) was an important contribution to West European integration. After the FRG joined it in 1949, this organization represented 17 states. The Marshall Plan was an important factor in the economic rehabilitation of West European countries, which had an opportunity on this basis to modernize all spheres of production thoroughly and in this way make rapid progress in their development, thus laying the foundation for subsequent major economic reforms.

At the same time, the first projects were prepared for the economic unification of Western European states. The economic aspect of West

European integration was constantly growing in importance. In 1952 the European Coal and Steel Association was set up (with France, the FRG, Italy and the Benelux countries as members) according to the plan of the French Foreign Minister, Robert Schuman. Finally, the European Economic Community, the leading integration body in Western Europe, was set up in 1957. At the outset its founding fathers planned that it would also deal with foreign policy issues, but those plans never materialized, primarily because of French opposition.

The EEC, or the Common Market, initially incorporated six member-countries: France, Italy, the FRG, Belgium, the Netherlands and Luxembourg. At the same time, a treaty was signed on the establishment of Euratom, an organization for joint action in the field of nuclear research. In 1959 Britain set up the European Free Trade Association (EFTA), intending it to be a counterweight to the EEC and a weapon in their rivalry with France. Later, however, Britain, Denmark, Ireland, Greece, Portugal and Spain joined the Common Market and under the 1965 Brussels Treaty, the leading bodies of a number of integrational organizations were merged. The intergovernmental 'European' bodies include: the European Council, the Council of Ministers of European Communities – a cumbersome organization, containing numerous committees, with a staff of several thousand; the Court of European Communities; the Economic and Social committees; and, finally the European Parliament, whose members have been elected since 1979 by the direct votes of people of the EEC member-countries.

The process of formation of European associations and organizations in the political and military spheres was also developing. In 1948, the Western Alliance was founded and included Britain, France, Belgium, the Netherlands and Luxembourg. In addition to the United States and Canada, the North Atlantic Treaty Organization (NATO), a military–political organization established in 1949, was eventually joined by all leading West European countries.

Thus, a broad and ramified network of West European bodies and organizations was formed during the 1950s, and the dreams of many generations of Europeans about European unity were being realized.

The formation of a new Europe was associated with the names of Jean Monnais and Robert Schuman of France, Alcide de Gasperi of Italy, Konrad Adenauer of West Germany and Paul-Henri Spaak of Belgium. They held different views of the goals and tasks of European integration. Jean Monnais, for instance, saw the new Europe as the incarnation of the ideas and ideals put forward by Rousseau and

175

Kant, and in the nineteenth century, by Coudenhove-Kalergi and Spinelli. Monnais' ideal was a Europe without borders, with guaranteed human rights and general democratic institutions. For Monnais, a united Europe should embody the ideas of West European liberalism. He proposed to set up a new Europe without Russia.

For Robert Schuman, Europe was primarily an economic unity. On his initiative various economic associations were set up, the first among them being the European Coal and Steel Association. In his declaration of 9 May 1950, Schuman pointed out that the establishment of an economic community gave a mighty impetus to the development of broader co-operation among European countries that had been separated for a long time. He regarded economic unity as an important factor in a new, vital and organized Europe, where the old French dream of a united Europe might be realized. It would be a continent of peace, security and co-operation.

De Gasperi, a leader of the Christian Democrats, regarded European federalism as a stage of transition to an open international community. He and his Christian-Democrat associates believed that 'small federations' (such as, for instance, Benelux) should serve as a point of departure in the formation process of the European Community for the future gradual transition to broader associations and organizations (like the United Nations) that would be able to ensure international co-operation. While speaking about Italy's place in the Committee of European Nations, de Gasperi constantly stressed the dual nature of his nation's functions on the international scene, for Italy, he said, was both a Mediterranean and a Danube basin power.

It should also be noted that Article 11 of the Constitution of the Italian Republic, the only European constitution of the post-war period (Article 11 was proposed by the Christian-Democrats), states that

> on terms of equality with other states Italy is ready to accept certain restrictions of its sovereignty necessary for the establishment of a system that would ensure the reign of peace and justice among the nations [and] promote the formation and operation of international organizations called upon to ensure the attainment of this goal. (*Constitutions of Bourgeois States of Europe*, Moscow, 1957)

Konrad Adenauer assessed the present and future of Europe in the context of Germany's status after its defeat in the Second World War. His ambition was to lift the restrictions imposed by the Occupation

176

Statute on FRG sovereignty and restore Germany's position in Europe (at least its Western part) and for the country to survive the tragedies of fascism and bankruptcy.

Adenauer viewed the Franco-German rapprochement and the participation of West Germany in the newly formed European institutions as the cornerstone of a new Europe. However, the West German Chancellor's pragmatism went hand in glove with his Europeanism. For him, the European tradition was not an abstract formality. German political thought and past ambitions with respect to Europe had nourished Europeanist concepts of the 1940s–50s. Adenauer often referred to the period of Bismarck's rule, and the heritage of the great nineteenth-century unifier of Germany was of great importance to the German Chancellor of the post-war period.

However, compared with other political leaders of post-war Germany, Adenauer was the least nationalistically minded and held the most advanced pro-Europeanist views, which was most vividly manifested in his polemic with Schumacher, his main political opponent. Schumacher regarded the idea of European integration with great suspicion and whenever possible stressed the German people's national interests and the priority of German statehood.

Although Adenauer's view of Europeanism was limited and, at times extremely narrow, in the first post-war years he did not rule out the possibility of the USSR, or some part of it, taking its place in a united Europe of the future. W. Weidenfeld, who supported Adenauer's political view of European problems, cited the question Adenauer asked in his speech of 5 May 1946: 'Why should not some of Russia's European republics join the United States of Europe?', although he also pointed out that pretty soon Adenauer changed his views and in his speech made in May 1947 he insisted on the thesis that 'Asia dominates Europe'. By late 1946 it had become clear that 'when Adenauer speaks about Europe he implies Western Europe'.

However, Adenauer had certain reservations when he mentioned Western Europe. Authors of publications about Adenauer have pointed out that the FRG–France–Great Britain triangle was central to his policial views, although at various periods he assessed its component parts differently. Thus, in 1946 he adhered to the idea that 'Britain and France should be Europe's leaders' and criticized those who preferred France alone, whereas in his address at an Inter-parliamentary Union session on 23 March 1949, in Berne, he stated unequivocally that 'relations with France are an important aspect of German foreign policy'. With the passage of time his pro-French orientation became the leading feature in his thinking.

Adenauer's attitude to the role of the United States in Europe was extremely controversial. On the one hand, he was inclined to regard Europe as a 'third force' placed between the two superpowers (for instance, he expressed this idea in his speeches at a congress of the Christian-Democratic Union in Rheinland-Pfalz in April 1950), whereas on the other, in talks with US politicians he seemed to support the idea that 'Americans are the best Europeans', clearly intimating that he attached more importance to Germany's relations with the United States than to those with its European partners.

In the last ten years of his service as chancellor, Adenauer's relations with the United States were considerably dampened, particularly after Dulles' death and John F. Kennedy's election as President. At that time he again put his stake on 'the French card' with the result that the Elisée Treaty was signed.

In general, in his interpretation of the European idea Adenauer identified it with the notions of 'Western culture' and 'Christian West' and responded to the 'threat' not only from Asia but also from Africa. On the whole, Adenauer's Europeanism was part of the general trend of European development, with West Germany, then in the process of its regeneration, included in a renovated Europe.

Paul-Henri Spaak, with his widely known projects of the war-time period, was an ardent advocate of European federalism. His Europeanism had always been affected by specific political practices and the way Europe was viewed by official circles.

On the whole, the views held by advocates of European integration and their actual policies were a happy combination of the specific post-war political realities and the old traditions. Apart from the official circles, there was a broad intellectual community which reflected the moods of the political and intellectual élite. The life and works of Denis de Rogemont, an outstanding Swiss historian and philosopher, are a relevant example. In his address to the European congress, held in The Hague, he said:

> By our joint efforts we shall be able to set up tomorrow the most significant political and economic structure of our times.
>
> Such a mighty community of free people will be something unprecedented in the history of humanity . . .
>
> The supreme European value will be man's dignity, and his freedom is his real strength.

Rogemont explained his vision and interpretation of the goals of a united Europe. He spoke about free circulation of people, ideas and goods. He hoped that the Code of a new Europe would guarantee human rights and freedom of the press and political opposition. He dreamed of a European Assembly where the various political forces of all European nations would be represented. Rogement's works were devoted to Europeanist ideas, dreams and realities. His was classical Europeanism, with human rights and the principles of equality, democracy, law and freedom forming its core. He carried on the traditions of the liberal ideas of the nineteenth and twentieth centuries.

In the late 1940s and 1950s a large number of conferences and forums were held in Western Europe, which stimulated the formation of new concepts of European cultural identity and the common principles of civilization. European development at this time can hardly be described as idyllic: numerous trends and varying views were advocated, with sharp clashes taking place among their supporters. Some of the conflicts of opinion were in evidence even in the process of formation of the European community or soon after, and the most fundamental of them were of a durable nature.

The fiercest debates were those about the nature of the European community: was it a Europe of fatherlands or Europe as a new fatherland? The old arguments between the advocates of stronger national statehood and those of a supranational Europe were manifested in the course of those debates. In the end, as a result of the old conflict between these trends and interests, the EEC countries rejected for the first stage of the Community both federative and confederate forms of co-operation.

In this instance the good intentions and interests of none of the West European leaders or political parties were of decisive importance. European history, including its post-war period, testified clearly that the upholding and strengthening of national statehood is an important element and any version of a supranational Europe was powerless to change this.

This factor was important for the future of West European integration as it set certain limits for the evolution of integration processes. In this context it was quite predictable that the economic and political rivalries among countries in integrated Western Europe sometimes continued. Many European countries were not prepared to sacrifice their own interests and age-old traditions, their political system and culture for Europeanist ideas. National awareness and culture were highly developed in West European countries.

In spite of these complications, integration processes went on at a rapid pace in Western Europe and were increasingly manifest in social, party and political affairs, as well as in foreign policy and the military sphere, although in the latter case there was considerable antagonism within the community. The European Community was quite successful in its economic rivalry with the United States: Western Europe outstripped the US in GNP, commodity exports and gold and hard currency reserves. In the political sphere, too, the United States was rapidly losing its former control over Western Europe, which had turned into an independent power centre.

In the 1950s–70s many new factors came to the fore in the system of West European integration. Although economic unity was progressing rapidly, including the customs policy and various other aspects, a considerable number of discussions were held about the establishment of new integration bodies or improving existing ones. Elections by direct vote were held for the European Parliament and the Council of Europe, and the EEC bodies, located in Brussels, were vested with broader powers and rights.

However, major complications now arose because of the stand taken by Britain. In the second half of the 1940s, Churchill's attitude and that of many British politicians made an important contribution to the development of the European idea. But Britain took an increasingly intolerant stand with respect to the EEC, refusing to join for a long time, and after having joined striving to retain its special status.

During the 1980s a fresh impetus was given to European unification. European integration started developing in a new direction and took new forms as a result of developments in Eastern Europe and the Soviet Union. After the downfall of the communist regimes, disbandment of the Comecon and cancellation of the Warsaw Treaty, the former members of the 'socialist community' were faced with new problems and priorities. Poland, Czechoslovakia, Hungary, Romania and Bulgaria rapidly joined the practice of contact with the system of West European integration (economic and political).

In spite of immense difficulties a similar process can be observed in the former republics of the Soviet Union. The Baltic states, the Ukraine, Moldavia, Byelorussia and, finally, Russia started rapidly advancing towards the united Europe. Although the EEC leaders are very cautious in their approach to the admittance of new members to the Community, largely due to economic considerations (the same level of economic development in all EEC countries is an essential condition of membership), there is no doubt that the absorption into the EEC of East European countries and the former Soviet Union republics is only a matter of time, for it is an objective process.

The end of 1991 was an historic landmark in European development for then a programme of guidelines for European development was adopted at a top-level meeting of the European Community, held in Maastricht, a small Dutch town. It will not be long before Europe truly becomes a continent without borders and customs barriers. The doors of European universities will be thrown wide open to students from all countries. The programme outlines new forms of division of legislative and executive power, as well as functions of the European Parliament and other European executive bodies.

In general, one might say that members of the EC have at last found a form of harmonizing national and pan-European interests on the basis of their experiences of the past three decades and with numerous discussions, and we are actually witnessing the process of materialization of the great idea of the United States of Europe. The EC has demonstrated its unity in economic, political and spiritual spheres. At the same time the national colours of the European states, both large and small, their historical traditions, inimitable original features and individual contributions to the European cultural heritage have been preserved.

Participants in the Maastricht meeting proved unable to overcome all their differences (largely associated with Britain's particular stand), although it is absolutely clear that Europe is on the threshold of a genuinely historic era when the plans and ideas of the great Europeans of past centuries will at last materialize.

However, the realization of this dream hinges not only on the integration of Western Europe but also on the new hopes for the formation of Greater Europe which is expected to incorporate Russia, the Ukraine, the Baltic countries and other states situated on the territory of what was once the Soviet Union.

At present there is a chance to put into practice François Mitterrand's idea for a European Confederation and the idea of a common European home, put forward by the former Soviet leader, Mikhail Gorbachev, both of which might help overcome the split of Europe and produce a radically new model.

Mitterrand's vision of Europe has been set out in many of his speeches and works. For instance, in his speech at the Council of Europe in September 1982, Mitterrand pointed out that Europe had the right to existence by becoming a free Europe and that this appraisal was embodied in the Council of Europe, which was the oldest European institution and was the organization uniting the greatest number of states.

Moreover, even at that time, when Mitterrand raised the issue of European unity he included the continent's Eastern part and outlined such fundamental factors as human rights and the cultural identity of

European civilization. Some seven or eight years later, after the development of the Helsinki process and the incipient collapse of totalitarianism in Eastern Europe, the French president began to offer energetic arguments in favour of the idea of a political confederation of Europe. In his New Year message in 1990, Mitterrand outlined new European guidelines to incorporate all states of the European continent in a permanent unity, based on mutual exchange, peace and security. Naturally, this would be possible exclusively after a multi-party system, free elections, a representative system of government and freedom of the press had become part of the reality in East European countries.

Later this idea was supported by many European leaders. Although in a somewhat modified form, the idea of confederation was also approved by the President of the European Community, Jacques Delors, who suggested that a federation of twelve be set up within the framework of the EC. Mikhail Gorbachev's concept of the common European home and François Mitterrand's idea of European confederation will go down in the European history of the 1980s as mutually complementary. In January 1990, French journalist Alain Dauvergne wrote:

> The West has nothing to say in response to Mikhail Gorbachev's idea of 'the common home', so after he had put it forward, silence fell. And now the time has come when the vacuum is filled – I mean François Mitterand's proposal of December for setting up a European Confederation and Jacques Delors's proposal of January 1 for a Federation of Twelve. They may even say that there are too many proposals now, but that would be wrong: the evolution of Europe – or Europes – in the past few months raises the issue of setting up a new system of organization on the continent and its component parts.
>
> The Moscow idea of 'the common home', first received as a piece of propaganda pure and simple, has been regarded as quite sensible since last summer. Six months later – a period packed with major events such as the election won in Poland by Solidarity and Ceaucescu's death – this idea became quite creditable. Quite unexpectedly, the idea of 'the common home', in other words, the Soviet concept of the European arrangement, attracted general attention. Mitterrand put an end to this kind of ideological monopoly by his New Year address. He thoroughly checked and corrected it with his own hand in his desire to find the right words which came as a result of his long deliberation over the destinies of East European countries and their evolution.

François Mitterrand, Mikhail Gorbachev, Vaclav Havel, Jacques Delors and Helmut Kohl symbolized the new realities of modern Europe. The new Europe is now rapidly taking shape, based as it is on All-European values, including those of the west and the east of the continent. This process rests on the age-old experience of European cultural identity. European politicians may now make use of the achievements of the Helsinki process, which has culminated in the adoption in 1990 of the Paris Charter for European development which outlines a model of the Europe of the future. The tempestuous developments of 1991, especially the break-up of the Soviet Union and the further evolution of Eastern European countries, gave new impetus to European development, confronting European politicians and the public with many new formidable problems and provoking new conflicts and outbursts of violence.

High on the agenda are the issues involved in setting up Greater Europe. This will hardly be an idyllic process, for Europe is faced with a great number of complicated and grave problems. It will take a lot of time, determination and patience to solve them, for they involve a wide range of trends and factors.

Experience has shown that unity can be found on the basis of variety of form and diversity of development. The solution of all the problems will serve as a necessary prerequisite for fashioning Europe's new structure at the close of the twentieth century.

22

NEW TRENDS IN THE DEVELOPMENT
OF EASTERN EUROPE AND RUSSIA

The mid-1980s ushered in a new stage in the development of Soviet foreign policy, including its attitude to Europe. First, pragmatic tasks were set for normalizing the situation in Europe and for large-scale arms cuts, as well as disarmament in general, within the framework of the Helsinki process which was under way throughout Europe. Next, it was necessary to supply theoretical substantiation to the process of new thinking for cardinal changes on a world-wide scale.

New tasks and priorities in Soviet foreign policy were inseparable from changes on the domestic scene. Proclamation of the priority of common human values led to cardinal changes in Soviet European policy and the Soviet stand on Europeanism – the civilizing dimension of the pan-European process – was accepted as a guideline. For the first time in the post-revolutionary era Soviet leaders started working with notions such as European civilization without adding critical comments about its 'narrow class nature' and lack of respect for the Marxist theory of social formations.

With the passage of time, a new vision of Europe was formed in the USSR. Europe, as Mikhail Gorbachev saw it, was a continent of peace, security, co-operation and good neighbourliness; it was totally unprecedented for a Soviet leader to speak about human rights and democratic values.

In the past Soviet representatives had stressed emphatically at various international forums that the bourgeois concept of human rights was 'limited' and 'harmful', asserting that socialist gains and the socialist ideal of man were the only true values, so it was exceptional for a communist leader to give priority to common human values rather than to socialist values and class struggle.

In his address to members of the European Parliament in Strasbourg in July 1989, Gorbachev described with the utmost clarity a new

Soviet view of Europe that could be interpreted as the USSR's reunion with Europe. He did not envisage it as an automatic process but spoke about the Soviet Union's new image – in fact, an entirely new world – which had for many decades been regarded as posing a permanent threat to European nations and European democracy.

The European concept set out by Gorbachev and Shevardnadze was the result of gradual evolution rather than a static concept. At first it was dominated by elements of foreign policy, with hardly any changes in other views and ideas. However, after the breakthrough of the mid-1980s, Soviet leaders took up the subject of democracy and human rights; Shevardnadze made reference to great European thinkers such as Rousseau and Voltaire in his speeches, and later there was a talk in Moscow about European democracy.

At that stage, democratic values were still seen from communist and socialist viewpoints, and Francis Fukuyama's words about the triumph of liberalism and the global retreat of communism were still regarded critically as obvious exaggeration and as the fantasy of the US establishment rather than reality.

In the initial years of *perestroika* the prevailing ideas were about re-structuring the socialist system and the USSR's reunion with Europe as a socialist state, with words such as 'renewal', 'reappraisal' and 'a new interpretation of socialism' widely used in the country. Gorbachev con-ducted a lively dialogue with the French President, the FRG Chancellor and the British and Italian Prime Ministers about the future of Europe. The Helsinki process was being further developed and was imbued with a new content. The notorious 'third Helsinki basket' was turned from a factor of confrontation into a sphere of broad co-operation and interaction. Meanwhile, European disarmament talks made rapid progress, paving the way for new European realities and contributing to a new vision of Europeanism in the late twentieth century.

Shevardnadze's speech in Vienna in late 1989 was a confirmation of the regenerated Soviet Union's readiness to accept the European realities. The Soviet Union unequivocally stated its desire to take part in the activities of West European integration organizations, such as the EC in Brussels and the Council of Europe in Strasbourg.

Curiously enough, purely functional interests were increasingly upheld in Western Europe, and apprehension was expressed in Paris, Brussels, Rome and Berlin about bureaucratic trends in integrated Europe, whereas in Moscow stress was laid on the values that inspired the founders and ardent supporters of Europeanism at earlier stages. One might say that Moscow was going through the earliest stage in the development of European ideas and concepts.

Moscow intellectuals regarded Europe as a dream and a symbol; the European idea which had for many decades been conceived without Russian participation – and quite often against it – was given a new interpretation, so Moscow was clearly inclined to become part of Europe and a co-owner of its cultural heritage and civilization. The process of transition to Europeanism, naturally, could not be easy, for both objective and subjective factors were contained in it. The trend for the revival of Russophile and Slavophile moods not only gained strength but also tended to become militant and uncompromising.

The natural process of renaissance of Russian culture, with many forgotten names – Berdyaev and Florensky among them – restored to the nation, at the same time led to the revival of old theories of Russian superiority and Russia's special mission in history, which was often discussed as being outside European history and European traditions. Extremist nationalist and chauvinist trends, like the notorious *Pamayat* (Memory), took shape in the country. Even if we ignore these extremist trends, it can still be acknowledged that a process of regeneration of old ideas and concepts was under way in the Soviet Union – which in the nineteenth century had led to an upsurge of antagonism in Russian society.

There were two parallel trends at the time: on the one hand, Oswald Spengler's *The Decline of Europe* was published in the USSR and, on the other, Danilevsky's *Russia and Europe* was offered to the Soviet readership. In addition, Soviet newspapers and periodicals carried articles and excerpts from books by Europeanists of earlier epochs such as Briand, Kant, Coudenhove-Kalergi, de Gaulle and Mitterrand.

Apart from the desire to enjoy the benefits of European values and the advantages of European democracy, Soviet people were increasingly eager to have access to the boons of civilization on a par with Europe. Carried away by the idea of attaining the level of Western prosperity, they were oblivious of the real contradictions of the European reality. In that context, the idea of reunion with Europe produced a dual effect: on the one hand, Soviet intellectuals wished to enjoy the benefits of freedom and democracy and, on the other, the broad masses strove to attain the level of European and US living standards and consumption.

At the same time, the mass media carried on a broad propaganda campaign about Russian exclusiveness, Russia's special mission and alien European influences. Contributing to this process was an unprecedented upsurge in religious observance and the increasingly privileged position enjoyed by the Orthodox Church. New interest in religion and the growing authority of the Church in the USSR meant that Orthodox ideas and dogma were often regarded as being diametrically opposite to Catholicism and the Western tradition. This, naturally, added to the appeal of the idea of Russian exclusiveness, providing, as it were, a theoretical basis for the arguments of critics of West European values, thus offering proof of their alleged unacceptability on Russian soil.

Every effort was made to smuggle in and spread the idea that since Christianity was not the only tradition represented in Russia, and as a large part of the population professed the Moslem faith, European Christian practices could not and would not be automatically transferred to a multinational country with such a plurality of religious denominations.

Thus it is clear that the development process of the European idea in the renovated Soviet Union was certainly not straightforward. Gorbachev's Europeanism was also contradictory and somewhat inconsistent. For the new Soviet leader, both the European spirit and the European soul were, in fact, non-existent. His ideas were dominated by foreign-policy factors and the desire to involve the country in democratic processes on the European model and to transform the USSR into a rule-of-the-law state.

However, the idea of restructuring socialism in the Soviet Union and 'the socialist community' countries was prominent in Kremlin policy before the end of 1989 and a section of the Soviet leadership still toyed with the possibility of bringing in 'socialism with a human face' on the 1968 Czechoslovakian model. Moreover, the Kremlin leaders, and Gorbachev for that matter, had no premonition of any imminent crisis; they did not realize that they were lagging behind in development processes. In this case, developments in Eastern Europe proved crucial.

The totalitarian Stalinist model of government, built up in Eastern and south-eastern European countries in the post-war period, sometimes clearly malfunctioned, even in the mid-1950s: events in the GDR in 1953 and in Hungary in 1956 testified that there were profound contradictions behind the respectable façade of those countries. It should be pointed out that, just like the Soviet leaders, the communist leaders of these countries had failed to prevail over history. The old and deep traditions of their former multi-party systems and democratic institutions had neither been forgotten by their people nor totally removed from their political practice. In Czechoslovakia, a country with the most advanced democratic

187

traditions because of their development in the period between the two world wars, opposition was brewing, albeit clandestinely. In Poland, the Church originally acted as a focal point for opposition, but later the opposition rallied around the well-known Solidarity worker movement. Hungary, for its part, had never forgotten the brutal suppression of the 1956 uprising.

In general, the rigid centralized model of government gave rise to distortions in economy and considerable deterioration in living standards, with the result that those countries' traditional contacts with Europe were interrupted. So the latent process of degradation of socialism was steadily developing and anti-Soviet feelings were mounting in those countries. The image of socialism lost its halo in many countries in Eastern, Central and south-east Europe.

For many years Soviet tactics towards its allies consisted of the suppression of all and every dissension; the allies had to obey without a murmur and be totally loyal in the ideological sphere. Moscow chose leaders for its East European allies to suit its own taste and set up a wide network of punitive bodies which acted in line with instructions from Moscow. The invasion by troops of the Warsaw Treaty country of Czechoslovakia in August 1968 to cut short the development of the Prague Spring process was a logical outcome of this policy.

One might say that in this way the Moscow *nomenklatura* took its revenge for the shock of Khrushchev's exposures. Since neo-Stalinist rule had been established in the Soviet Union comparatively easily, party leaders believed that any attempt at 'revisionism' abroad would be equally easily crushed. However, the invasion had far greater consequences than had been expected, for it was actually in August 1968 that the dissident movement was born in the USSR which grew into a substantial factor of the Soviet reality in the 1970s and the early 1980s. On the other hand, the invasion of Czechoslovakia had thoroughly compromised the image of socialism Soviet-style among millions of people in Eastern Europe, thus making the abyss that divided Eastern from Western Europe even wider and the contrast between socialism and democracy more vivid.

Organizations of socialist integration assumed an increasingly autarchic nature, contributing still further to the stagnation of the socialist economy. In this situation, Dubček's idea of socialism with a human face seemed to offer a way out of the totalitarian blind alley, and opposition forces regarded it as the only chance of giving a new lease of life to the socialist idea, that is, to produce a combination of socialism and democracy.

188

However, the brutal suppression of the Prague experiment not only cut short the process of reform but also struck a heavy blow at the idea of changing communism through reform. In fact, further developments revealed that the idea of socialism with a human face no longer served as an inspiration to democratic circles in East European countries.

The policy of *perestroika* in the Soviet Union had a great impact on the socialist countries' position. This process took various forms in various states. The ruling *nomenklatura* in the GDR, Czechoslovakia and Bulgaria desperately opposed any reforms, whereas in Hungary and Poland society developed at a rapid pace, and there the process of deep-going reforms was stepped up. However, there, too (just as in the Soviet Union), initially it was planned to introduce exclusively cosmetic changes, with the obtaining structure and order left intact.

But this state of affairs could not have existed for ever, and it is to Gorbachev's credit that he not only permitted but also accelerated the development of processes that were under way in the Eastern European countries. Apart from general support for those processes, Moscow stated unequivocally that the multi-thousand-strong Soviet troops stationed in Poland, Czechoslovakia, Hungary and especially in the GDR would not interfere in the developments which were taking place. There was a world of difference between this Soviet stand and the one adopted in 1968. Thus, the Brezhnev doctrine of limited sovereignty was brought to an end. The autumn of 1989 saw an avalanche of crumbling totalitarian regimes in the former Soviet satellites, which were overthrown in a matter of weeks – and sometimes in a few days. Just as had been predicted by some analysts, this process did not develop on a socialist basis: in a comparatively short period all their socialist structures were swept away. A few months later it became obvious that communism had collapsed and that the communist parties had lost popular support and their former unlimited power monopoly.

In that context, Eastern European countries approached Western Europe and the United States with a request to be admitted to the bodies and structures of West European integration. As a consequence, Europeanist ideas were revived in a number of former socialist bloc countries. This was most vividly manifested in Czechoslovakia. President of the Czechoslovak Federal Republic Vaclav Havel became a symbol of the new East European Europeanism. Havel's Europeanism dates back to an earlier period, as is known, that is, before he came to power. At first, he focused his works and speeches on Central Europe which, he believes, should form a new historical, cultural and political community, with Czechoslovakia, Poland and Hungary as its nucleus. However, developments in Eastern Europe took a dramatic turn with, among other things, tensions coming to a head in relations between Czechia and Slovakia and civil war breaking out in Yugoslavia. Nevertheless, Havel's idea of a Central European alliance was not committed to oblivion, but assumed new features and dimensions, albeit seemingly prompted by foreign policy, rather than historico-cultural, considerations.

After the 1989 'velvet revolution' in Czechoslovakia, Havel wrote and spoke largely about Europe as a whole. In a certain sense he became a symbol of the new Europe that has risen from the ashes of the communist regimes of the former socialist community. Czechoslovakia's new policy was based on democracy and the European tradition. As distinct from the pragmatic and functional tasks and interests of the bodies of West European integration, Havel embraced the democratic aspect of Europeanism. It was probably only natural that new ideas were supplied by Eastern Europe which was coming back to democracy.

The 1989 revolutions in Eastern Europe, which stepped up the process of *perestroika* in the USSR, served as precursors of the bankruptcy of communist ideas and regimes as a whole. In this context, the process of Germany's reunification was of crucial importance to present-day Europe.

The GDR had long been regarded in the USSR as the advanced guard of socialism. Soviet propaganda constantly operated with terms such as 'a frontline state' and 'a symbol of socialism in Europe'. This line also corresponded to the ideological tasks of the GDR leaders. They were reputed to be the most ardent advocates of the East–West confrontation and of the 1968 invasion of Czechoslovakia, since they were the most dogmatic interpreters of Marxist principles and ideas. Even after it had established lively economic and political contacts with the FRG, ideological pressure on the GDR was unremitting.

The GDR leaders regarded the German state as an incarnation of Marxist ideas; the idea of two German nations, which ran counter to the German people's historical experience and traditions, was formulated in the GDR. Even after the prospect of a measure of compromise between the USSR and Western powers became real, the GDR leaders rejected out of hand any versions of Germany's unification or a rapprochement of the two German states. Even in the period of *perestroika* the USSR still clung to the idea that Germany's reunification would take a long time, and involve numerous transitional stages. This was probably in harmony with the vision of *perestroika*, based on the concept of preserving the Soviet Union as an undivided unit and the existence of the socialist community.

In that situation, too, the GDR leaders stubbornly opposed profound *perestroika* processes, which only contributed to the erosion processes that were under way in the GDR. At this juncture it is to Gorbachev's credit that he realized the historical inevitability and just nature of the demands for German unity, and gave the green light to the process of reunification of the two German states. However, as at the previous stages, the German issue became a decisive, influential factor on developments in the USSR.

At one stage Germany's reunification became a bone of contention between the main advocates and opponents of the foreign policy line pursued by Gorbachev and Shevardnadze. It also became a factor in the opposition of the military, the old party apparatus and all conservative forces to the foreign policy and reforms of the Soviet leadership.

Apart from the Soviet leaders' policy, also of decisive importance was the irreversible nature of the trend for German reunification that developed against the backdrop of the total collapse of the socialist community. The division of a great European power was an historical anomaly. Sooner or later Germany would have to be reunited – and it happened simultaneously with the collapse of the communist regime.

After Germany's reunification had become an accomplished fact, it became clear that it had largely come as a consequence of the new thinking in Soviet foreign policy and renunciation by the Soviet Union of its former imperial mentality. Germany's reunification has brought about a new stage in Soviet–German relations.

New vistas are now opening up in Soviet–German economic cooperation. The new situation makes it necessary to review many long-standing and traditional problems in German–Russian relations, which presupposes taking into account the political situation in Europe and throughout the world. New spheres and forms of relations with Germany, as well as the new contours in the world political system, are taking shape.

The ever-deepening pan-European process is an inalienable element of stability, and in this context, Germany, Russia and other European countries are working out mechanisms, obligations and guarantees for stability in Europe. The bankrupty of communist regimes in Eastern Europe, the disbandment of the Comecon, the cancelling of the Warsaw Treaty and the reunification of Germany have changed the post-war map of Europe. The world political system, established as a result of the Yalta agreements, is now in fact non-existent. The era of confrontation and balance of blocs is over; Poland, Czechoslovakia, Hungary, Romania and Bulgaria are now going through the process of adapting to the West European realities and regard themselves as part of both old and new Europe.

The old concept of the hostile enemy is losing its grip on Europe, which has been given a new lease of life with the new unity. However, the tempestuous course of events and great upheavals in the east of the continent in late 1989–early 1990 did not bring the whole process to a conclusion.

The abortive putsch staged in the USSR in August 1991 gave a powerful impetus to further developments in the USSR. The break-up of the USSR was completed during the next few months. The communist empire, which has been the source of great tensions in the last seventy years, has crumbled. New independent states are now in the process of formation in its place. The next few years will show how long the economic and other contacts formed during the past decades will ensure some kind of unity or co-operation among the republics of the former Soviet Union. At present, however, we are witnessing the redrawing of the geopolitical map of Europe: the Baltic states are engaged in the restoration of their pre-war status; an independent Ukrainian state is being formed in the political fore-ground of Europe; and complicated processes are under way in Moldavia and the Caucasus.

The eternal theme of Russia and Europe is again looming large on the European horizon. As the main legal heir of the USSR, Russia is also subjected to geographical changes. Now that it is separated from Eastern and Central Europe by a group of independent states (the Ukraine, Byelorussia, Moldova and the Baltic states), this cannot but affect the solution of many political issues. Thus, the subject of Russia and Europe still assumes great importance not only as a specific political reality in the world but also as a historico-cultural community carrying the problems of the unity and identity of European culture, traditions and civilization.

23

CONCLUSION

Europe has entered into a further stage of its development. The break-up of the Soviet Union, the collapse of communism in Eastern Europe, the unification of Germany and the end of the Cold War era have all contributed to radical changes in its post-war structure and in the system of international affairs. The old concept of security 'from whom and from what?' and 'for whom and for what?' is being gradually ousted by the formula of security for all. Leaving behind the era of confrontation, military conflict and ideological hostility, Europe is entering the epoch of interdependence, co-operation and good neighbourliness.

There is not only a widespread realization of the need for unity but also a readiness to accept the fact that European unity can be attained only on the basis of conformity of civilization and historico-cultural universal human values. Democratic rights and institutions, human rights, freedom, self-determination and independence are becoming the substance and basis of European values. It is probably the first time in history that Europeanism, based precisely on those principles and postulates, unites all Europeans, from the Atlantic to the Urals.

Europeans are now faced with the task of working out new principles of security and European structure, and are being called upon to ensure peace, stability and the prosperity of Europe at the start of the twenty-first century. The concepts of a common European home or of a pan-European confederation, the new stage in West European integration and the economic, political and cultural requirements reflect the European historical realities of the late twentieth century.

Many elements of the European idea now have new components. Discussions about the term 'Europe' are currently being held. There is the concept of Europe as the territory stretching from the Atlantic to the Urals, or the concept of Europe stretching to Vladivostok and to San Francisco, within the framework of the Helsinki process. Sometimes the old interpretation of Europe – from Brest to Brest –

is reanimated. In all these cases the concept of Europe incorporates political, economic and military–strategic aspects.

The substance of the modern interpretation of the concept of Europe consists in the fact that disputes are no longer about its purely geographic aspects, although there are some nuances even in this case. A booklet entitled *Bruxelles – le centre de l'Europe* is available in bookstores in Brussels, whereas in Paris they toy with the idea of Paris as the centre of Europe. In the past few months there has been talk about Prague as the centre of Europe. However, the political aspect of the concept of modern Europe is much more important than these geographical disputes. The idea of Europe as an actual community, including the continent's West and East as well as Russia, is increasingly being established in the world.

A further problem, that of 'Russia in Europe', is by no means new. It was the topic for heated discussions in the nineteenth century between the Westerners and the Slavophiles in Russia, and caused a substantial split in Russian society. In the West it used to be widely asserted that classical Europe did not incorporate Russia and even in the twentieth century the USSR was excluded from Europe. Today, plans for European development and a new European order are simply unacceptable without Russia.

In Russia the issue of interdependence and mutual relations between Russians and other nationalities residing on Russia's territory is especially acute. In this context, the factor of the historico-cultural and civilization identity of Russia and Europe is of primary importance. This problem is complex, for Russia belongs in Europe and at the same time not only in Europe – a sizeable part of it is situated in Asia. It is not accidental that in our times special interest is shown in the theories of Eurasia and the Eurasian idea, as well as in the concept of Russia as a synthesis of both great civilizations.

With this in mind, we are now even more justified in speaking about the historico-cultural identity of Russia and Europe. At present there is a rare opportunity in Russia to assert such fundamental Europeanist principles as human rights, freedom and independence, the rule-of-law state and the civic society.

However, Europe needs not only spiritual unity but also political community and structure. The new realities of modern Europe serve as a basis for European unity, and for a new European structure. It is too soon as yet to offer any theories of what the new Europe will be like in the twenty-first century: whether or not Eastern Europe and Russia will accept the institutions and forms of West European integration, or whether a confederation of all European states will be set up that would incorporate Russia, the Ukraine, the Baltic states and other independent states which were part of the Soviet Union.

Debates are now in progress in an integrated Western Europe between those who regard European unity as a process of the establishment of numerous institutions and managerial bodies and those who believe that a united Europe will represent a triumph of the European spirit, with its own identity of culture and civilization, the embodiment of age-old European traditions, and the realization of the ideas which have inspired the best European minds.

The European idea now seems to have a new lease of life. Although it is interpreted in a variety of ways in London, Berlin, Warsaw, Paris and Moscow, and national and social conflicts are still part of the picture, there is now a historic chance to realize European unity on the basis of a vast variety of special national features, different historico-cultural, economic and political backgrounds, and, at long last, to discover the coveted common denominator that has been sought by Europeans throughout the many centuries of the Old World's existence. Meanwhile, today's discussions about the relations between Russia and Europe and the exceptional mission of Russia are a continuation of the old debates of 'Westerners versus Slavophiles'. At the same time they are a result of the recent conflicts and contradictions of the various political forces and the search for a new civilization model for post-Communist Russia. Undoubtedly, the fact that Russia and the states of the European Union will benefit equally from the partnership and the co-operation will have a significant stabilizing effect in Europe and the world.

BIBLIOGRAPHY

Achiezer, A.S. *Rossia: critica istoricheskogo opyta.* T. 1–3. Moskva, 1991.
Baranovski, V.G. *Evropejskoe soobshchestvo v sisteme mezhdunarodnykh otnoshenij.* Moskva, 1986.
Brugmans, H. *L'idée européenne, 1916–1966.* Bruges, 1966.
——, *L'idée européenne, 1920–1970.* Bruges, 1970.
Chabot, J. *L'idée d'Europe unie de 1919 à 1939.* Grenoble, 1978.
Civilizatsii. Vyp. I. Moskva, 1992. Vyp. II. Moskva, 1993.
Dahrendorf, R. and Th.C. Sorensen. *A Widening Atlantic? Domestic Change and Foreign Policy.* New York, 1986.
Defarges, Ph. *L'Europe et son identité dans le monde.* Paris, 1983.
Delmas, C. *La civilisation européenne.* Paris, 1980.
Duroselle, J.B. *L'idée d'Europe dans l'histoire.* Paris, 1967.
Europe: Dreams, Adventure, Reality. Brussels, 1987.
Europa: Testi e documenti per una storia dell'unita europea. Palermo, 1987.
Evrazia. Moskva, 1992.
Evropa kak kulturnaja obschchnost. Moskva, 1991.
Evropa v mezhdunarodnykh otnoshenijakh, 1917–1939. Moskva, 1979.
Evropejskij almanakh: Istoria, Tradicii, Kultura. Vyp. 1–4. Moskva, 1990–93.
Foerster, R.H. *Europa: Geschichte einer politischen Idee.* München, 1967.
Gruber, E. *L'idée européenne.* Paris, 1971.
Istoria Evropy. T. 1–3. Moskva, 1987–93.
Propiläen Geschichte Europas. T. 1–6. Frankfurt am Main, 1976–79.
Ranimer l'Europe: Regard dans le miroir d'autres civilisations. Paris, 1984.
Russkaja idea. Moskva, 1992.
Tchoubarian, A.O. *Evropeiskaja ideja v istorii.* Moskva, 1987.

DATE DUE

AUG − 4 1995	

UPI 261-2505 G   PRINTED IN U.S.A.